BAND SAW HANDBOOK

Mark Duginske

 Sterling Publishing Co., Inc.   New York

Dedication

This book is dedicated to my parents, who recently celebrated their fiftieth wedding anniversary in good health.

Edited by Michael Cea

Library of Congress Cataloging-in-Publication Data

Duginske, Mark.
    Band saw handbook / by Mark Duginske
       p. cm.
    ISBN 0-8069-6398-0
    1. Band saws. 2. Woodwork. I. Title.
    TT186.D84 1989   89-35457
    684'.083—dc20   CIP

Copyright © 1989 by Mark Duginske
Published by Sterling Publishing Co., Inc.
387 Park Avenue South, New York, N.Y. 10016
Distributed in Canada by Sterling Publishing
% Canadian Manda Group, P.O. Box 920, Station U
Toronto, Ontario, Canada M8Z 5P9
Distributed in Great Britain and Europe by Cassell PLC
Artillery House, Artillery Row,
London SW1P 1RT, England
Distributed in Australia by Capricorn Ltd.
P.O. Box 665, Lane Cove, NSW 2066
Manufactured in the United States of America

Contents

Acknowledgments

During the three years that I worked on this book, I had help and suggestions from a large number of people. I would like to thank these people for their help. I hope that I have not forgotten to mention any of them.

First of all, I would like to thank my wife, Kate Morris, for her help and patience during this long process. She did a great job of editing, and contributed helpful suggestions. As his summer job during high school, my nephew, Chris Morris, helped me by doing some of the drawings and much of the photography. David Morris and my brother Gene also helped with the photography. Mike Cea of Sterling Publishing skilfully edited the book.

I would especially like to thank my father, whose years of practical experience make him a well of knowledge. Jack Turley contributed a section on blade tension, a complex and difficult subject. Joe Roposa edited the chapter on blade tension and had helpful suggestions. Peter Segal and Henry Lanz made important technical contributions.

A number of companies and individuals were extremely helpful; these include the following: Charlie Nurnberg of Sterling Publishing; Garry Chinn of the Garrett Wade Co.; Gene Sliga and Lou Brichner of Delta; Allen Nielson of Ryobi; Tim Baldwin of Shopsmith; Chuck Olson of Olson Saw; Jim McMahan of Doall; Chris Bagby and Brad Pachard of Highland Hardware; Jesse Baragon of Eagle Tool; Jill Goldman of DonJer Products; Dick Burrows of Fine Woodworking; Paul Thoms and Dale Zimmerman of the Woodworkers Store; Doug Hicks of Woodsmith Publishing; INCA of Teufental, Switzerland; Stan Black of Trendlines; New Milford Specialties Co.; Jim Forrest of Forrest Manufacturing; Kasco; Brad and Paula Witt of Woodhaven; Paul Starret of AMI; Rick and Ron Bechen of Workbench Tool Co.; Ken and Barb Burch of The Hardwood Connection; International Marine Publishing Co.; Dick Johnson of Johnson's Workbench; Sun Designs; Stan Austin and Beau Lowerr of the Wisconsin Woodworkers Guild; and Better Built Corp.

I would also like to thank the following individuals: Pat Spielman, Toshio Odate, Sharon Grossman, Tom Klosinski, Dan Szitta, Postal Lapinski, John Cosperdot, Jim Langlois, Doug Bootes, Tom Stender, Chris Schwamb, Bill Stankus, Don Misoni, Stuart Braunstein, Ed Hinza, Joni Lew, Neil O'Reily, Jim Kirschner, Elizabeth Doherty, Bob Umnus, Dean Slinde, Fall Wing, Glen Elvig, Yvonne Barnes, Wayne Francis, Louisa Bonnie, Rick Hartom, Tom Gabriel, and the late Bill Rogers, whose support and generosity will always be appreciated.

Introduction

The ancient craft of woodworking is now enjoying an unparalleled rebirth in popularity, for it provides the participant with both practical and emotional fruits. As our society becomes increasingly complex, woodworkers can still enjoy the straight cause-and-effect results that wood offers. Woodworking provides contact with a natural material—something that is often lacking in our busy plastic world.

Woodworking is also beneficial in the economical sense. Many people now make all or some of their furniture and gifts. In many cases, the home workshop also provides a means of income.

Aesthetically, woodworking has something to offer to all age groups. When a child plays with a wooden toy, he uses his creativity to its utmost without the hindrance of batteries and gimmicks. For adults, the rewards from woodworking are immediate, but also long-lasting. The things that our fathers and grandfathers have made from wood are treasured today by us. The things that are made today will be appreciated years from now.

The modern woodworker needs tools that are simple yet versatile. These tools should do a large variety of jobs without expensive or complex jigs. There is no operation more basic to woodworking than sawing, and the versatile band saw can do all types of sawing. It will cut wood thick or thin and square or round. It will cut both curves and straight lines. It will resaw thin veneer and make tight scroll-saw-type cuts. A skilled user can quickly turn a humble log into four perfectly matched Queen Anne chair legs. And with a simple band saw jig (like the one described in Chapter 15), he can cut through dovetails for a box or a drawer precisely and efficiently with a minimum of setup. In fact, a band-sawn dovetail box can be finished before a router jig can be properly adjusted for the same operation. The band-saw dovetail jig doesn't cost anything either, just a little time and some scrap wood.

There are many reasons why a band saw should be the first power tool a person should learn to operate. To use a term coined in computer jargon, the band saw is user friendly. It is quiet and easy to use. Women often comment that it reminds them of a sewing machine. It can also be used for a wide range of functions.

One huge advantage to using the band saw is *safety*, which should always be the first consideration in any sawing operation. The band saw is infinitely safer than the table saw or radial saw. The blade is easily covered by the guard. The cutting speed is slow and the noise level is low. Noise causes operator fatigue, which encourages accidents.

When you make a rip cut with a table saw, and especially a radial arm saw, the circular saw blade applies a force on the wood in the direction of the operator. The average rim speed of a ten-inch circular blade is 110 miles per hour. If the circular blade binds or is pinched by the wood, the board flies back at the operator with lightning speed. This dangerous situation, called "kickback," is the cause of a large percentage of serious sawing accidents.

Dangerous kickbacks cannot happen with a band saw. The band saw blade applies a force directly towards the table, literally holding the wood down as it is cutting. For this reason, many experienced woodworkers rip short, narrow, or warped boards only with a band saw. This safety feature is particularly attractive for the beginning woodworker, as well as children, women, and older people, who have a slower reaction time. When safety is considered, a well-adjusted band saw will often be the tool of choice.

The design of the band saw is very simple, as the tool has few working parts. The flexible band or blade has cutting teeth on one edge. The blade is held under tension by two wheels. As the wheels rotate, the blade also rotates and cuts through the wood. The narrow blade allows the wood to be rotated during the cut, producing a curve. The blade will also cut straight. The cutting principle is the same for a 1/16-inch blade cutting tight scrolls as it is for a giant 16-inch blade cutting logs into planks. A chain saw uses a similar principle—a chain with cutting teeth replaces the toothed saw blade.

As mentioned, there are many advantages to using the band saw. The one drawback is the fact that the blade, thrust bearings, and guides have to be adjusted, and the wheels aligned. This takes time and patience. In fact, it actually takes more time to learn how to adjust the band saw than it does to use it.

Correctly adjusting the band saw does not take much skill. Once you understand the step-by-step sequencing involved, you will be on your way to mastering the art of band saw tuning, and will not be as reluctant to change blades.

Two chapters in this book are devoted to the principles involved in aligning band-saw wheels, tracking the blade, and adjusting the thrust bearings and guides. Another examines blade tensioning. The correct amount of tensioning is essential when using the band saw to make accurate cuts. The troubleshooting information and advice that is included will be particularly helpful to the self-taught woodworker who often feels very isolated because he has no one to talk to, or worse, to listen to.

Much of the book focuses on the many jobs the band saw can be used for—cutting curves, circles, and straight lines, to name just a few—and the shop-made jigs that can be used to facilitate these jobs. Commercially available jigs are very limited in scope. If you are truly interested in getting the most out of your band saw, you will have to invest some time and energy into making your own jigs and fixtures. A final chapter offers a wide range of projects that should inspire you to become a more skilled band-saw user, and thus a better craftsperson.

—Mark Duginske

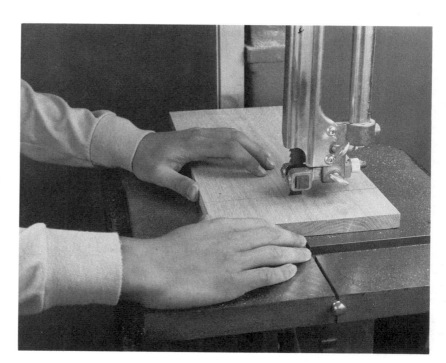

Illus. 1. Crosscutting freehand with a band saw.

BAND-SAW FUNDAMENTALS

1
Historical Overview

We live in a time of very rapidly changing technologies. New, exotic materials are now being cut with high-tech diamonds, lasers, and very sophisticated saw blades. The band saw is perhaps the most versatile cutting tool. New band-saw blades, accessories, and techniques are constantly being developed to make this tool even more versatile. A cutting technique that cannot be accomplished with a band saw today may be possible next week. It is important to realize that the band saw and our abilities to use it are evolving.

The development of the band saw can be found in the evolution of saws in general. Man's first cutting tools were sharp stones. With time, the importance of the serrated cutting edge was realized and the technique for making these serrations evolved into an art.

The next major development of the saw occurred at approximately 5000 BC, when metal was first used. Copper was tried first, but it proved to be too soft. When tin was added to the copper, the harder alloy of bronze was created. Illus. 2 shows a bronze saw used by the Egyptians from approximately 3200 to 500 BC. It is interesting to note that these saws were used on the pull stroke like the present-day Japanese saws.

The first iron saws emerged on the scene approximately 1400 BC. The greater durability of iron added to tooth strength and longevity. Iron was also stronger in thin sections, which allowed for a narrower kerf or saw cut.

The bow saw was first used in approximately

Illus. 2. An Egyptian using a bronze saw about 3200 BC.

900 BC. This is a saw in which a narrow blade is held taut in a bow-shaped frame. At about the same time teeth were set, which allowed curves to be sawed with narrow blades. By 100 AD the "buck saw," which used a tension rope, was in

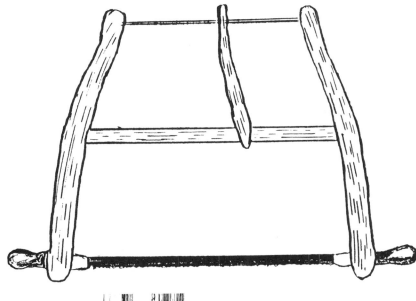

Illus. 3. A Roman buck saw from about 100 AD. The basic design has not changed since then, although the blade has been greatly improved.

Illus. 4. A drawing of a water-powered saw mill. A dam was used to capture the water and sometimes to float the logs. (Drawing courtesy of International Marine Publishing Company, Camden, Maine 04843)

common use throughout the Roman Empire. (See Illus. 3.) The basic design of the buck saw has changed very little since then.

Despite the fact that water-powered grist mills were used throughout the Roman Empire, no known attempt was made to use water power as a source for sawing wood. The first attempt at a water-powered saw was tried in Germany in the 4th century. This attempt was unsuccessful be-cause the blades used then dulled so quickly. For the next thousand years, logs continued to be cut with the tedious pit saw.

By the 14th century, the art of blade making had developed to the point that water power was now practical. During the 15th century, water-powered mills became common throughout Europe. By the 16th century, the Dutch had developed wind-powered mills.

The New World, which was chronically short of skilled labor, was quick to use powered devices whenever possible. Water-powered saw mills were in use in colonial Virginia by 1640. Water power became so important in the New World that finding a suitable mill site was often the first criteria in starting a new settlement. (See Illus. 4.)

There was much experimentation with the processing of raw materials before and during the Industrial Revolution. Sawing wood was a basic need, and much attention was given to developing new methods and techniques. Towards the end of the 18th and beginning of the 19th centuries, the circular saw was developed simultaneously in England and the United States. (One of the American inventors was a woman who belonged to the Shaker community.) The circular saw with its rotating blade was quickly put into use. The power could be easily transmitted through a simple drive belt. This made it easy to use with various drive sources, including the steam engine.

Most of the early power-driven saws consisted of a relatively narrow blade held in a frame. The frame was powered to go up and down, and to cut on the downstroke. In 1808, William Newberry of England patented the first "band saw," as he called it. (See Illus. 5.) The blade was attached at the two ends, creating a loop or circle. The looped blade was suspended over two rotat-ing wheels. As the wheels rotated, the toothed band or blade also rotated, creating a continuous sawing action.

Newberry's band saw was similar to the band saw used today. All of the principles and parts were workable. The only real problem with it was the blade. Blade development was still too primitive to make a workable band saw blade. Plagued by blade breakage and unsatisfactory welding methods, the earliest band saw was impractical.

In 1846, a French woman, Mlle. Crepin, perfected and patented a method of brazing band saw blade ends. At about the same time as the welding breakthrough, steel makers also made another important contribution. They developed a technique for rolling spring steel. These two advances made band-saw blades more dependable and practical to manufacture.

The band saw continued to be improved after better blades were developed. Illus. 6 shows a patent drawing for a French band saw circa 1855. By 1860, the band saw was developed to the point where it was practical for everyday use. It continued to be developed throughout the last half of the 19th century. Illus. 7 shows a three-wheel band saw circa 1888. Giant band saws were developed for use as sawmills. The narrow kerf made the band saw mill less wasteful than circular saw mills. (See Illus. 8.)

By the turn of the century, the band saw had

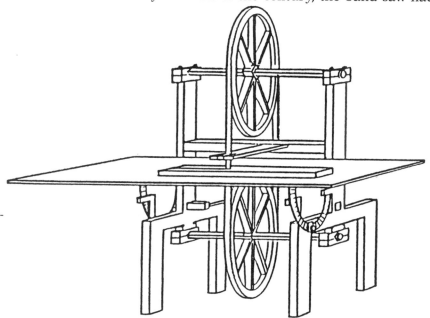

Illus. 5. Patent drawing of the first band saw designed by William Newberry of England in 1808.

become an integral part of the woodworking industry. Initially, the tool was developed for industrial use. After the turn of the century, smaller, less expensive, models became available. These were used by small professional shops and contractors. Although gingerbread decoration on houses was not as popular as it had been earlier, there were still multiple uses for the band saw in house building. The consumer market developed quickly as serious amateurs realized the efficiency of the band saw.

In the following chapters, you'll discover the many woodworking applications the band saw can be used for. It is its versatility that has helped make it one of the most indispensable tools used in the home workshop today.

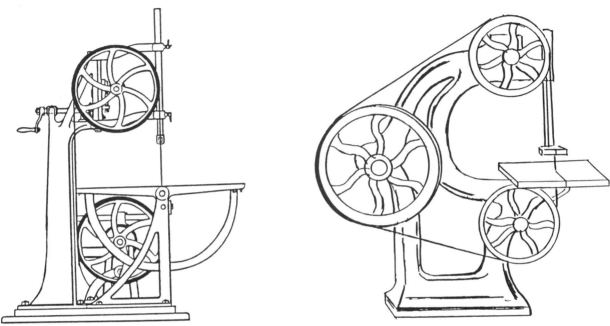

Illus. 6 (above left). Patent drawing for a French band saw made in 1855. Band-saw development continued in France after a French woman perfected the technique for brazing blades. Illus. 7 (above right). One of the first three-wheel band saws circa 1888.

HENRY DISSTON & SONS, INC.

LEFT-HAND

BAND SAW MILL

CUT NO. 1.

Illus. 8. Disston was the largest saw maker in the world at the turn of the century. It made large circular and band-saw mills in both right-hand and left-hand models.

2
Basic Information

Band-Saw Parts and Characteristics

It is important that you familiarize yourself with the parts of the band saw and how they function. (See Illus. 9.) Each manufacturer and each section of the country uses different terms for band saw parts. What follows are the generally accepted terms, which are those that will be used throughout this book.

Wheels

The blade is suspended over the two wheels. As the wheels rotate, the toothed blade also rotates, creating the downward cutting action. The wheels are usually covered with a piece of rubber called a tire. The tire cushions the blade and protects the teeth from contact with the metal wheel. (See Illus. 10.)

The bottom wheel is the drive wheel. It is attached to the power source either directly or through a belt. The bottom wheel powers the

Illus. 9. Shown are the parts of the band saw and the generally accepted terms used to describe them. The parts are called by different names. For example, the column is often called a post.

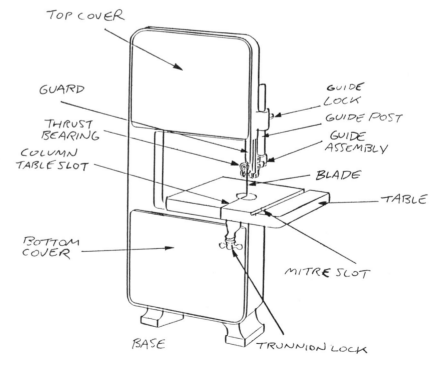

BAND SAW TERMINOLOGY

TOP COVER

GUARD

THRUST BEARING

COLUMN

TABLE SLOT

BOTTOM COVER

GUIDE LOCK

GUIDE POST

GUIDE ASSEMBLY

BLADE

TABLE

MITRE SLOT

BASE

TRUNNION LOCK

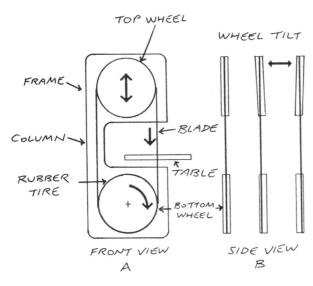

Illus. 10. The top wheel has two functions. It is used to tension and to balance or "track" the blade. Tracking is done by tilting the top wheel, as shown in B.

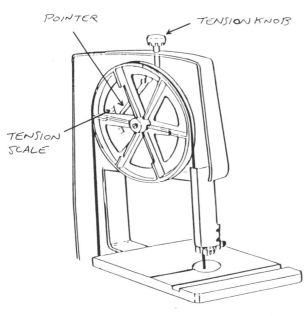

Illus. 11. The tension knob raises the top wheel to tension the blade. As the tension is increased, the pointer gives a reading on the tension scale.

blade and pulls it downwards through the workpiece. The top wheel has two functions, and is adjustable for each one. One function is balancing or tracking the blade on the wheels. The top wheel has an adjustable tilt mechanism that is used to balance the blade. (See Illus. 10B.) The other function is to tension the blade. The wheel moves up and down. Upward adjustment tensions the blade. Illus. 11 shows the tension knob that raises the top wheel to tension the blade. As the blade is tensioned, the pointer gives a reading on the tension scale.

Frame

The wheels, table, top and bottom guide assemblies, and most of the other important parts attach to the frame. There are various styles of frames, and each manufacturer makes its frame differently.

Frames are either one-piece castings or of the skeletal type. One-piece castings are one large casting that provides both the main framework and cover for the back of the wheels. (See Illus. 12A.) Skeletal frames are simply frameworks that are either cast or welded. (See Illus. 12B.) A separate piece of sheet metal is attached to the frame to safely cover the back of the saw. (See Illus. 12C.) This protective cover is called a wheel housing.

Illus. 13 shows a modern Sears band saw with a one-piece casting. The ribs in the casting are for strength. Illus. 14 shows a 14-inch Delta band saw that has a skeletal framework and wheel covers. Band saws made years ago had a skeletal framework that didn't have wheel housings; the wheels were left exposed. You can make wheel housings out of plywood if you have an old saw that didn't come with any protection.

The frame of the metal-cutting band saw is designed to be very rigid. The metal-cutting blades require extremely high tension to cut efficiently. For this reason, the column is quite thick; it allows absolutely no deflection of the frame under high tension. (See Illus. 15.) High-quality metal-cutting band saws are often made of a huge one-piece casting that ensures rigidity. The frame on smaller wood-cutting band saws is sometimes cast in two pieces and then bolted together. (See Illus. 16.)

Cover

Covers protect the operator from the wheels and the blade. If the blade breaks, the pieces of blade are contained by the covers. The covers are either of one or two pieces. Some are hinged

Illus. 12. Band-saw frames are either one-piece castings or skeletal framework that is either cast or welded.

ONE PIECE CASTING

SKELETAL FRAME

WHEEL COVERS

a.

b.

c.

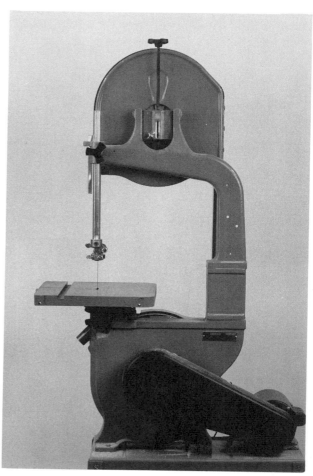

Illus. 13 (above left). Many band saws are now made with one-piece castings. Shown here is the inside of the Sears band saw. Illus. 14 (above right). This Delta 14-inch band saw has a cast-iron frame with wheel covers attached for safety. A similar design is used on the Taiwanese saws.

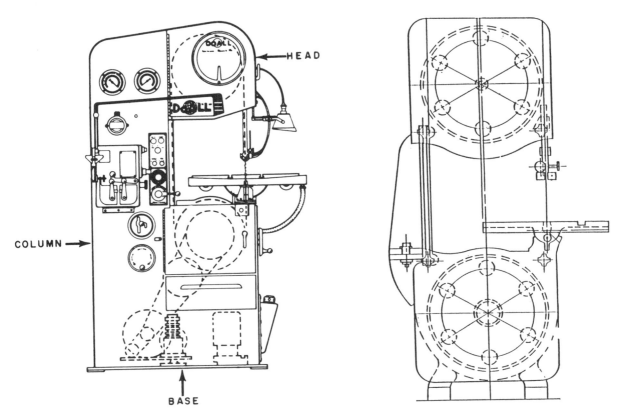

Illus. 15 (above left). A drawing of a metal-cutting band saw. The massive column guarantees absolute rigidity under high tension. (Drawing courtesy of Doall) Illus. 16 (above right). A drawing of a band saw with a two-piece casting. The head and the base are made of two separate castings and are bolted together at the base of the column.

Illus. 17. Hinged covers allow for easy access to the inside of the band saw. Shown here is a band saw with a two-piece hinged cover. (Photo courtesy of Delta)

(Illus. 17); some are attached with knobs or clips. The two most common materials used for covers are plastic and metal. Plastic is quieter and less susceptible to vibration.

Size

Band-saw size is measured by the width of the throat, which is the distance between the blade and the column or post. (See Illus. 18.) This measurement is slightly less than the wheel diameter on two-wheel band saws. A two-wheel band saw with 16-inch wheels will have a throat width or size of about 15½ inches. This is because about half an inch is taken up by the guard on the column side of the saw. In the past, band-saw size was determined by wheel size, and this means of classification is sometimes still used today.

Band-saw manufacturers have recently begun to make more three-wheel models. Three wheelers were designed to increase the throat width, which is very useful in some instances. Early three-wheel models had a reputation for short blade life because of the very small wheels that were used. The newer models, especially the larger saws, seem to be improved in this area.

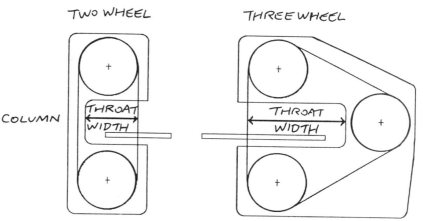

Illus. 18. The size of the band saw is determined by the width of its throat.

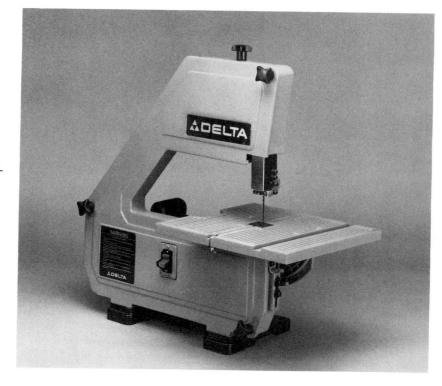

Illus. 19. Shown here is one of the popular small band saws now available. It has a three-wheel design that allows for a wide throat capacity.

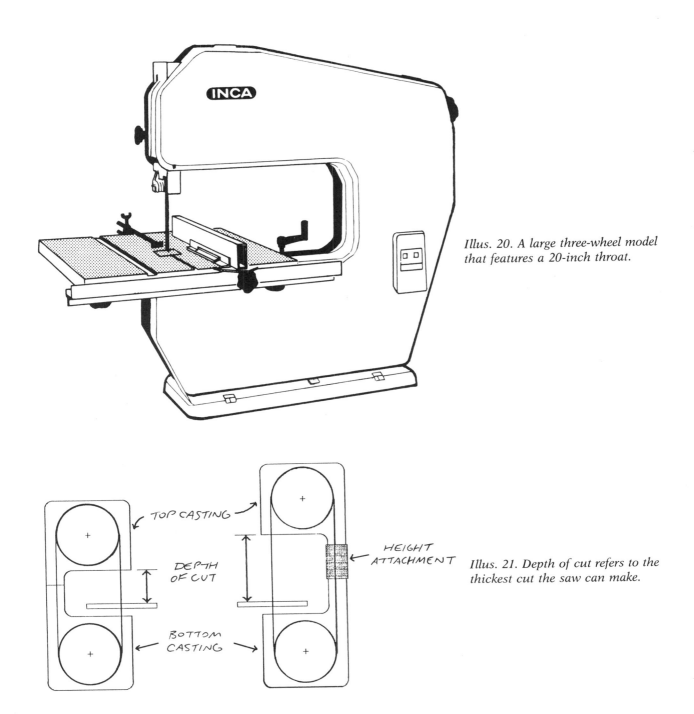

Illus. 20. A large three-wheel model that features a 20-inch throat.

Illus. 21. Depth of cut refers to the thickest cut the saw can make.

Yet, the blade life of a three wheeler may not be quite as long as a two wheeler. There is a tradeoff between blade life and throat width. (See Illus. 19 and 20.)

DEPTH OF CUT

Another way of determining band-saw size is to measure the "depth-of-cut" capacity of the saw.

This refers to the thickest cut the saw can make. This distance is usually about 6 inches on consumer-grade saws. (See Illus. 21.)

Height Attachment The height attachment is an accessory that increases the depth-of-cut capacity. Some band saws have a frame made of two castings. The height attachment bolts between these two castings and effectively raises the top casting. (See Illus. 21.) This helps to increase the depth of cut to either 10 or 12 inches. This extra height is useful for resawing.

The height attachment requires a longer blade. The power of the saw should be increased to 1½ horsepower to adequately resaw either 10 or 12 inches of hardwood. A speed-change mechanism, usually step pulleys, should be added to give a range of speeds for thick work. Increasing the depth of cut without increasing power and speed selection won't always give satisfactory results.

Table

The workpiece rests on the table as it is fed into the blade. The table surrounds the blade. A large hole in the middle of the table around the blade allows the operator to make adjustments below the table. This hole is covered by the throat plate. (See Illus. 22.) The throat plate is either plastic or metal. A plastic plate is quieter and won't cause any damage if the blade accidentally touches it. An alternative is to make your own out of wood or plastic. The plate should be level with the table. If it is too high, the work will catch on it. If it is too low, the work could get caught in the hole.

TABLE SLOT

A slot in the table allows the blade entry into the middle of the table. (See Illus. 23.) There is usually a mechanism to keep the two separated halves of the table in line with each other. It may be a bolt, pin, or a screw. Some manufacturers use the front rail. Make sure that you align the saw table halves. If you are negligent, you risk the chance of the two halves warping in opposite directions, causing an uneven table.

Illus. 22. The parts of a typical band-saw table.

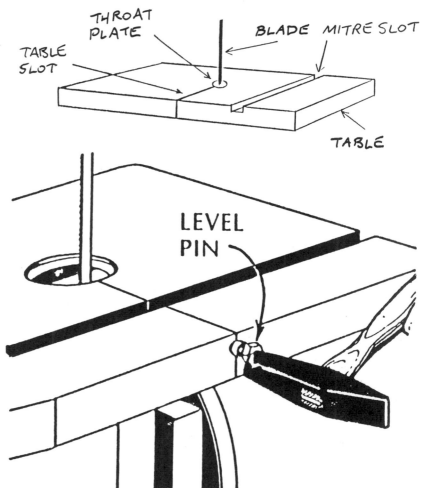

Illus. 23. Band saws have a mechanism for aligning the table on each side of the slot. Shown here is a level pin. The pin is gently tapped into the hole, forcing the two sides into proper alignment. To remove the pin, turn it with a wrench.

TABLE TILT

The table on a band saw is designed to tilt, which means that it can make bevelled or angled cuts. The table tilts away from the column up to 45 degrees. (See Illus. 24B.) On some models, it also tilts towards the column up to 10 degrees. (See Illus. 24C.) This added feature may be handy at times, but it is not a necessity. Underneath the table there is an adjustable bolt or screw to help level the table back to 90 degrees after the table has been tilted.

TRUNNIONS

The table is attached to two semicircular metal pieces called trunnions. (See Illus. 25.) The trunnion mates with another semicircular piece at-tached to the bottom of the table. This mechanism allows the table to angle. After the table is adjusted to the desired angle, it is locked in place with the trunnion lock. A scale and a pointer register the angle of tilt. The pointer and the levelling bolt should be adjusted for an accurate 90 degrees. The best way to do this is to use an accurate square. (See Illus. 26.)

MITRE GAUGE SLOT

Most saws have a mitre gauge slot. (See Illus. 26.) This slot runs parallel to the blade and accepts the mitre gauge bar, which is usually used for crosscutting. The mitre gauge slot is very useful for owner-built jigs. Many jigs are designed to

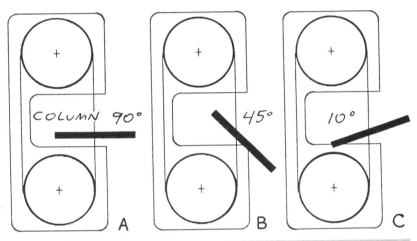

Illus. 24. The band-saw table tilts away from the column up to 45 degrees. On some saws, it also tilts towards the column up to 10 degrees.

Illus. 25. Shown here is the front trunnion on a Taiwanese band saw. The trunnion should be cleaned and lubricated often if the table is tilted frequently. Avoid grease as a lubricant because it traps sawdust. A lubricant such as Teflon works well.

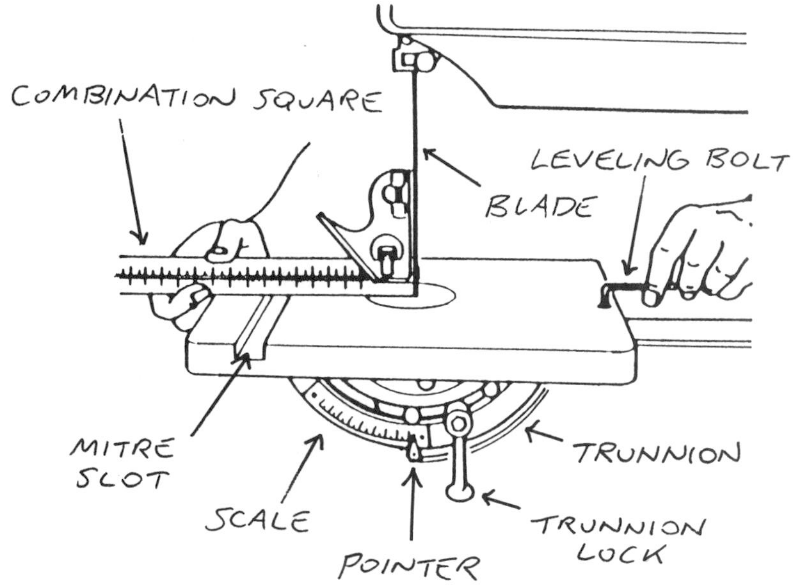

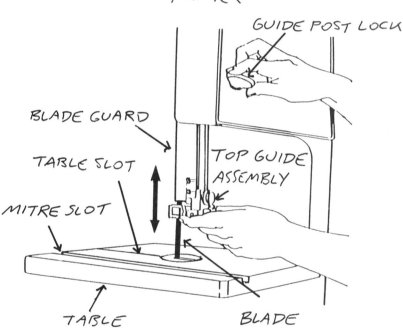

Illus. 26. The top and bottom of the band-saw table. The squareness of the blade and the table should be checked often.

Illus. 27. The upper guide assembly is adjustable up and down. The blade guard is attached to the front of the assembly. For safety and performance reasons, lock the assembly approximately ¼-inch above the workpiece.

operate parallel to the blade, and the mitre gauge slot provides the most logical path.

GUIDE ASSEMBLY

There are two guide assemblies, one below the table and one above the table. The top assembly is attached to a metal rod called the guide post. The whole upper guide assembly is adjustable up and down. (See Illus. 27.) The guide-post lock screw locks the post at the desired height. The blade guard is attached to the front of the guide post. To adequately protect the operator from

the blade, the bottom of the upper guide assembly should be positioned above the workpiece about ¼ inch. This position protects the operator and adequately supports the blade, which decreases the likelihood of undesirable blade flex.

Each guide assembly consists of two guide blocks that are located on each side of the blade. The blocks hold the side of the blade in position. Each assembly also houses the thrust bearing, which keeps the blade from being pushed rearward when the saw is cutting. (See Illus. 28.) The blade guard is attached to the blade assembly.

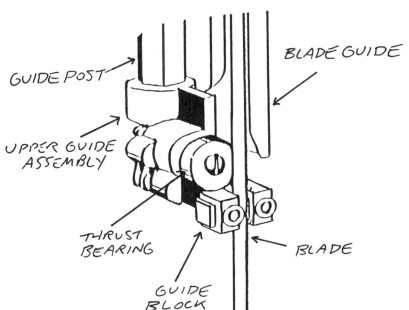

GUIDE POST

BLADE GUIDE

UPPER GUIDE ASSEMBLY

THRUST BEARING

BLADE

GUIDE BLOCK

Illus. 28. A closeup of the upper guide assembly.

Motor

Power is important. It is better to have power to spare than to be underpowered. Having enough power is especially important when cutting thick stock. Power is usually transferred from the motor to the band saw through a belt-and-pulley-system. Speed change is made possible with the use of a step pulley system. High-quality belts and pulleys should be used to lessen vibration.

Two European saws, the Inca and the Minimax models, use direct-drive motors. (See Illus. 29.) They both run very smoothly and are very quiet because the vibration of the belt and pulley is eliminated. They are also as powerful as band saws with a belt-and-pulley system.

The average consumer saw in this country comes with a ½ horsepower motor, which is barely adequate. It is worth the extra money to buy a more powerful motor if it is offered as an option. The better motors have ball bearings, which are more expensive than lower-quality sleeve bearings. TEFC (totally enclosed fan-cooled) motors will last longer in a dusty shop environment than a model with a ventilated housing.

Dust is very hard on motors. It is a good idea to blow the dust off a band-saw motor occasionally. This will help prevent the motor from overheating.

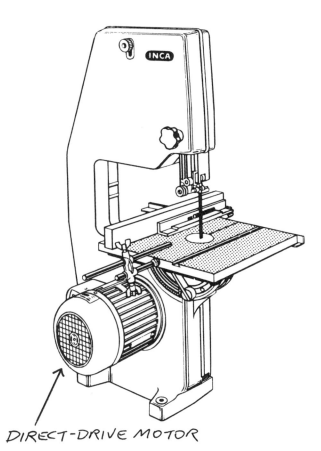

DIRECT-DRIVE MOTOR

Illus. 29. On some saws, the motor is attached directly to the saw. This eliminates the belt-and-pulley mechanism and helps to make the saw portable.

Speed

Band-saw speed is determined by how many feet the blade travels in one minute. This is termed *feet per minute*. The average band saw runs between 2,600 and 3,100 feet per minute and is adequate for most woodworking operations. Some large industrial saws cut at speeds of up to 5,000 FPM. Thick stock is usually cut better at faster speeds because the sawdust is cleared more efficiently.

The rate at which the wood is fed into the blade by the operator must correlate with the speed of the blade. The faster the blade travels, the faster the wood is cut and the sawdust is cleared. Do not feed the wood more quickly than it can be cut with the blade.

It is very important to match the blade, material, and the speed when cutting any material. This may take some experimentation. When a band saw is used to cut metal, the FPM is between 40 and 400, depending on the type of

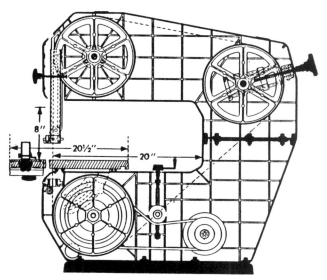

Illus. 31. On some saws the bottom wheel is a giant step pulley. An idler wheel is used to tension the belt.

metal and the blade. This is a relatively slow speed. Some band saws called Wood and Metal band saws have a speed range of 40 to 3,000 FPM. Some manufacturers such as Sears sell a converter to lower the speed for metal cutting on band saws that do not have this kind of range. You can change the speeds on most saws by changing the belt on step pulleys. (See Illus. 30.)

Be extremely careful when cutting metal. The sparks can ignite the sawdust inside the machine.

Switch

You can turn the band-saw motor on and off with a switch. On some models, the switch is attached to the saw. On other models, it is on the stand. There are safety devices designed on some switches. The Sears band saw, for example, has a removable plastic key. (See Illus. 32.) Unauthorized use of the saw cannot take place unless the plastic key is used. If children may be tempted to turn on the band saw, make sure that you use some kind of a protection. A locked electrical panel box protects the entire shop.

Band-Saw Styles

There are three basic styles of band saws. Large industrial saws—called floor models—have big

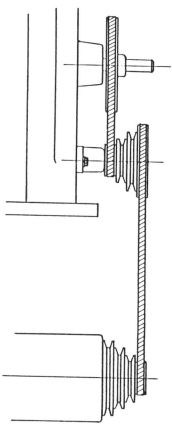

Illus. 30. A step-pulley system is the usual means of changing the speed of the blade.

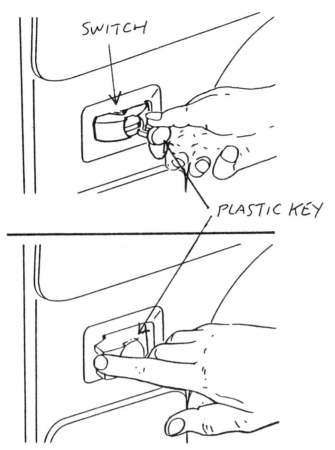

Illus. 32. This switch—which is used on a number of Sears tools—functions as a safety device. It will not operate until the plastic key is in place.

wheels that are contained in a large cabinet. These cabinets rest directly on the floor. (See Illus. 33A.) Stand-Mounted saws are bench-style saws that are mounted on their own wood or metal stands. (See Illus. 33B.) The stand is separate from the machine and usually contains the motor and drive belt. Bench-top saws rest on top of a table. (See Illus. 33C.) They have the advantage of being compact. Some bench-top models are designed to be portable.

Left- and Right-Hand Saws

Band saws are termed either right hand or left hand. (See Illus. 34.) These terms refer to the orientation of the table and wheels, and have nothing to do with the operator being either right-handed or left-handed. If you are making straight cuts and you are right-handed, you may prefer to have the rip fence on the right side of the blade. This is the usual procedure on the table saw. You can do this on either type of band saw, but it is more convenient on the "left-hand" model. The left or right orientation doesn't make a great deal of difference because you can get use to the saw either way.

Band-Saw Design Variations

Newberry's simple idea of using a continuous narrow steel band as a cutting device was a good one. Today, it is used in various forms to cut everything from tomatoes to huge pieces of hardened steel. Thus far, I have discussed the "scroll-type" band saw. The following is information on other variations of Newberry's ingenious idea.

Metal-Cutting Saws

There are two general types of band saws; vertical and horizontal. Each term is self explanatory. (See Illus. 35.) Horizontal saws are used for metal cutting and are known as "cutoff" saws. (See Illus. 36.) The blade is twisted by the saw guides so that a workpiece of any length can be cut off. The wheels are mounted horizontally and are usually angled at 45 degrees. They usually are flanged. A flange is a flat metal rim opposite the teeth that supports the back of the blade under the heavy feed pressure common with metal cutting. The blade width on flanged wheels is fixed, not optional. The blade is wide enough to be well-supported by the wheel with the teeth just barely off the wheel.

Some of the inexpensive horizontal saws are hinged, and can thus be converted to a vertical mode. (See Illus. 37.) When they are used in the vertical position, a small auxiliary table is used to support the workpiece. These saws have become quite popular because they are versatile and fairly inexpensive.

Metal-cutting saws are also classified as horizontal or vertical. They can only be used in either a vertical or horizontal mode. Vertical saws are used for either straight or curved cuts and are called contour saws. (See Illus. 38.) Horizontal saws are used strictly for cutoff work. Some are adjustable for cutting angles; these are called angle saws. (See Illus. 39.) Both styles, especially the horizontal saws, often have pumps and a collection pan for reusing the cutting fluid that is often used in metal cutting.

There are hand-held portable band saws, designed for cutoff work on construction sites. (See Illus. 40.) These saws are small enough to carry and to work with comfortably, and are used mostly for metal cutting. Some have an optional stand, so the front of the saw is hinged.

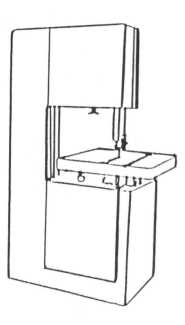

FLOOR MODEL
A

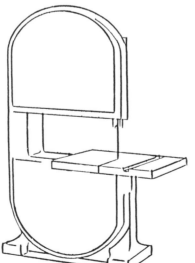

STAND MOUNTED
B

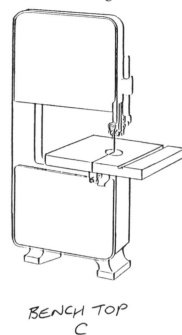

BENCH TOP
C

Illus. 33. Three basic styles of band saws.

LEFT- RIGHT ORIENTATION

Illus. 34. Band saws are described as either right-hand or left-hand.

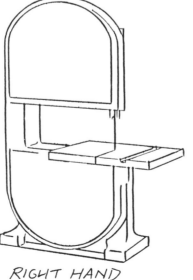

RIGHT HAND

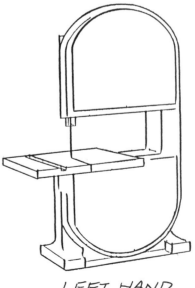

LEFT HAND

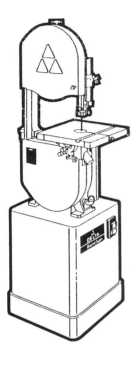

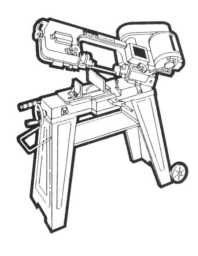

Illus. 35. Vertical band saws are used to make straight or curved cuts. Horizontal band saws only make straight cuts and are often used to cut long pieces to length.

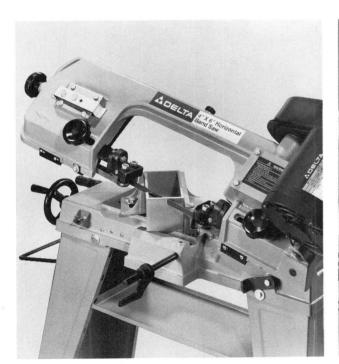

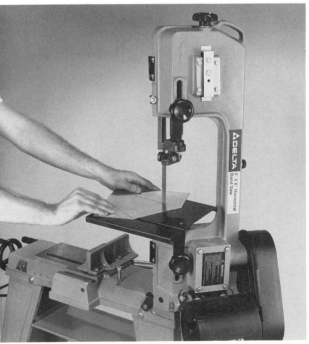

Illus. 36 (above left). On a horizontal band saw, the blade moves rather than the workpiece. A vise is used to hold the work secure. Illus. 37 (above right). On some of the smaller horizontal saws there is a design option that allows the operator to use the saw in the vertical position. A small auxiliary table is used to support the work.

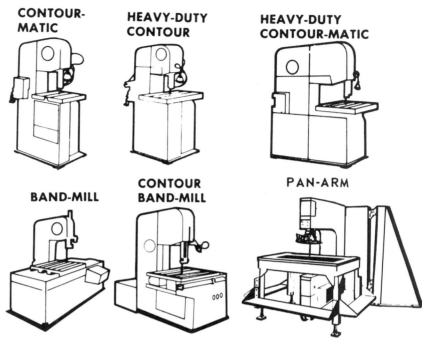

CONTOUR-MATIC **HEAVY-DUTY CONTOUR** **HEAVY-DUTY CONTOUR-MATIC**

BAND-MILL **CONTOUR BAND-MILL** **PAN-ARM**

Illus. 38. Professional vertical band saws are made in a variety of designs. Shown here are some of the designs made by Doall.

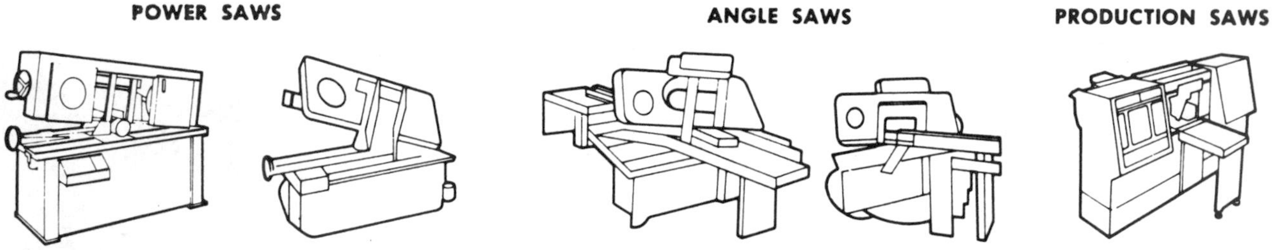

POWER SAWS **ANGLE SAWS** **PRODUCTION SAWS**

Illus. 39. Professional horizontal metal-cutting saws are large and heavy. Both horizontal and vertical saws have pumps for circulating cutting fluids, which are often used for metal cutting.

Illus. 40. A hand-held portable band saw.

Production Saws

Production saws are very large and expensive saws that are used for production. The horizontal production saw is similar to the other horizontal saws, but it is more sophisticated. The vertical production saw is unique. The blade is twisted like the horizontal saw so that the blade is 90 degrees from its natural position. The saw is mounted on a carriage that allows it to move forward into the work somewhat like a radial arm saw. (See Illus. 41.)

Band-Saw Mills

VERTICAL BAND-SAW MILLS

Vertical band-saw mills are now widely used throughout North America. The band mill has replaced circular mills because the thinner blade wastes less wood and requires less horsepower. The wheels are between 5 and 12 feet in diameter, and the bottom wheel is often placed below ground level. This allows the log and the carriage that holds the log to be at ground level. The carriage runs past the saw on a track similar to a small railroad track. (See Illus. 42.) After each cut, the top section of the carriage and the log are moved closer to the saw for the next cut. Some blades have teeth on both sides, and the cut is made with both the forward and rearward carriage movements.

Illus. 43 shows a vertical mill at Johnson's Lumber in Charlotte, Michigan. The bottom wheel is below ground level. Illus. 44 shows the carriage and log during the cut; they are in a different position from that shown in Illus. 43. Illus. 45 shows the blades used on the vertical mill. They are 11 inches wide when they are new, and are reground until they are 7 inches wide. Each new blade is extremely expensive. These blades have teeth on both sides; the tooth opposite the cutting tooth is called a "sliver tooth." It is used to cut any slivers that could dislodge the blade as the carriage and log return.

Illus. 41. The vertical production band saw has a blade that is twisted at 90 degrees. It cuts as it moves forward, similar to the way a radial arm saw blade cuts.

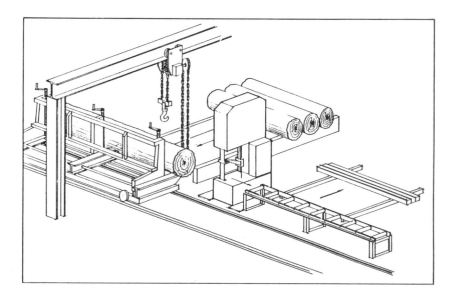

Illus. 42. The layout of a typical band-saw mill. The carriage which holds the log moves on small track that's similar to railroad track.

Illus. 43 (above left). The six-foot band-saw mill at Johnson's Lumber Company, in Charlotte, Michigan. Illus. 44 (above right). The band-saw mill making its initial cuts. The log will be rotated between cuts until it is square; then the rest of the cutting will be completed.

Illus. 45. The person in the middle of the photograph gives scale to the size of the blade. Mills like those in Johnson's Lumber Company have one person who works fulltime taking care of the blades.

HORIZONTAL BAND-SAW MILLS

Horizontal band-saw mills are popular in England and on the Continent. The British manufacturer Forrestor exports many large mills to Third World countries. The largest Forrestor mill will cut a log five feet in diameter. It runs on a track similar to a small railroad track. The log lies on the ground and the saw moves, thus eliminating the expensive carriage. (See Illus 46.) The logs are cut "through and through" and dried in a stickered pile that keeps them together. (See Illus. 47.) In Europe whole trees are sold intact, assuring the buyer that the grain will match. Illus. 48 shows the band saw cut-pattern perpendicular to the edge of the tree.

Portable, Horizontal Band-Saw Mills American manufacturers have started making smaller horizontal band-saw mills. These saws are large enough to do heavy-duty work, yet are small enough to be portable. The average saw mill will cut about 1,000 board feet of lumber in one day. These mills now range from small portable ones to those with built-in trailers with hydraulics for lifting rotating logs.

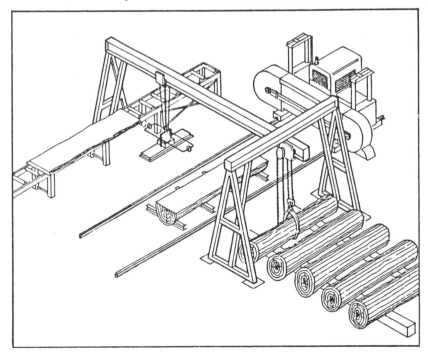

Illus. 46. The horizontal mill runs on a small track. The mill moves, rather than the log. This is advantageous when cutting wide logs.

Illus. 47. Large horizontal mills make parallel cuts. The logs shown here have been cut and are being stickered to dry. This is how many exotic species are exported. The trees are sold as a whole unit.

Illus. 48. A band-saw mill cuts a line that's perpendicular to the edge of the board. Here is a closeup of the lumber shown in Illus. 47.

Illus. 49 shows my friend Tom Gabriel cutting an oak log with his Kasco mill. The saw runs on a track similar to that on the Forrestor model. The track is levelled at each new location. Tom can place his mill on a trailer and move it in about half an hour.

The Kasco is a basic band mill—it has only what is needed to perform the operation. This means that there is not a lot that can go wrong with it. The Kasco mill is powered by an 8-horse-power Briggs and Straton motor.

Portable band-saw mills have become very popular with cabin builders. You can process the logs with parallel cuts like those made on a log cabin or cut the logs into dimensional lumber.

The Kasko band-saw mill isn't the only saw on the market. Laskowski Enterprises of Indianapolis produces the Woodmizer band-saw mill,

which is made in three models. The Woodmizer saw features power feed and power return. The heavier-duty version has a 16 horsepower engine and can be expanded to 32 feet. A smaller 5 horsepower model is made by W. K. Ross of West Hampstead, New Hampshire. This 5-horsepower model can cut a log 17½ inches in diameter and 16 feet, 9 inches long. You can provide your own track if you wish. The sizes and specifications on these saws are subject to change, so it is best to send for the latest literature.

A newcomer to the band-saw scene is The Lumber Company, manufactured by Delta International. This band-saw mill is unique in that it is lightweight and "portable." It weighs about 165 pounds. Rather than a "track," the saw rides on the log. The first cut is made with a rail with metal brackets provided by Delta. (See Illus. 50.)

Illus. 50 (above left). The first cut with the Lumber Company band-saw mill is made with a straightedge framework. The straight edge guarantees a straight cut. The metal frame crossmembers are provided by Delta. Illus. 51 (above right). After the first cut, the saw rests on the log for the rest of the cuts. By resting the saw log on a smaller log, the operator can utilize gravity during the cut.

The rest of the cuts are made with the saw riding on the log. (See Illus. 51.) The saw can cut a thickness of ⅛ to 5 inches and handle log diameters up to 23 inches. A 1½-inch Stellite-tipped blade is used. The band saw is powered by a 5 horsepower gas motor. An optional stand converts it to the vertical position.

The latest entry into the portable band-saw market is the Ripsaw, which is made in Massachusetts. It is designed to be used by one person. It weighs 38 pounds and is available as either gas- or electric-powered. (See Illus. 52.) The electric motor is 2.3 horsepower. The gas motor is 2.4 horsepower and has two cycles.

Illus. 52. The Ripsaw weighs 38 pounds and is powered by a gas or electric motor. It rides along the top of the log.

Illus. 53. This chain saw with a lumber-making frame is being used to quarter-saw an elm log. The kerf is very wide because the cut releases tension in the log and each quarter warps outward. The chain saw wastes about ³⁄₈ inch of wood per cut.

Illus. 54. Here the Ripsaw is being used to "slab" the quarters, a technique that produces highly desirable quarter-sawn wood. The band saw does not waste nearly as much wood as the chain saw.

Illus. 55. The bevel band saw is also called the boat builder's band saw. Its tilting blade makes it easier to make the long-angle cuts needed in boat building. (Photo courtesy of Pat Spielman)

The Ripsaw makes cuts 9 inches high and 10 inches wide. This means that you can process a log that is 14 inches in diameter. It has a narrow kerf (.070 inch), so there is not a lot of wood wasted. It is a tool that would complement a large chain-saw with a lumber-making frame. Illus. 53 shows such a chain saw quartering a large log. The ripsaw is then used to process each quarter section of the log. (See Illus. 54.) The ripsaw cuts about as quickly as the chain saw, but only wastes about one sixth of the wood.

Bevel Band Saws

The bevel band saw is similar to a large band saw except for the table. The saw is unique because the table is stationary and the blade tilts to cut angles. (See Illus. 55.) It is similar to a tilting arbor table saw.

The bevel band saw has been used extensively in boatbuilding. It is used to make curved cuts on the large timbers used for shipbuilding and boatbuilding. Some models have a powered tilt mechanism that allows the cut angle to be changed slowly during the course of a long cut. Some models have powered rollers in the table to help move heavy workpieces. These models, however, are becoming rare.

The huge commercial bevel band saw has declined in popularity, as there are now far fewer large wooden boats being built. It is interesting to note, however, that the latest Sears model is a bevel-style band saw.

Resaws

Resawing is the process of ripping a board on edge into two pieces. The band-saw mill is used to cut logs into large pieces that are later resawed into smaller pieces. The term resaw usually refers to the center resaw. (See Illus. 56.) The band saw used for this operation is a large, vertical single-purpose saw. It usually has wheels 3 to 4 feet in diameter and uses a 3- to 5-inch blade. (See Illus. 57.) On large resaws, the bottom wheels may be partially buried in the ground. These saws often have an adjustable power-fed mechanism, usually two rotating rollers on each side of the blade. Smaller versions by Hitachi and Ryobi have blades 3 inches wide. (See Illus. 58.)

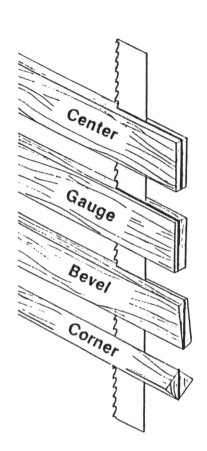

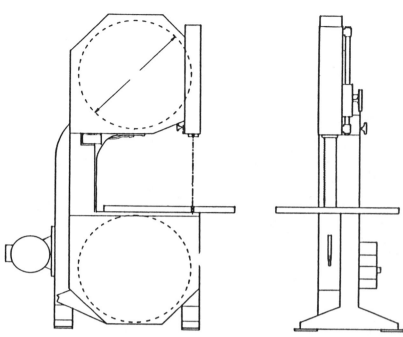

Illus. 56 (left). Most resawing is done in the center of the board. Bevel sawing is used to make siding. Gauge and corner sawing are used for special applications. Illus. 57 (above). Commercial resaw band saws have wheels 3 to 4 feet in diameter, and blades 3 to 5 inches wide.

Illus. 58. The Ryobi resaw band saw is a smaller version of the commercial models. It takes a 3-inch blade.

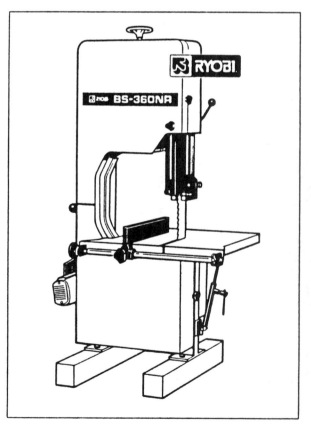

ALL ABOUT BLADES

3

Blade Basics

The band saw is named after the type of blade that is used on the saw. The blade is a continuous metal band. (See Illus. 59.) The ends of the band are joined at the "weld." Teeth are formed on one side of the band, which is suspended around the wheel. As the wheel rotates, the blade also rotates and provides the cutting mechanism. This allows for efficient continuous cutting. (See Illus. 60.)

The blade is narrow enough so that the work can be rotated around it. The ability to turn the work around the blade is called unrestricted machine geometry. (See Illus. 61.) The blade can be

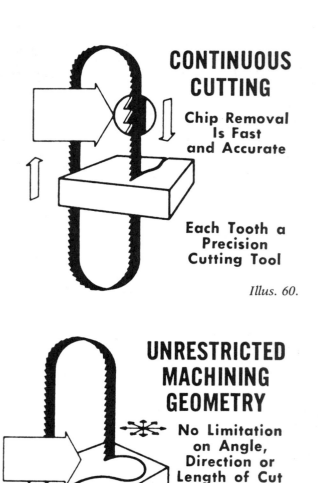

CONTINUOUS CUTTING

Chip Removal Is Fast and Accurate

Each Tooth a Precision Cutting Tool

Illus. 60.

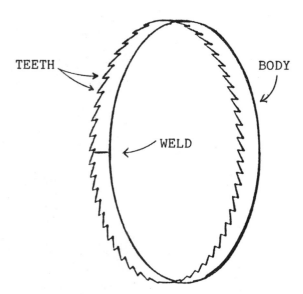

TEETH

BODY

WELD

Illus. 59. The band saw is named after the band blade. The band ends are joined at the weld. The endless loop is a continuous cutting tool.

UNRESTRICTED MACHINING GEOMETRY

No Limitation on Angle, Direction or Length of Cut

Built-in Tool Holder

Illus. 61.

used for straight or curved cuts, which makes the band saw the most flexible of cutting tools.

The band-saw blade is easy to use and safe. The downward cutting action of the blade holds the material securely on the table. The workpiece cannot bind and be "kicked back" at the operator, as occurs when a circular saw blade is used. (See Illus. 62.)

SIMPLE FIXTURING

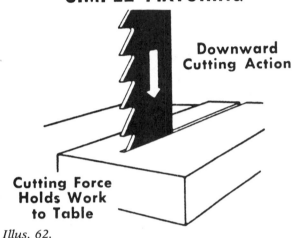

Illus. 62.

Because the blade is narrow, it requires less power. A well-tuned consumer-grade band saw can easily saw 6-inch-thick wood. There is also less material waste. (See Illus. 63.) You can easily follow the cut line, and remove whole sections at a time. (See Illus. 64.)

LESS HORSEPOWER

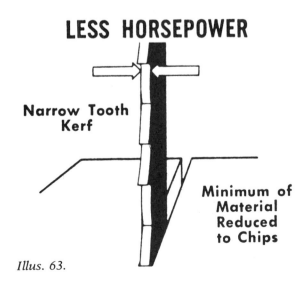

Illus. 63.

LEAST MATERIAL WASTE

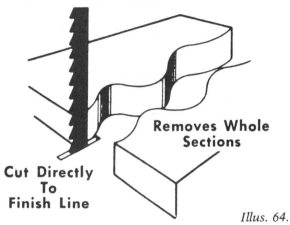

Illus. 64.

A band-saw blade must flex around the wheel, yet remain perfectly straight in the cut. It must be strong enough to tolerate the tension required to achieve these two requirements without breaking. The teeth must be hard enough to cut, and the body flexible enough to twist slightly when cutting tight curves. The blade must do all of this at 30 miles per hour.

Band-saw blades are now made in over 500 different variations. New blades are constantly being developed in order to efficiently cut modern high-tech materials. The band saw is very adaptable. It is capable of an incredible array of cuts when a variety of jigs and fixtures are used. It is used in industrial settings to cut a large number of materials. (See Illus. 65.) With attachments, the band machine can file, sand, or polish.

The band saw is often perceived as a tool that cuts less accurately than table or radial arm saws. Yet, band saws are used in industry to cut large pieces of hardened materials very accurately. The band saw can cut very accurately, but only if the saw is accurately aligned, which is also true of the table and radial arm saws. In fact, a well-tuned band saw is often preferred for cutting joinery that has to be precisely made.

If woodworkers believe that the band saw cannot cut accurately, it is only because they have not taken the time to make it cut accurately. Following is blade information that is essential in ensuring that the band saw cut as efficiently and accurately as possible.

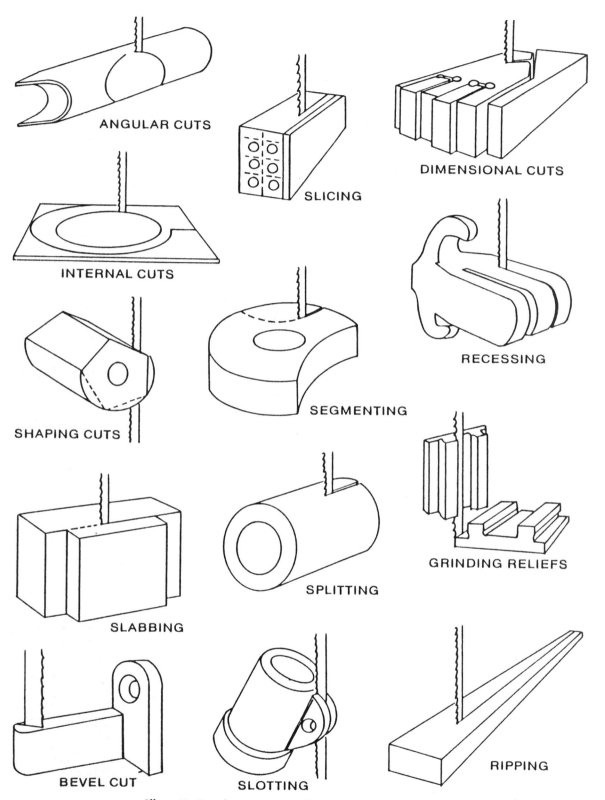

ANGULAR CUTS

SLICING

DIMENSIONAL CUTS

INTERNAL CUTS

RECESSING

SHAPING CUTS

SEGMENTING

SLABBING

SPLITTING

GRINDING RELIEFS

BEVEL CUT

SLOTTING

RIPPING

Illus. 65. Band saws are used in industrial settings for a variety of applications that have to be precise.

Terminology

To use the band saw correctly, it is important that you select the best blade for a particular application. Blades are selected by metal type, width, thickness, set, pitch, tooth form, and length. Changing one factor can greatly alter the cutting characteristics of the blade.

It is important that you understand clearly what different band-saw terms mean. Manufacturers, tradesmen, engineers, and craftspeople don't always use the same terminology. For example, blade thickness is now defined by the actual thickness of the blade. A blade that is .025 inch thick is called "twenty-five thousandths." In the past, blades were sized by a "gauge" system similar to how sheet metal is still sized, and today the terms gauge and thickness are often used interchangeably. The gauge number used, however, isn't the same as the actual thickness of the blade. Some older woodworkers still refer to the gauge system; consequently, younger people don't know what they are talking about.

To standardize our vocabulary, the following terms will be used throughout the book:

BODY—The band material without the teeth. It is pliable enough to tolerate the constant flexing cycle.

TEETH—The teeth do the cutting. On some blades, the teeth are hardened. Some teeth are made of a harder material than the blade.

GULLET—The space between the teeth that holds the sawdust during the cutting process.

BACK—The back of the blade contacts the thrust bearing during the sawing process. On some saws, the back of the blade is hardened for cutting metal, which requires heavy-feed pressure.

PITCH—A term used to describe how many teeth there are per inch of blade. It is usually referred to as Teeth per inch (TPI).

TOOTH SPACING—Refers to how far apart the teeth are. "Fine" refers to many teeth. "Coarse" refers to few teeth.

KERF—Width of the saw cut.

WIDTH—The distance from the front to the back of the blade. The wider the blade, the greater the beam strength. Beam strength is a term used to describe resistance to deflection.

SET—Bend of the teeth. Set is measured at the widest point. The more set, the wider the kerf.

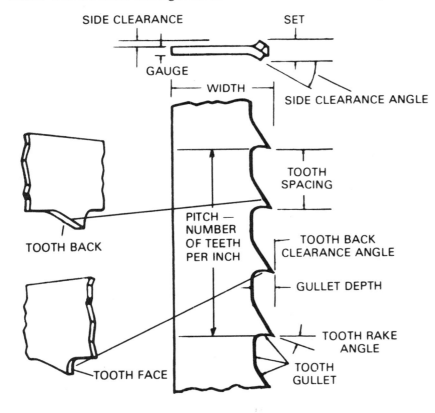

Illus. 66. Blade terminology.

With the teeth set, the blade cuts a kerf wider than the body of the blade.

GAUGE—A term that refers to the thickness of the band.

SIDE CLEARANCE—The difference between the body of the blade and the kerf. It is determined by the amount of blade set. It prevents binding in the kerf and allows the workpiece to be rotated around the blade, creating a curve.

GULLET DEPTH—The distance from the point of the tooth to the back of the gullet. The greater the depth, the greater the gullet's capacity to hold sawdust.

BODY WIDTH—The blade width minus the gullet width. It is the functional width of the blade and determines the beam strength.

GULLET CORNER—The corner of the gullet. The sharper the corner, the greater the likelihood of premature breakage. Gullet corners are usually rounded for this reason. Blades usually break at the gullet corner.

TOOTH POINT—The point of the tooth is the cutting or scraping edge. It does the most work and suffers the most wear during the sawing process.

RAKE ANGLE—The angle of the tooth face in relationship to the tooth back.

All these factors will be thoroughly explored in the sections that follow.

Saw Teeth

There are two major categories of saw teeth. One type was developed for crosscutting, the other for ripping. Crosscut teeth cut with their outside edges or tip. Rip saw teeth cut with their whole point.

Band-saw teeth are similar to saw teeth used for ripping. This tooth style is efficient, particularly at the high speed of the band-saw blade. The shape of the tooth is good for cutting thick stock without binding. If a smooth cut is desired, smaller teeth (more teeth per inch) and a slower feed rate can be used. This is especially true for crosscutting. By choosing the right band-saw blade for the material, you can get a variety of desired effects: speed, smoothness, accuracy, etc.

It takes skill and the right touch to operate the band saw. It is especially important to be able to feel when the saw is cutting at maximum capacity. Increased feed pressure at this point doesn't increase efficiency; it can actually have negative effects, such as slowing or actually stopping the machine. One thing to consider when the tooth is cutting and filling the gullet completely is that the tooth cannot cut any faster because the gullet cannot carry the sawdust away any faster. It must be remembered that sawdust takes up roughly four times as much space as solid wood.

Ideally, each tooth should be exposed to the material at a smooth, even rate. The tooth will start to cut at the top of the material and continue to the bottom, removing its share of the waste. Each tooth should still have some room in the gullet at the end of the cut. That means that the saw should not be cutting at maximum capacity, which would completely fill each tooth gullet. (See Illus. 67.)

When you feed too much material into the teeth, you often get vibration and chatter. This is particularly true with thick stock. If you completely fill the gullet, the saw momentarily stops cutting (though only for a micro second). When fresh teeth get their chance to bite into the material, they all bite at once; this creates a vibration or chatter. Some sawdust can escape rearward in between the teeth into the kerf, but it isn't enough to prevent chatter.

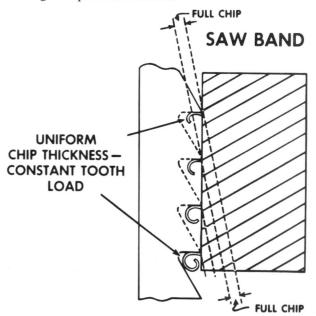

Illus. 67. Each tooth should be exposed to the material at a smooth rate. The tooth starts cutting at the top, and removes its share of the material.

The operator's goal should be to feed each tooth enough, but not too much. Ideally, each individual tooth must do an equal share of the work. This results in an effective cut.

Pitch

There are two systems for measuring pitch (tooth spacing): either in points per inch or teeth per inch (TPI). TPI is the more current means of measurement, and thus the one that will be used. The only difference between the two systems is that there is always one more point than tooth per inch. (See Illus. 68.)

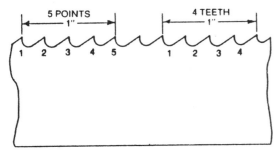

Illus. 68. Tooth pitch, or tooth spacing, is given in either points per inch or teeth per inch (TPI). TPI is more commonly used.

The size of the tooth determines the TPI. The smaller the tooth, the greater the TPI. The distance between teeth can be found by dividing the pitch or TPI into the number 1. For example, a 4 TPI blade has teeth spaced ¼ or .250-inch apart.

A blade with a regular (standard) tooth form is available in pitch from 4 to 32 TPI. Skip and hook blades which have fewer teeth than a blade with a regular tooth form, usually have a TPI of 1 to 8. (See Illus. 69.)

The TPI of a blade is usually associated with blade width, but not always. It is most common for wide blades to have fewer teeth and narrow blades to have more teeth. Wide blades are available with many teeth per inch, but this isn't usual. The word *coarse* is used to describe a blade with four teeth or fewer per inch. The word *fine* is used to describe a blade with more than 10 TPI. (See Illus. 70.)

The smoothness of the cut and the speed at which the material is cut is determined by the blade pitch. The coarser the blade, the faster but rougher the cut. The fewer the teeth engaged in the work, the higher the cutting efficiency. This is because the penetration capacity of each tooth is greater if the feed pressure is distributed over a fewer number of teeth. Simply put, each tooth is pushed harder into the stock.

A blade with a coarser pitch is more productive and also has a larger gullet, which allows space for the increased sawdust. This is especially important when ripping or resawing because cutting with the grain produces sawdust that has a lot of bulk. The large gullet of the tooth on a coarse blade has the capacity to hold more sawdust. The large tooth cuts fast with less friction, causing less heat. This is especially important when cutting thick stock.

It is important that the pitch is not too coarse because this can lead to premature dulling of teeth, especially when cutting hard material. Rather than getting a good bite, the tooth slides off the material. This causes the tooth to wear rather than cut efficiently. (See Illus. 71.)

Finer blades make a slower and smoother cut. Each tooth takes a smaller bite. This causes an increase in heat and friction and an increased probability of filling the gullet to capacity. Finer-pitched blades are often the best choice for crosscutting because they give a smoother finish. Crosscutting doesn't produce as much sawdust, and the sawdust that is produced is finer. The capacity of the smaller gullet isn't taxed as heavily when crosscutting.

When choosing blade pitch, you want to choose the right compromise between a coarse and fine blade. (See Illus. 72.) This depends on a

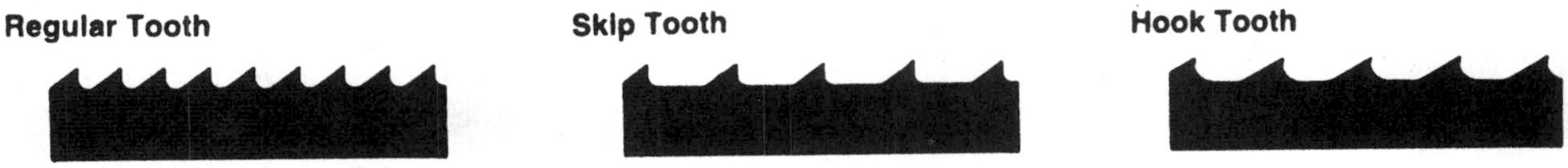

Regular Tooth   **Skip Tooth**   **Hook Tooth**

Illus. 69. A blade with a regular tooth pattern has more teeth than blades with other patterns. Blades with skip and hook teeth have less teeth because of the wide space between the teeth.

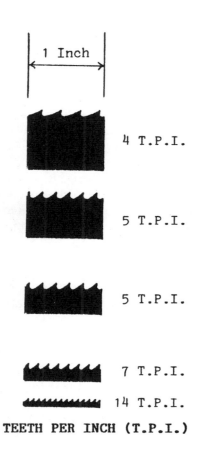

1 Inch

4 T.P.I.

5 T.P.I.

5 T.P.I.

7 T.P.I.

14 T.P.I.

TEETH PER INCH (T.P.I.)

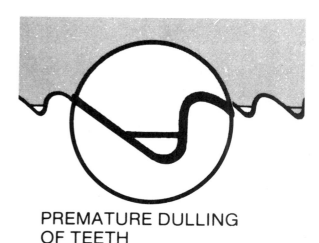

PREMATURE DULLING OF TEETH

Illus. 70 (left). It is common for wide blades to have fewer teeth than narrow blades, which often have many teeth (fine). Illus. 71 (above). If a blade has a pitch that is too coarse, the teeth will dull prematurely. The blade will slide off of the material rather than make an efficient cut.

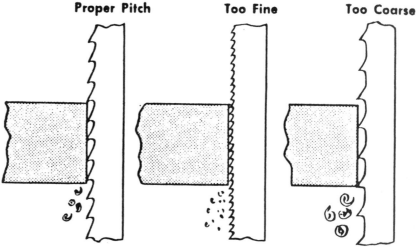

Proper Pitch   **Too Fine**   **Too Coarse**

Illus. 72. If you want to make the most efficient cut, make sure that you use a blade with the proper pitch.

number of factors, including the hardness, thickness and consistency of the material. Thin material requires a fine pitch, and thick material requires a coarse pitch.

Hard material requires a finer pitch than softer material, which is usually cut fairly easily with a coarse blade. (See Illus. 73.) If the material is thick and hard, the pitch should be finer than if the material is soft. The final finish of the material should be considered. The finer the pitch, usually the better the finish; this, however, is just a general rule. There are exceptions.

Blades of each width are made with a variety of pitches. This allows the user a choice of pitch and width in the same blade. A good example of this is the very useful ⅛-inch blade. Illus. 74

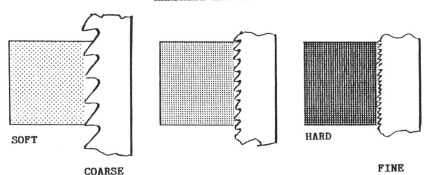

SOFT

COARSE

HARD

FINE

Illus. 73. Hard material requires a finer pitch than soft material.

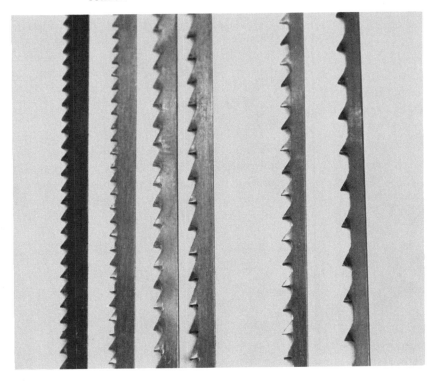

Illus. 74. A variety of tooth pitches are available for each blade width. The blades shown here are ⅛ inch wide. The blades on the left have regular teeth, and one on the right has skip teeth.

shows six different pitch choices for the ⅛-inch blade. Narrow blades usually have a finer pitch. Often, however, it is handy to have a narrow blade with coarse teeth. Wide tooth spacing on a narrow blade would require the whole width of the blade to form the teeth. The skip-tooth blade is useful here because its teeth are spaced far apart, yet the blade body is still strong. Skip-tooth blades would be good for thick work such as cutting a cabriole leg.

Choosing the Correct Pitch

For general-purpose sawing, the coarser saw blade is desirable. A blade with a TPI of 3 to 5 will give a satisfactory cut, but where a very smooth cut is required a TPI of 6 or 7 is better. At least three teeth should be in the stock being cut. For example, you would need a blade with at least 3 TPI to cut a piece of 1-inch thick lumber. Use a finer blade if you desire a smoother cut, but never a coarser one. If, for some reason it is necessary to use a fine blade to cut thick stock, be sure to feed the work into the blade very slowly. This allows enough time for all the sawdust to be ejected from the cut. (See Illus. 75.)

Each tooth should take an equal bite of the material. This helps make the cut smooth. If there are only one or two teeth touching the ma-

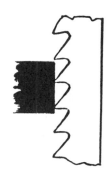

Illus. 75. A blade that has three to five teeth per inch in the stock will give a satisfactory cut. If it has more teeth per inch in the stock, it will give a smooth finish. At least three teeth per inch should be in the stock at all times during the cut.

terial, the blade chops through the material and makes a pounding cut. Rather than the teeth making a smooth transition in and out of the material, they tear their way through the cut. If the material is hard, like metal, it can actually hurt the tooth, or even worse, strip it off of the body. (See Illus. 76.) The next time the blade contacts the material, more teeth may be stripped off. (See Illus. 77.) The blade may also break or buckle.

Illus. 76. Here one tooth has been stripped off the blade body.

Illus. 77. If one tooth is stripped off, more teeth will be stripped as the saw continues to cut. Once tooth stripping begins, the blade is ruined.

Blade Set

Most saws are designed to cut a kerf (saw cut) wider then the saw blade. This is accomplished because the teeth used are bent or set so that the front of the blade is wider than the back. (See Illus. 78.) The difference between the body of the blade and the kerf is called side clearance. (See Illus. 79.) Side clearance prevents the blade from binding in the saw kerf, which would cause friction and create heat. Side clearance is especially important for the band saw because it allows the workpiece to be rotated around the blade, creating a curve. (See Illus. 80.)

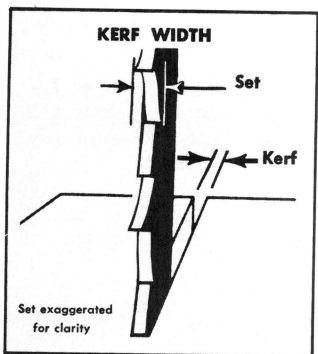

Illus. 78. The teeth on a band-saw blade are set, which creates a saw kerf that is wider than the saw body.

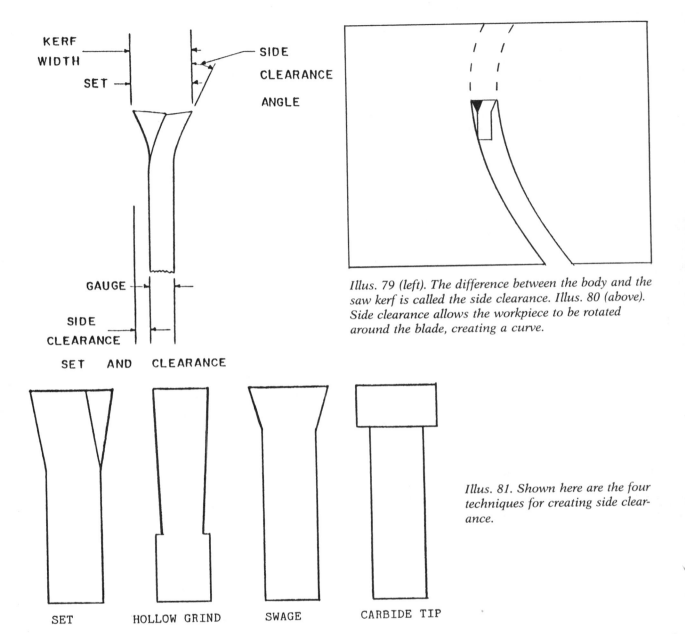

Illus. 79 (left). The difference between the body and the saw kerf is called the side clearance. Illus. 80 (above). Side clearance allows the workpiece to be rotated around the blade, creating a curve.

Illus. 81. Shown here are the four techniques for creating side clearance.

There are four factors that create side clearance. Each factor causes the cutting edge to be wider than the body of the saw. They are as follows:

1. *A blade with set teeth.* This type of blade is the most commonly used on band saws. The alternating teeth are bent in opposite directions, creating a kerf wider than the body.
2. *Hollow grinding.* This is used on circular saw blades for fine cuts. It is not commonly used for band-saw blades.
3. *Swaging.* This is a technique that flattens the tooth end, making it wider. It is commonly used on large band-saw mill blades.
4. *Insert teeth.* Insert teeth such as carbide teeth are welded to the blade. Expensive band-saw blades have insert teeth.

Blades are set according to blade thickness, width, and tooth size. A thick blade will have more set than a thin blade; thus, the kerf will be wider. The amount of set is usually proportionate to the thickness of the blade body. The set is usually about 25 percent of the blade thickness. A blade that is .020 inch thick would have each tooth set at about .005 inch. The body plus the set (.005 in the opposite direction) would give a blade a kerf of .030 inch. (See Illus. 82.)

The middle third of the kerf is cut by every tooth. The outside portions are cut by the group of teeth "set" in that direction. (See Illus. 83.) Each material being cut has different set requirements. Green wood, for example, requires more set than dry wood. Thick material also requires more set.

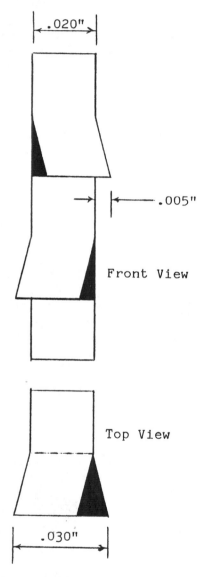

BLADE THICKNESS AND SET

Illus. 82. The set takes up about 25 percent of the blade's thickness. A blade that is .020 inch thick will cut a kerf that's .030 inch.

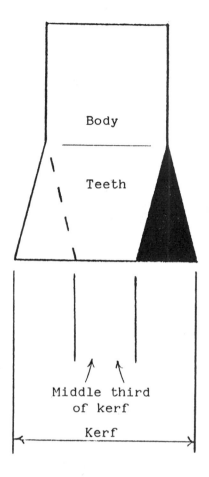

Illus. 83. The middle third of the kerf is cut by every tooth. The outside thirds are cut by the teeth set in that direction.

Set is not a separate option. It comes standard with the blade that you choose. Set must, therefore, be one of your considerations when you decide which blade to use.

Set and Curves

The band saw is the tool of choice for cutting curves. This is accomplished by a combination of two factors: kerf width and blade width. Because the band-saw blade cuts a wide kerf, the workpiece can be rotated around the narrow blade, which creates a curve. The amount of curve possible is determined by the width of kerf and the width of the blade. The narrower the blade and the wider the kerf, the tighter the curve that can be made. (See Illus. 84.) This is discussed in detail on page 56.

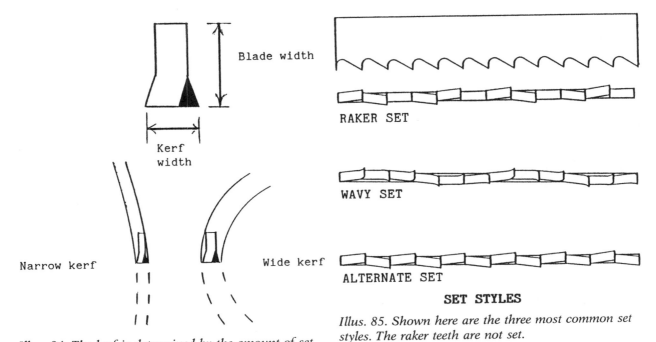

Illus. 84. The kerf is determined by the amount of set. The wider the kerf, the tighter the turn.

RAKER SET

WAVY SET

ALTERNATE SET

SET STYLES

Illus. 85. Shown here are the three most common set styles. The raker teeth are not set.

Set Styles

The set of a blade's teeth is an important factor in band-saw performance. Different materials and procedures require a variety of set styles. There are three general set styles: alternate, raker, and wavy. (See Illus. 85.) The average woodworker uses blades with alternate and raker teeth.

There are other blades with sophisticated set styles that are used primarily for cutting metal. Some of these designs are patented by their manufacturers and are used for interrupted cuts for materials such as pipe and I-beam, where vibration is a serious problem. These blades are generally called variable-set blades. (See Illus. 86.)

ALTERNATE SET

Alternate-set teeth are called a variety of other names, including regular set, straight set, and ETS (Every Tooth Set). Every tooth is set alternately left and right. The cut is smooth because each tooth cuts along the kerf. Blades with alternate-set teeth are used for wood, plastic, nonferrous metals, and even meat. They are used when an exceptionally smooth finish is required and for short, accurate cuts such as those needed for woodworking joints.

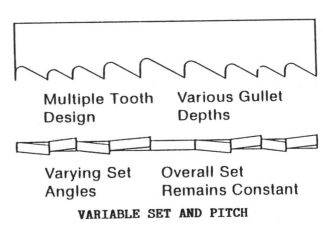

Multiple Tooth Design   Various Gullet Depths

Varying Set Angles   Overall Set Remains Constant

VARIABLE SET AND PITCH

Illus. 86. Blades with a variable set and pitch are used to cut metal. These types of blades are less prone to vibration.

RAKER SET

A blade with a raker set follows the following pattern: two teeth are set in opposite directions and the third tooth (the raker) remains unset. The raker-set style provides optimum chip clearance on thick stock. It is used for long cuts and is recommended for profile and contour cuts. Because it only has two-thirds the number of teeth cutting the kerf sides, it is not as smooth as the alternate-set type. It is used with horizontal band saws in production settings to cut thick sections of metal. It is used with vertical band saws for contour and friction cutting.

Although the usual raker pattern has every third tooth unset, it is becoming more common to use every fifth or seventh tooth as the raker.

WAVY SET

A blade that has teeth with a wavy set has groups of teeth set to the left and to the right; these groups of teeth are separated by unset raker teeth. This forms a wavy pattern. This is the usual pattern of teeth on hand-held hacksaws. Blades that have teeth with a wavy set are generally used for cutting thin metal sections, pipe, tubing, and structural shapes. They are not used for wood. Each successive tooth takes a small bite, which minimizes tooth damage. This means that you can cut a wide range of material and thickness with the same number of teeth per inch. This type of blade is used in situations where blades with raker teeth would be damaged and as a general-purpose cutoff blade on horizontal saws.

VARIABLE SET

Blades that have teeth that are not evenly spaced are called variable set. Variable-tooth spacing is used to dampen harmonic vibration when a band saw is used to make interrupted cuts such as those on heavy pipe or I-beams. This is a metal-cutting design used when the wavy or

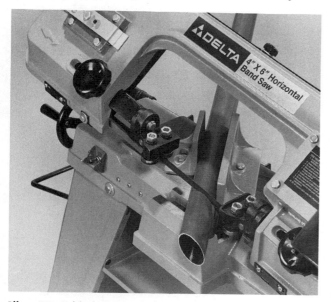

Illus. 87. A blade with a wavy set of teeth is similar in design to a hacksaw blade. It is often used to cut pipe.

raker designs vibrate too much. Since each tooth in the pattern has a different size, it requires a different amount of set. On most variable designs, the overall amount of set stays the same.

Tooth Angle

One of the most important factors to affect the cutting performance of a saw blade is the angle at which the point of the saw tooth contacts the material. This will determine how aggressively a blade will cut and how well it will perform. This angle of entry, called tooth angle, is similar to the angle of a chisel or a plane. Changing the angle changes the cutting performance.

Traditionally, the angle is changed according to the hardness and thickness of the material. A woodworker may have three ripsaws, each filed at a different angle to accommodate the hardness of various species of wood in his locale. Hard woods require less angle (a blunter point) than soft woods. In fact, woodworkers in different regions gear the cutting angles of their saws to the native woods of that area. Japanese handsaws, for example, have sharper angles because Japanese woods are usually of a softer variety. (See Illus. 88.)

The angle for ripping is different than the angle for crosscutting.

The tooth angle on a band-saw blade is also called the "rake angle" or "hook angle." The tooth angle is the angle of the point created by the intersection of the tooth face and the tooth back. (See Illus. 89.) If the tooth face is at 90 degrees to the blade body, it is called a "neutral hook" or a "zero-degree rake." Often, it is just called a "rake." The standard tooth and the skip tooth both have a zero-degree rake. (See Illus. 90.) (See the next section, Tooth Form, for more information on standard, skip, and other types of teeth.) If the angle is more pointed, it is called a "positive hook" or simply "hook." The hook-tooth blade is named for its positive hook angle. If the tooth face slants the opposite way, it is called a negative angle.

The hook tooth (positive hook) is either 5, 7, or 10 degrees to the blade. The distinctions in the amount of angle are more important when metal is being cut instead of plastic or wood. The 10-degree hook is the most common type of tooth used for metal-cutting. The lower angles are used if the material is hard.

The micro-hook tooth has a 0-degree rake, and a distorted point that has a small hook. This tooth design is for high-volume production sawing on automatic machines. It has a very tough

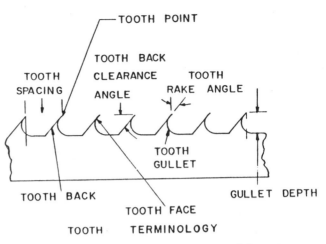

Illus. 89. The tooth angle is the angle of the point created by the intersection of the tooth face and the tooth back.

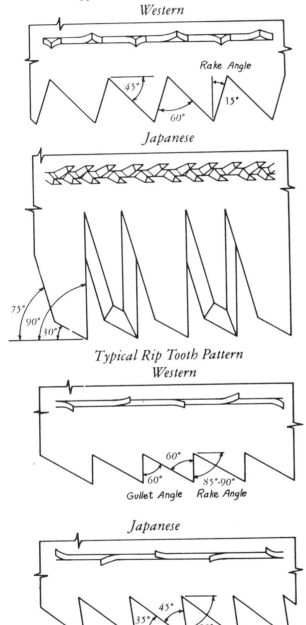

Illus. 88. A comparison of Japanese and Western saw teeth patterns. (Drawing courtesy of Garrett Wade Company)

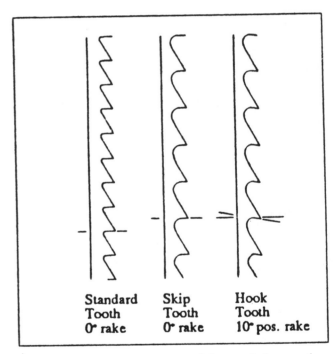

Illus. 90. Standard and skip teeth have a 0-degree rake angle. Hook teeth have a positive angle, which is usually 10 degrees. (Drawing courtesy of Tony Dileo)

high-speed-steel M42 tip. Its high expense keeps it in the high-production arena, where it is used to cut large pieces of very tough alloys.

The difference between hook and rake (neutral-angle) teeth is how they cut. The rake tooth cuts with a scraping action. This requires a fair amount of pressure (commonly called feed pressure) to feed the material into the blade. The finish is smooth. The hook tooth digs into the wood with the hooked tip, pulling itself into the work. It cuts faster and requires less feed pressure. The cut is usually rougher than that by the rake tooth.

Another distinction between rake and hook teeth is the amount of heat they generate. The scraping action of the rake tooth produces more heat. With some wood such as cherry, this heat buildup can "bake" the pitch onto the tooth face. If this happens, it would be wise to use a blade with fewer teeth. The heat buildup is more common with small blades such as ⅟₁₆- and ⅛-inch blades because they retain heat. The small blades don't have large bodies to draw heat off the tip.

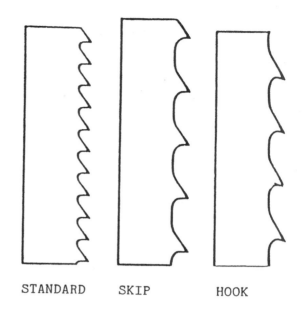

STANDARD   SKIP   HOOK

TOOTH FORMS

Illus. 91. Blades with skip and hook teeth have half as many teeth as those with standard teeth. This means that they cut more efficiently but not as smoothly as blades with standard teeth.

Tooth Form

Tooth form is a term used to describe the shape of the tooth and the gullet. It is perhaps the most important characteristic of the blade because it determines the ability of a particular blade to do various procedures well, including the following: ripping, resawing, crosscutting, cutting curves smoothly, cutting end grain smoothly, cutting circles, and cutting green wood.

There is no magical blade that does everything well. In fact, some blades do specific jobs rather poorly. Therefore, it is important to understand the strong points of each blade. Switching to the appropriate blade in the middle of a project can save hours of finishing time.

Initially, the teeth on the band saw were similar to the teeth on the frame saw. The tooth and gullet are still the same size. This tooth-gullet design makes up the standard form that is still popular today. (See Illus. 91.) With the speed and efficiency of the band saw, the tooth is easily filled to capacity, especially when used to cut thick work. A blade with skip-tooth form has every other one of its teeth missing. The teeth have a bigger gullet, and thus more capacity to carry sawdust. (See Illus. 92.)

The next type of blade developed was the hook-tooth blade. The tooth angle was changed to a positive angle. The gullet was also rounded. This increased the cutting efficiency, and allowed for

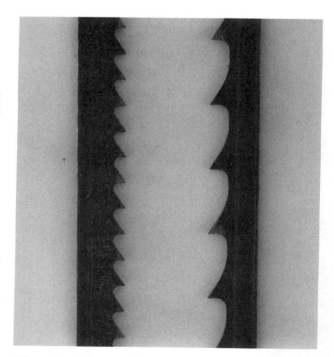

Illus. 92. Shown here are two ¼-inch blades. The skip-tooth blade on the right has half as many teeth as the standard-tooth blade on the left. Both blades have a 0-degree rake. Their teeth are at 90 degrees to the body.

less feed pressure, less tension, and longer blade life. (See Illus. 93.)

The hook-skip design combines the hook of the hook tooth and the gullet of the skip tooth. (See Illus. 93.) It was designed to cut as efficiently as the hook-tooth blade and leave as smooth a finish as the skip-tooth blade.

The variable-pitch design has teeth that progressively change in size. (See Illus. 94 and 95.) This design is used in metal-cutting for architec-

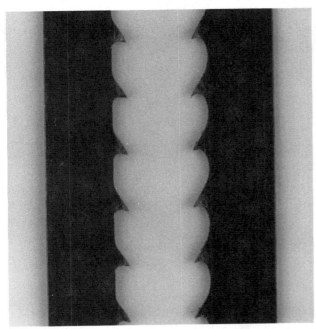

Illus. 93. Both of the blades shown here have hook teeth. The hook-skip teeth on the blade on the left have straight gullets like the teeth on skip-tooth blades. The hook teeth on the blade shown on the right have rounded gullets.

REGULAR TOOTH FORM—VARIABLE PITCH

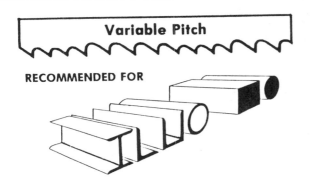

Illus. 94. The variable-pitch blade was developed for cutting structural shapes.

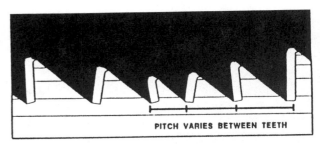

Illus. 95. The pitch of a variable-pitch blade changes from one tooth to the next. This dampens vibration that is common when structural shapes are being cut.

tural beams, pipe, etc., where vibration is a problem. The varying pitch dampens vibration.

Following is a closer look at each of the blade forms just described.

Standard-Tooth Blades

The standard-tooth blade is also called by a number of other names, including a "regular" or "precision" blade. The teeth on a standard blade are similar to the rip teeth on a handsaw. The teeth and gullet are the same size. The tooth is flat across the tip. It has a zero-degree rake angle and is available in all three set styles, alternate set being the most common. When a standard blade with an alternate set is used at a slow feed speed, it gives the smoothest finish of any band-saw blade. It is recommended for intricate curves and straight cutoff work.

One disadvantage of the standard-tooth blade is the closeness of the teeth and, consequently, the small gullet. In thick wood it is easy to over-feed (feed too quickly) and clog the teeth by completely filling the gullet. This is especially true if the material is gummy, such as cherry wood or aluminum.

Another disadvantage is that the scraping action of the zero-degree rake can cause the blade to become hot. This is compounded by the fact that a standard-tooth blade has more teeth than other types. The more teeth, the more heat that is generated. Unless a slow feed is used, the cut can "follow the grain" and be deflected by the grain pattern. This is more likely with dull teeth.

Skip-Tooth Blades

The skip-tooth blade, as the name implies, has every other tooth missing. This creates a large gullet and fewer teeth. The fewer the teeth, the more efficient each tooth is and the faster the cut. However, though the skip-tooth blade is efficient, it does not cut smoothly.

The skip-tooth blade is available in both alternate and raker set. Raker set is the most common and is preferred when cutting thick stock. Because of its efficiency, the skip-tooth blade requires very little set. In fact, some skip-tooth scroll-saw blades are not "set" at all. Like the teeth on a standard-tooth blade, the teeth on a skip-tooth blade have a 0-degree rake angle.

The tooth rake and the large flat gullet tend to "break up" chips. This is important when cutting thick material at a fast rate. This makes the skip-tooth blade a good choice for cutting aluminum, copper, magnesium, and soft brass because it won't clog or gum up the blade. It is good at removing large wood chips, and is especially good on soft woods. Because it tends to run cooler than the regular blade, it is often the blade of choice for plastics. The cooler cut decreases the likelihood of the plastic melting back together after the cut is made.

The skip-tooth blade has a shallower gullet. This means that more metal exists in the blade. This permits a coarser pitch (fewer teeth) to be put on a narrower band. You get greater gullet capacity without weakening the band. The greater band thickness allows more tension to be placed on a narrower band, thus achieving more beam strength.

Some woodworkers believe that skip-tooth blades last longer without breaking. This may be because the fewer the teeth, the less heat generated. Heat decreases blade life. It may also be because the gullet corner is not as sharp as that on a standard tooth blade. The blade usually breaks at the gullet corner.

The skip-tooth blade has some disadvantages. Although it cuts smoothly with the grain, it does not always cut smoothly when crosscutting. The harder the wood, the less smoothly it cuts. The finish is improved when the feed rate is slowed down.

A narrow skip-tooth blade has a tendency to "flutter." The term flutter is used to describe harmonic vibration. Illus. 96 shows the effect of flutter on the wood. The gentle diagonal curve pattern to the left of the blade is the telltale sign of

Illus. 96. When a blade vibrates during the cut, it is called harmonic "flutter." The diagonal pattern shown to the left of the blade is a sign of flutter.

harmonic vibration. Harmonic vibration is discussed on pages 66 and 67.

The forte of the skip-tooth blade is making straight and curved cuts, especially with the grain. If you practice and have patience, the result can be a finish that's quite good. Pay close attention to the feed rate because the skip tooth may be the most speed-sensitive of the tooth forms. A slow rate will produce a fairly smooth finish, but a fast rate can produce a very rough finish. Illus. 97 shows a mahogany cabriole leg being made with a narrow skip-tooth blade. On softer woods like mahogany, the finish is quite good. Illus. 98 shows a 5-inch cone in elm being cut with a narrow skip-tooth blade. The finish on harder wood like elm is slightly rougher than that on soft wood.

Hook-Tooth Blades

The advantage of the hook-tooth blade is that the teeth bite more aggressively into the material. The tooth spacing is the same as that for the skip-tooth blade. The tooth angle, however, is a positive one and can be 5, 7, or 10 degrees. The harder the material, the less the angle. Most blades available have teeth at 10 degrees. The hook-tooth blade can have alternate or rake set teeth. The positive hook angle and the generous gullet size is good for long cuts in wood because the tooth and gullet design resist clogging. The

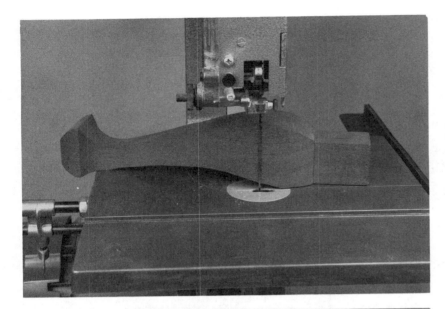

Illus. 97. A ⅛-inch skip-tooth blade works well on thick wood that isn't too hard. Here a 6 TPI skip-tooth blade is being used to cut a mahogany cabriole leg.

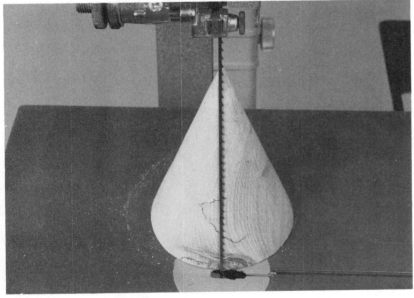

Illus. 98. A narrow skip-tooth blade can make tight turns in thick stock. This coarse, ⅛-inch blade is cutting a 5-inch elm cone.

hook-tooth blade is good for soft metals, especially aluminum, bronze, and magnesium. It is also the blade of choice for many plastics and most fibrous compositions.

The teeth on the hook-tooth blade have the same spacing as those on the skip-tooth blade, but the gullet design is different. The gullet on a hook tooth has a round back. This is especially important when metal cutting because round chips are produced. (See Illus. 99.) The round gullet is the perfect receptacle because the chip curls as it is being cut. It is good for thick wood, especially resawing, because of its capacity to hold sawdust. (See Illus. 100.) The design is especially good for green wood because the sawdust doesn't get packed into the gullet and stay there. (See Illus. 101.)

The hook tooth has some advantages that are subtle but very important, especially when the blade is being used to cut thick stock. Because of its positive rake angle, the hook tooth pulls itself into the stock. This means that less feed pressure is required. Less feed pressure places less force on the band and decreases the likelihood of blade deflection. The less the potential for blade deflection, the less tension is needed. Avoiding

Illus. 99 (above). This close-up shows a hook-tooth blade cutting metal. The round gullet curls the chip. This is important in metal cutting. Illus. 100 (right). Resawing with a ½-inch, 3 TPI hook-tooth blade. This blade or a 3 TPI hook-skip-tooth blade are the best blades for resawing. The blade you use will depend on the power of the machine and the species of wood.

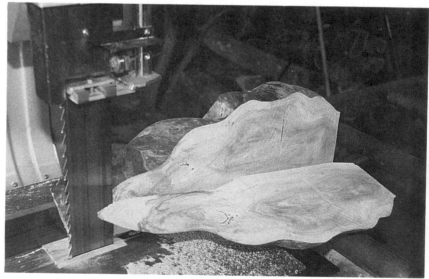

Illus. 101. The blade shown here is being used to cut green elm burl. A blade with hook teeth is best for green wood because its gullets have enough space to hold the wet sawdust.

excessive tension helps the blade last longer. Standard- and skip-tooth blades both require more tension than a hook blade of the same size. The hook-tooth blade is the least likely of all the blades to break because of its round gullet.

Because of the efficiency of the hook design, the tips of the teeth stay cooler. This also adds to blade life. The hook-tooth blade will usually out-last a skip-tooth blade of the same size because its teeth cut rather than scrape.

Because of the speed at which the hook-tooth blade cuts, it requires more power. A hook-tooth blade being used to resaw 6 inches of hard wood requires a band saw of at least ¾ horsepower. It will easily stop if it is used with a band saw that has ½ horsepower.

Hook-Skip Blades

A hybrid blade was developed when hook teeth were combined with skip-teeth gullets. Hook-skip blades are called various names, including "cabinetmaker-band" and "furniture-band" blades, because they are often used in the furniture industry. Every fifth tooth is a raker.

The teeth on hook-skip blades are not quite as aggressive as hook teeth. This makes the hook-skip blade easier to control when feeding, an advantage for people who don't have a lot of band-saw experience. The finish left by the hook-skip blade is quite good, usually smoother than that left by the hook-tooth blade. In fact, it is the smoothest of the resawing finishes.

Because the hook-skip blade is not as aggressive as the hook-tooth blade, it requires less power. This is especially important when cutting thick stock with a consumer-grade band saw, because most are underpowered. A saw with a ½-horsepower motor will usually do better with a hook-skip blade than with a hook blade.

Variable-Pitch Blades

Variable-pitch blades have a specialized tooth form designed for cutting metal. Conventional blades have a consistent number of teeth per inch. These blades are best at cutting solids of consistent density where vibration and noise are not usually a problem.

Variable-pitch blades have teeth spaced along the blade in a harmonically derived ratio designed to tune out vibration. The blade has a coarse pitch that gradually changes to a fine pitch and then back to a coarse pitch. The pattern was originally designed for interrupted cuts such as tubing, box channel, I beam, etc. It is now used on some solid shapes and very hard materials.

Blade Thickness

The thickness of band-saw blades is determined by the thickness of the blade body. (See Illus. 102.) Blades vary in thickness from .014 to .042 inch. The usual progression is .014, .018, .020, .022, .025, .032, .035, and .042 inch. The thickness is now given in thousandths of an inch. In

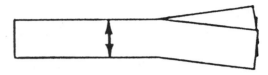

Illus. 102. Blade thickness is the thickness of the blade body. If the body is too thick for the wheels, the band will break prematurely.

the past, the Stubbs and Birmingham gauge systems were used. Even though those systems are now passé for band-saw blades, the word gauge (gage) is still used when referring to blade thickness.

Make sure that you select a blade of the proper thickness. Possibly as much as 75 percent of blade strain occurs when the blade revolves around the wheels and straightens out again. This continual flexing of the blade causes metal fatigue and failure. Fatigue is the tendency of a metal to break under continued flexing that's considerably below the maximum tensile strength.

The thickness of the blade required depends upon the diameter of the wheels and the work to be done. Thick blades will withstand more strain from cutting than thin blades, but will break more easily from the bending action, especially when run on small wheels. Each revolution flexes the blade to near the elastic limit of the steel, which causes the metal to fatigue and break quickly. Thinner blades are preferable to heavy blades when the work is light.

Manufacturers recommend the following blade thicknesses and the appropriate wheel diameters:

WHEEL DIAMETER	RECOMMENDED BLADE THICKNESS
4-6 inches	.014 inch
6-8 inches	.018 inch
8-11 inches	.020 inch
11-18 inches	.025 inch
18-24 inches	.032 inch
24-30 inches	.035 inch
30 inches over	.042 inch

Most blades have a standardized thickness. Blades ½ inch wide or less are .025 inch thick; those ⅝ and ¾ inch wide are generally .032 inch thick; and those 1-inch wide are .035 inch thick.

Small-wheeled saws such as the very popular bench-top three-wheel models require thin blades. A blade .014 inch thick is best, and one .018 inch thick can be used for thicker work.

As a general rule, saws with wheels between 10 and 18 inches in diameter—which are the most common saws—should be equipped with blades .025-inch thick and under. This thickness usually limits the blade width to ½ inch. If thicker blade stock is used, the flex life of the blade is usually fairly short.

Blade Width

Blades are designated by the width of the band. This measurement is taken from the back of the blade to the front of the blade. (See Illus. 103.) The width of the blade is usually the first piece of information given about a blade. An example is the blade often used for resawing and cutting thick stock, the ½-inch, 3 TPI hook-raker.

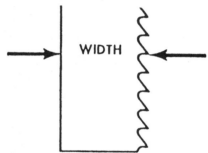

Illus. 103. Blade width is measured from the tips of the teeth to the blade back.

Band-saw blades are available in sizes from ¹⁄₁₆ inch all the way up to 16 inches for giant band mills. The blades available for vertical band saws range from ¹⁄₁₆ to 1½ inches. Consumer-grade band saws will usually handle a blade from ¹⁄₁₆ to ¾ inch. When you use blades with narrow widths, you do not get a choice of form or set. The ¹⁄₁₆-inch blade only comes in the standard form. The ⅛-inch blade comes in six different pitch sizes. The ³⁄₁₆-inch and larger blades are available in just about any combination of set, form, and pitch. The great variety available allows you to choose the exact blade type in the width that you need for a specific purpose.

The width of the blade should be your first consideration when choosing a blade. It is an indication of the blade's ability to cut contours and to maintain accuracy and sawing rates when straight cuts are being made. For straight cuts, the widest blade possible should be used. The wider the blade, the greater the beam strength, and the greater the blade's ability to resist deflection. For contours (curves), the radius of the smallest arc in the pattern determines the width of the blade. Use the widest blade that can cut the desired curve. (See Illus. 104.) It is a good idea to have a wide variety of blades on hand. This gives you the most choices possible.

Contour Sawing

Contour sawing is a term for cutting curves. The band saw is the tool of choice for cutting curves because the work can be slowly rotated around the small blade, creating a curve in the saw cut. The size of the radius that can be cut by a blade is determined by the ratio of the *width of the blade to the width of the saw kerf*. A smaller radius is cut by either increasing set or by reducing blade width. Doing either will increase the cutting angle of the blade, and thus its ability to rotate in its own kerf. Since you generally do not have the option as to which blade set to use, the minimum radius that can be cut is determined almost entirely by the width of the blade.

The width of the blade determines how much the stock can be rotated before it binds in the kerf. When wide blades are used, the workpiece can be turned very little before it binds. When narrow blades are used, the workpiece can be rotated quite far before it binds, thus creating a smaller radius. (See Illus. 105.)

When the blade binds, its back (opposite the direction of the rotation) rubs against the kerf. It also binds in the middle of the blade in the direction of the rotation. If you continue to rotate the wood after it binds, you will start to twist the blade. If you twist it too much, you will hear a squealing noise before the blade breaks. If your saw is underpowered, it may stop when you twist the blade. Try not to twist the blade. If you cannot make as tight a curve as you would like, back up and try again. If a curve is so abrupt that you have to repeatedly back up and try again, either change to a narrower blade or a blade with more set. Blades with a raker set are best for tight curves.

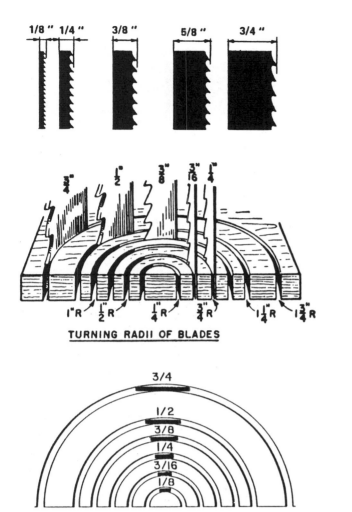

TURNING RADII OF BLADES

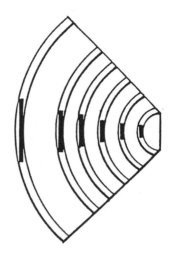

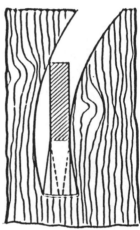

Illus. 104. A small blade can cut tighter curves than a large blade. This drawings shows the tightest curve that can be cut with each blade.

Illus. 105. During a sharp turn, the back of the blade rubs against the kerf. Trying to turn the blade more tightly at this point will only twist the blade. Twisting the blade should be avoided.

Straight Cuts

The strength of the band saw is in the narrow blade design. The relatively narrow blade allows curves to be cut as the workpiece is rotated around the blade. The narrow blade, however, can also be a disadvantage. If the blade doesn't stay straight, the cut doesn't stay straight either. A cut that doesn't stay straight is referred to in a number of terms. When a cut drifts to one side, it is called a "lead." (See Illus. 106.) Wander is when the blade first leads in one direction and then in another. (See Illus. 106.) A barrel cut occurs when the cut becomes round when thick stock is being cut. (See Illus. 106.)

Getting your saw to cut perfectly straight isn't as simple as it sounds. It would be wonderful if all you had to do to make a straight cut was to put on a wide blade and crank up the tension. However, there are a number of factors that influence straight cutting. These include the following: blade width and sharpness; wheel alignment and design; the setup of the guides and bearings; feed rate and technique; fence alignment; the blade teeth used (set and pitch); the tension used on the band saw; and how the band saw tracks.

Blade width is one of the most important factors to be considered. It is often relative to other

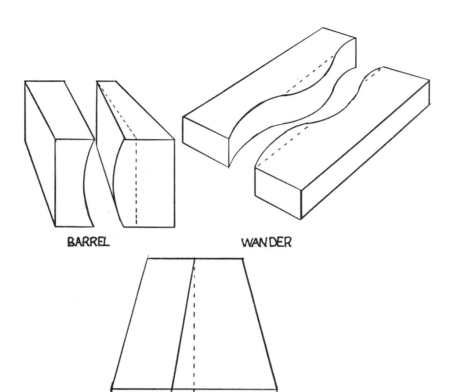

Illus. 106. Lead, wander, and barrel cuts.

BARREL

WANDER

LEAD

factors. If your saw is well aligned and tracked correctly, you can use a wide blade. If your saw is not perfectly adjusted, you will find that your wide blades may not cut well no matter how much tension you use. In this situation, you may find that you get better performance from blades with a narrower width.

When the band saw doesn't saw straight, it is usually because the blade is not staying straight during the cut. This is called deflection. Depending upon the width of the blade, it can either deflect rearward or sideways. (See Illus. 107 and 108.) Sideways deflection is most common with wide blades. Rearward deflection is most common with narrow blades. Medium-sized blades can deflect in both directions, which causes a rotation of the blade.

Pay attention to the cut and try to determine what is happening when the blade doesn't give a straight cut. Illus. 109 right shows the beginning of a barrel cut. By the end of the cut, the kerf is no longer straight from top to bottom. (See Illus. 109 left.) Blades of different widths will flex/de-

flect in different ways. By the end of the barrel cut, the blade shown in the illustration, which is ½ inch thick, has flexed sideways. It is too thick to be able to flex any other way unless there is a lot of distance between the thrust bearings.

You must remember that the band-saw blade is a metal band first and a saw blade second. Each blade will have different characteristics depending on the thickness and width of the band.

Narrow blades—those ⅛ inch and smaller—are like wires and can be flexed in any direction. Under sawing stress, they will flex straight rearwards in line with the cut. The cut will remain straight. It may seem unlikely that a narrower blade will make a better-quality cut than a wide blade, but it is true in some situations. With practice, the amount of rearward blade flex can be controlled and used to good advantage to create very accurate cuts. (See Illus. 110 and 111.)

The medium-sized blades between 3/16 and ⅜ inch flex the most. These blades simultaneously deflect, or turn, sideways like large blades and rearwards like small ones. The body of the me-

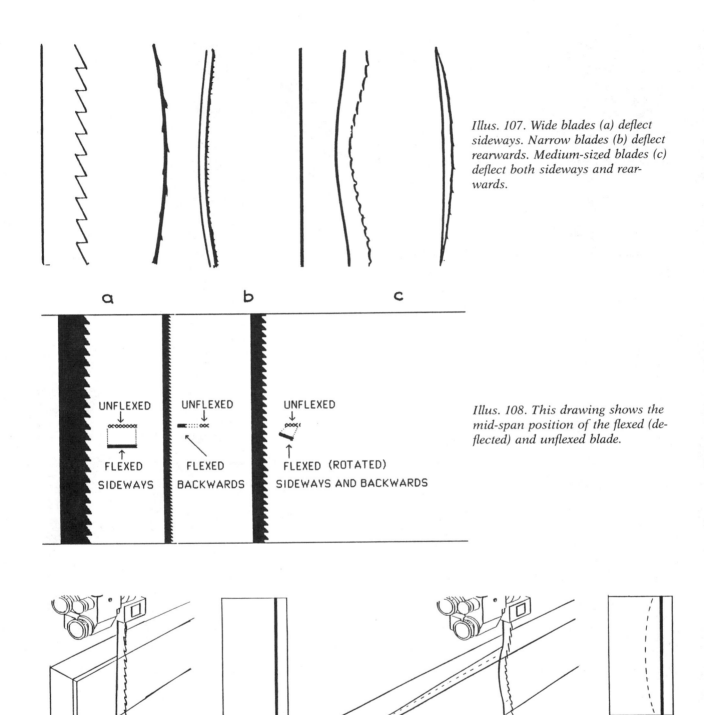

Illus. 107. Wide blades (a) deflect sideways. Narrow blades (b) deflect rearwards. Medium-sized blades (c) deflect both sideways and rearwards.

Illus. 108. This drawing shows the mid-span position of the flexed (deflected) and unflexed blade.

Illus. 109. When a barrel cut occurs, the blade initially cuts straight. By the end of the cut the blade has flexed sideways, creating a rounded cut.

Illus. 110 and 111. The ¹/₁₆-inch blade flexes straight rearwards in the cut. With practice, you can learn to cut very accurately with the rearward deflection of the blade. The curl cut off this 2-inch piece of hard maple is a uniform .004 inch thick.

dium blade is too wide to flex straight back, so the blade rotates to the side. The body of the rotated blade will rub against the work, pushing the blade even farther sideways as the cut progresses.

Beam Strength

Beam strength is a term that describes the ability of a band-saw blade to remain straight or to resist deflection. This quality is determined by the combination of blade width and thickness, and the amount of tension applied to the blade. Sufficient beam strength in a blade is necessary in order to cut at a maximum feed rate with a minimum of breakage and inaccuracy caused by flex or deflection. (See Illus. 112.) Blade flex/deflection is the result of not having enough beam strength. The greater the feeding force, the greater the beam strength required. Since the feed pressure is applied by the operator, it is adjustable. Beam strength is covered in detail on pages 155 and 156.

Problems with Wide Blades

Wide blades also have some distinct disadvantages. For example, they are more sensitive to wheel misalignment. They are less flexible because they are stiffer. This stiffness can cause instability when they are used with crowned wheels, which is the type of wheel used on most American consumer saws. The lack of surface

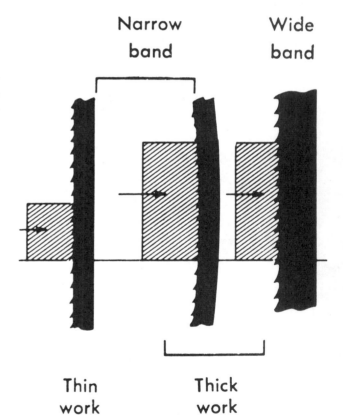

SAW BLADE BEAM STRENGTH

Narrow band   Wide band

Thin work   Thick work

Illus. 112. Beam strength is a combination of blade width and blade tension. If the beam strength is not sufficient, the blade will deflect during the cut.

area between the blade and the crown can cause the blade to sway on the crown. This is discussed at length on page 113.

Blades that are over a ½ inch wide are more than .025 inch thick. These blades are often too thick for wheels that are smaller than 18 inches in diameter. A thick blade flexing over small wheels can fatigue the blade and cause early breakage. For this reason, the ½-inch blade is probably the largest blade that can be used practically on many saws.

Blade Metallurgy

Originally, band-saw blades were handmade and expensive. People were trained to resharpen the blades. As cheap blade production developed, the importance of sharpening the blade decreased. Early blades were softer and were resharpened by hand with a file. Because early band saws ran at lower speeds, any imperfections in the blade were not very serious.

Today's blades are harder and require specialized equipment to make and grind them. Although some people make equipment to regrind their own blades, grinding equipment is not commercially available at a reasonable price. The blade can be resharpened by hand, and with practice, one can master the technique.

Some blade manufacturers offer a sharpening service for their expensive metal-cutting blades. As a rule, it is very difficult to find a professional sharpener who will refile or regrind a woodcutting band-saw blade. They usually say that it isn't worth it, that it would cost more to sharpen a blade than to buy a new one. Consequently, many woodworkers have a pile of blades that are too dull to use, yet they cannot bear to throw them away.

Following is an exploration of how different band-saw blades are made, and the factors that play vital roles in the life of a blade.

Blade Life

There are two distinct factors that must be considered when you are discussing blade life: the blade body and the tip of the tooth. These are the two blade parts that suffer the most from wear. When the tip becomes too dull, the usable life of the blade is over. The same is true if the blade breaks. Welding the broken blade and sharpening the tooth tip will extend the usable life of the blade. However, this is not usually cost-effective except in production settings.

Ideally band-saw teeth should be close to the end of their usable life cycle when the blade body breaks. The body shouldn't break when the teeth are still sharp. The blade body has to be flexible to withstand the constant flexing-straightening cycle. If it is too hard, it will be brittle and break too easily.

The teeth, on the other hand, have to be hard. The harder they are, the more resistant they are to wear and heat. Cutting produces heat. The harder and thicker the material is, the more heat that is produced. When metal is being cut, a coolant is often used to help dissipate the heat buildup. (See Illus. 113.) Extreme heat is destructive to the tooth tip, decreasing its ability to stay sharp and resist wear.

Illus. 113. When cutting metal, use a liquid coolant to dissipate heat and remove the waste material.

Destructive heat buildup is not usually a problem with the band saw unless it runs for a long period of time. Small blades such as ⅛ or ¹⁄₁₆-inch blades suffer more from heat buildup because they don't dissipate heat as well as larger blades. The large blade body can absorb heat off the tooth.

The Rockwell Hardness Scale is a means of measuring material hardness. Metals are measured on the Rockwell Subgroup C scale (usually abbreviated Rc), so this is the means used to indicate the hardness of band-saw blades. When the resistance to indentation is measured, the hardness of the material is determined. The higher the number, the harder the material. A tooth measured one point greater than another tooth on the Rockwell Hardness Scale is 100% more abrasion-resistant. In the following pages, you will come across references to the hardness of band-saw blades that are based on the Rockwell C Scale.

The performance of all cutting tools can be measured by the tool's ability to cope with the following: (1) heat, (2) shock, (3) abrasion, and (4) flexing. *Flex life* is the ability of the band-saw blade to withstand repeated flexing around the

Illus. 114. Some situations such as when you are making double cuts create shock and vibration. One of the considerations in choosing a blade for the cut shown here is the ability of the blade to withstand shock.

wheels of the band-saw machine without breaking. Resistance to shock is its ability to withstand impact blows caused by the vibrations inherent in cutting. (See Illus. 114.)

Abrasion resistance is an inherent characteristic of the material used to make the cutting tool, and the heat treatment to which this material may be subjected. The durability of a cutting tool is determined by its abrasion resistance and its hardness after heat treatment. (See Illus. 115.)

Red-heat hardness is the cutting tool's capacity to tolerate the heat generated in the cutting operation without destroying the tool's cutting ability. High red-heat hardness allows faster tool speeds, heavier feeds, and faster cutting rates. (See Illus. 116.)

Abrasion resistance and red-heat hardness are very important in metal cutting and not as important in wood cutting.

Spring-Steel Blades

Originally, band-saw blades were made of spring steel. Spring-steel blades are usually silver in color and are still somewhat popular. The teeth and body have the same hardness—Rc 36-42. This is not particularly hard. However, the blade is soft enough to be flexible, thus avoiding band breakage. It is hard enough to be used on soft woods, but dulls fairly quickly on hard wood, especially thick hard wood.

The spring-steel blade was suitable for old band saws that ran at much slower speeds. With new band saws, which run at higher speeds, the teeth are too soft to stay sharp for a long period.

In the old days, it was standard practice for people to refile their own blades when they got dull. Spring-steel blades were refiled 20-30 times. Woodworking factories usually had a person who filed blades full time. Today it is hard, if not impossible, to find someone who will still sharpen band-saw blades because blades are now relatively inexpensive in relationship to wages and overhead.

The spring-steel blade illustrates the problem common with many tools: how to make them hard without sacrificing their toughness. If the metal is too hard, it becomes brittle. This is especially true with the blade body because of the flexing cycle. So the bodies of some spring-steel blades are kept flexible because they are left soft, while the teeth are hardened. (See Illus. 117.) Harder teeth stay sharp longer.

There are a number of techniques for hardening the teeth. The tip can be induction-hardened with an electrical current or "flame"-hardened with heat. First, the teeth are cut in the soft body; then they are finish-ground and set. The last stage is the hardening process.

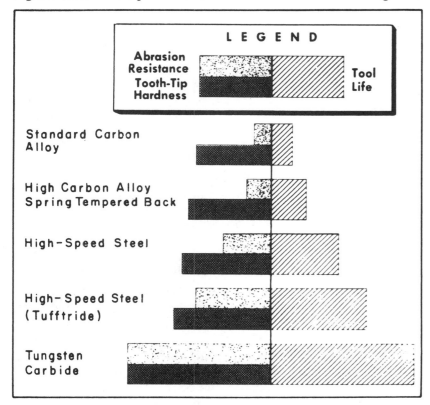

Illus. 115. The durability of a cutting tool, especially in metal cutting, is determined by its abrasion resistance. Abrasion resistance is not the same as hardness.

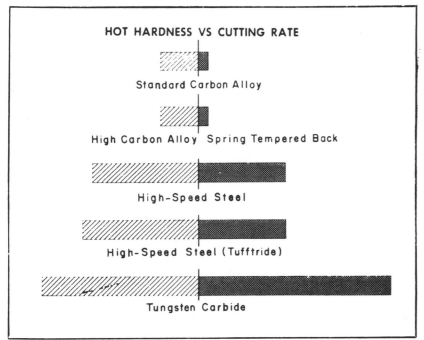

Illus. 116. Hot hardness is the measure of the cutting tool's ability to withstand heat. This is especially important in metal cutting. High-speed steel can withstand heat of up to 1100 degrees F.

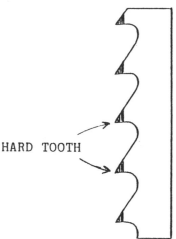

HARD TOOTH

Illus. 117. The teeth on some spring-steel blades are hardened. This makes them last longer, which is especially important when they are used to cut hard wood.

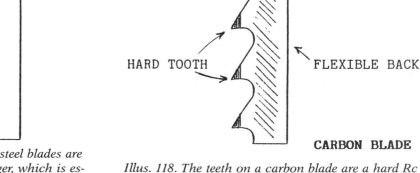

CARBON BLADE

HARD TOOTH   FLEXIBLE BACK

Illus. 118. The teeth on a carbon blade are a hard Rc 64. The flexible back is a softer Rc 28–34. This softer back extends the flex life of the saw.

Carbon Blades (Flex-Back)

The weakness of the spring-steel blade is two-fold. It has limited abrasion resistance and red-heat hardness. To increase its cutting ability, changes were made that included increasing the carbon content and thus making the teeth harder. These blades are called carbon blades. They are usually black in color. By 1939, the carbon blade was developed to the point that it was practical to use for metal cutting.

The teeth of the carbon blade are hard. They measure 64 on the Rockwell C Scale (Rc 64). (See Illus. 118.) This is about the hardness of a good chisel. When the teeth are hardened this much, their wear resistance and red-hot hardness are greatly increased. The teeth of a carbon blade can withstand heat up to 400 degrees F. This is important when cutting metal because high temperatures are generated. It is less important when cutting wood unless the blade is used in constant day-long production or to cut exotic woods, which are usually rather hard and have minerals that are very abrasive.

The back of a flexible or "flex-back" carbon blade is soft and more flexible (Rc 28-34) than the back of a spring-steel blade. The teeth are hard and durable and the blade's body is soft enough and not too brittle. These are the type of blades usually used for woodworking and for cutting soft metals.

Carbon Blades (Hard-Back)

The back of the carbon blade used in industrial settings has a hardness of Rc 43-47. (See Illus. 119.) This is important when metal cutting. The increased hardness increases the tensile strength of the blade. This allows the blade to tolerate the high tension used for metal cutting. The hard back increases the beam strength, which helps the blade resist deflection under the heavy sawing pressure (feed pressure) that is used in a production metal-cutting situation. It also prevents "mushrooming" at the back of the blade that occurs if the back is too soft. (See Illus. 120.) This "mushrooming" is also called cold-forming. If a blade is going to be resharpened, its ability to resist cold-forming is especially important.

The hard back prevents "work hardening," in which the back of the blade becomes brittle and starts to crack. If a blade starts to crack or break from the back, it usually means that the back is too soft or that too much feed pressure is being used.

A hard-back blade does not stretch as much as other blades when it gets warm. It works best on a large saw with large wheels. The hard back decreases the blade's flex life. Because of the additional heat-treating, a hard-back carbon blade is more expensive, which means that it is usually used in a commercial or professional setting, particularly the metal-cutting trade. The hard-

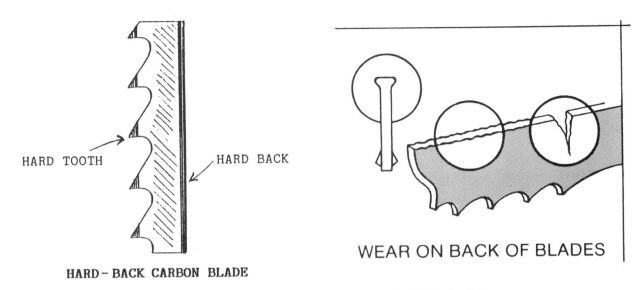

HARD TOOTH   HARD BACK

HARD-BACK CARBON BLADE

WEAR ON BACK OF BLADES

Illus. 119 (above left). The hard-back carbon blade is used to cut metal. The back of the blade is hardened to Rc 43–47. Illus. 120 (above right). The hard back prevents the premature wear that can occur on the back of the blade because of the heavy feed pressure common in metal sawing.

back blade isn't especially important for woodworking, and isn't worth the extra expense. A "flex"-back blade is sufficient.

Bi-Metal Blades

The bi-metal blade was developed during the 1960s for cutting various types and shapes of metal. (See Illus. 121.) The blade looks like a carbon blade, but is usually a uniform medium grey in color. (See Illus. 122.) Like the carbon blade, it has hard teeth and a softer body. A piece of cobalt steel (high-speed steel) laminated to the body forms the teeth. (See Illus. 123.) The back is usually measured at Rc 47-51, and the tips at Rc 66-69. A blade this hard is useful for extremely high temperatures of metal-cutting because it will withstand temperatures of up to 1100 degrees F. The blade rarely reaches 300 degrees F. when wood is being cut. The bi-metal blade can withstand much higher tension than the carbon blades. The high tension increases beam strength. This is useful in metal cutting because so much feed pressure is used. Bi-metal blades are designed to be used at 400 feet per minute for maximum blade life. A woodcutting saw runs at about 7 times that speed, or approximately 2,800 feet per minute.

Illus. 124 shows the piece of high-speed steel that forms the tip of the tooth. It forms about

half of the tooth. Carbide (Illus. 125) or stellite (Illus. 126) are also laminated to the body to create a bi-metal blade.

Recently one metal-cutting blade, the high-speed-steel, bi-metal blade, has been acclaimed by some blade manufacturers and venders as the ideal blade. Some boast that it can do for the band saw what the carbide-tipped blade has done for the table and radial saws. However, this type of blade has some drawbacks. The bi-metal blade fatigues if it is run too fast. This causes the body to break, which, at the speeds used for woodworking, can present a problem. The lack of fatigue resistance leads to problems when this blade is used with small wheels. The best-sized wheels for a bi-metal blade are 18 inches in diameter or larger.

The bi-metal blade is designed to withstand extremely high tension. This is important when metal is being cut on large band saws. The blade can tolerate the maximum tension that can be generated with a consumer band saw. The carbon blade and the consumer band saw are quite well matched for each other. If the carbon blade is overtensioned, it will break, almost like a shear pin. This blade breakage spares any permanent damage to the machine.

Because the bi-metal blade is able to tolerate high tension, the operator will not be privy to the warning signs that indicate an overtensioned blade may break. As a result, he can actually overtension the bi-metal blade past a safe limit on the consumer band saw, and temporarily or permanently twist the frame. Excessive tension can ruin or damage key parts of the band, peel tires off, damage the wheel, and break the shafts. Shafts on band saws break more often than is thought.

When the bi-metal blade is used on a woodcutting band saw, it can vibrate or "flutter," a phenomenon called harmonic vibration. Most blades vibrate under certain situations influenced by a combination of factors such as blade speed, tension, feed pressure, and the workpiece material being cut. Harmonic vibration roughens the cut and slows the cutting process. If it continues for a long time, it shortens blade life.

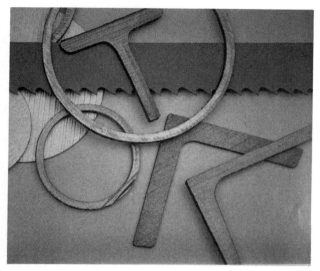

Illus. 121 (above left). Bi-metal blades are used to cut all kinds and shapes of metal. Illus. 122 (above right). The blade on the left is a spring-steel blade. The carbon blade in the middle and the bi-metal blade on the right have the same hook-tooth configuration.

Illus. 123. The bi-metal blade is made by laminating a high-speed steel strip to a spring steel back. Then the teeth are ground.

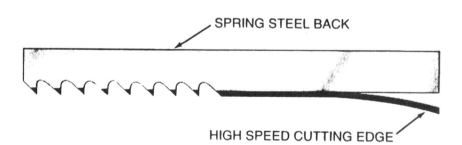

SPRING STEEL BACK

HIGH SPEED CUTTING EDGE

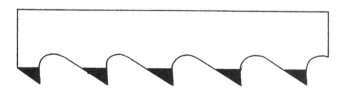

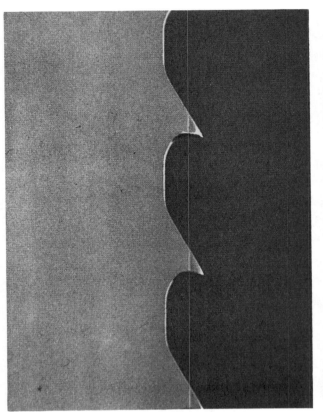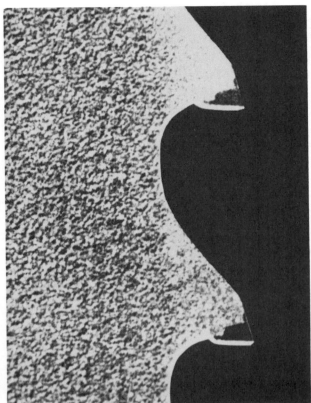

Illus. 124 (above left). A bi-metal blade with high-speed-steel hook teeth. Illus. 125 (above right). Carbide teeth are individually welded to the band.

Illus. 126. The stellite teeth on the Ryobi resaw stay sharper longer when it is used to cut green wood.

It can cause the teeth to greatly outlast the body. The bi-metal blade is quite stiff and hard. More tension has to be applied to the blade to curtail its tendency to vibrate.

Vibration is a particular problem with the ½-inch blade because most of these blades are .035 inch thick. This makes them very stiff; they require a great deal of tension to maintain smooth sawing. Blades this thick are recommended for saws with large wheels.

The bi-metal blade isn't as sharp as the carbon blade because a sharp edge isn't recommended for metal cutting. This may also add to its tendency to vibrate. The bi-metal blade may be most applicable in situations that require abrasion resistance, such as when cutting plywood, particle board, fibreglass, and exotic woods which have a high mineral content.

There are other disadvantages to using bi-metal blades. The woodworking industry has not found bi-metal to be cost-effective. Local saw-sharpening shops that rely on repeat business often don't recommend them for woodworking because they have had too much negative feedback from woodworkers who have tried them. And, bi-metal blades cost three to four times as much as the average carbon blade.

Using a bi-metal blade is not necessarily the best way to get the most out of your band saw. This can be achieved through a combination of good blade selection, proper tracking and wheel alignment, and good operating technique.

Special-Purpose Blades

There are a number of blades that are designed to cut a particular type of material or to make a specific type of cut. (See Illus. 127.) These blades are described below. Please note that sometimes the word band is used instead of blade. This is because in these cases the product is known by that designation.

Ply-Core Band

This band is designed specifically for plywood, especially for thick stacks of plywood. These blades are thick (.032-0.42 inch), and must be used on large band saws. These blades have coarse teeth with hard tips and a flexible band.

Furniture Band

As the name implies, this blade is used by furniture manufacturers to smoothly cut contours and shapes. Most of these bands have hard edges and are of the flex-back type. These blades usually have hook-skip teeth. They either have alternate-set teeth or a raker tooth every fifth or seventh tooth. Those used for large commercial saws are usually .032 inch thick. Furniture blades are available in widths of ¼, ⅜, and ½ inch.

Friction Band

Friction sawing is a unique metal-cutting technique. (See Illus. 128.) The blade runs very fast, up to 15,000 FPM. It is designed for very large saws because blade length is important for dissipating heat. The high speed of the friction-cutting blade creates heat, which melts the material in front of the blade. Thin material or odd-shaped metals may be friction-sawed when conventional methods fail. Friction sawing is suitable for material up to ½ inch thick. It is a technique that is used for cutting composite or complex materials such as high-strength steels, gratings and screens.

Illus. 127. There are now a number of blades made for one specific purpose. Most of these are blades that are used in the industrial sector.

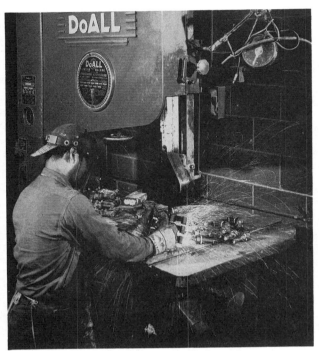

Illus. 128. In friction cutting, a high blade speed is used to produce heat. This softens the metal and makes it easier to remove with the saw teeth.

Illus. 129. The meat-cutting blade is thin enough to decrease waste, yet wide enough to have additional beam strength. The blade shown here is a skip-tooth blade.

Foundry Band

A foundry blade is very thick, usually about .050 inch, so it must be used on machines with at least 36-inch blades. This blade has an extremely heavy set that discourages binding or pinching. It is used for cutting waste off castings. It usually has a pitch of 3 TPI, and a raker set of hook teeth.

Meat Blade

Meat is usually cut with a thin, wide skip-tooth blade. (See Illus. 129.) This thin blade with a wide body wastes little material and has good beam strength.

Special-Purpose Bands

The band saw can be used with other blades besides the traditional blade with teeth.

Sanding Band

The blade can be replaced with a sandpaper band. There is usually a platen to hold the sand-

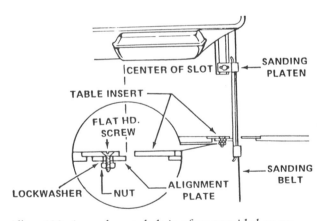

Illus. 130. A sandpaper belt is often provided as an accessory with consumer-grade band saws. A platen is used to support the sanding belt.

paper in place. (See Illus. 130.) Most consumer-grade band saws have this option.

Polishing Band

Another type of band that is useful is one for polishing objects. This is usually reserved for large industrial saws. Like the sanding band, it is used with a platen.

File Band

The band file is an industrial item. Short pieces of file are attached to a flexible band. (See Illus. 131.) A variety of band-file types are available.

Grit-Edge Blades

These blades have a metal band without teeth. Instead, a "grit" composite is fused to the front of the blade. The composite is either gulleted or continuous. (See Illus. 132.) The material used is either tungsten carbide or diamond. Following is a list of materials that can be cut with a grit-edge blade. Illus. 133–135 should include some of these materials being cut.

Fibreglass (all types)
Foamed glass
Carbon and graphite
Friction materials
Glass
Graphite epoxy

Hardened steel
Low-density ceramics
Honeycomb
Tires
Composites
Titanium
Beryllium

Cast iron
Nickel-base superalloys
Iron-Base superalloys
Fibre-reinforced cement

Round Bands

Round bands are used on specially designed band saws. There are two types of round bands. One is a spiral band. (See Illus. 136.) The other is a round grit band. Both are made by Doall. The

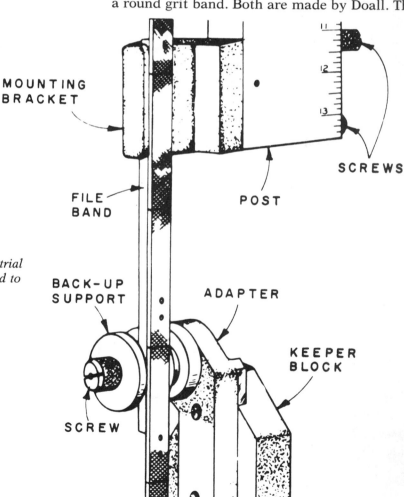

Illus. 131. File bands are used in industrial settings. Short pieces of file are attached to a flexible band.

grit used is either made of aluminum oxide, diamond, or borazon. This allows cutting from all directions, not just the front of the blade. This is particularly useful when using CNC equipment (computer controlled equipment) to guide the material.

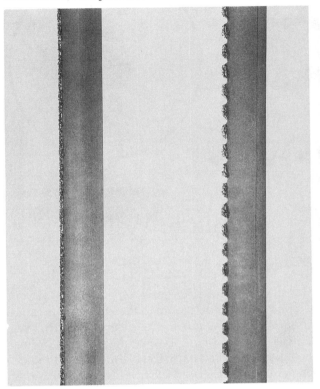

Illus. 132 (above left). Grit-edge blades have coarse-composition grit instead of teeth. The grit is either continuous, as shown on the blade on the left, or gulleted, as shown on the blade on the right. Illus. 133 (above right). Cutting fibreglass honeycomb.

Illus. 134 (above left). Cutting silica phenolic fibreglass. Illus. 135 (above right). Cutting high-alloy cast-iron pipe.

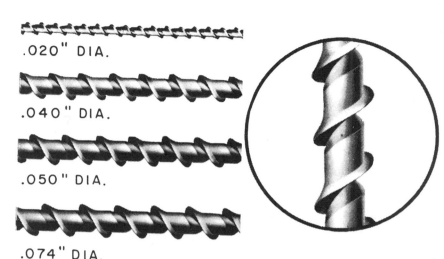

.020" DIA.

.040" DIA.

.050" DIA.

.074" DIA.

Illus. 136. Spiral bands are round and can cut from any direction.

Knife Bands

The knife band doesn't have teeth. Like a knife, it either has a straight blade, a scallop, or a wavy edge. These blades give a clean cut without sawdust or waste. They are used on a number of materials, including the following:

Foam rubber	Frozen food	Plastics
Cork	Metals	Coils
Rubber	Cardboard	Paper
Cloth	Sponge	Insulation

The straight knife band is perhaps the most useful of the knife bands. It is useful for cutting cardboard, foam (Illus. 137), and plastic mesh (Illus. 138).

Blade Weld

When to Weld the Blade

There are three occasions when the blade is welded. It is welded to form the continuous band after the blade is cut to the desired length. (See Illus. 139.) The blade is rewelded after it breaks to make it usable again. (See Illus. 140.) It makes sense to reweld a blade if it is in good shape. If, however, the blade is work-hardened, it will quickly break in another place. The third time a blade is welded is when it is used to make interior cuts. This often happens in metal working. The blade is purposefully sheared, threaded

Illus. 137 (above left). Foam is cut very cleanly with a straight knife band. Illus. 138 (above right). Plastic mesh—which is very hard to cut with a traditional blade—can be cleanly cut with a knife band.

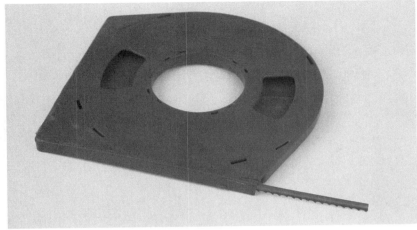

Illus. 139. Bands come in rolls of 100 or 250 feet.

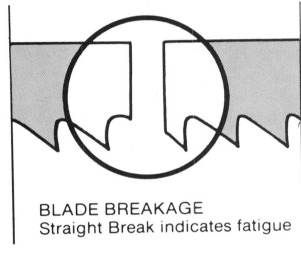

BLADE BREAKAGE
Straight Break indicates fatigue

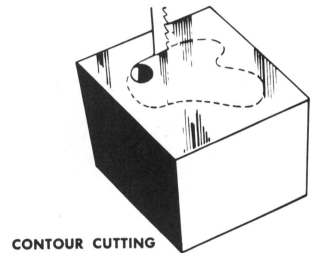

CONTOUR CUTTING

Illus. 140 (above left). Blades can be rewelded if they break. If the blade is in good condition, it makes sense to reweld it. If it has broken from metal fatigue or from work hardening, it will break again soon. Illus. 141 (above right). When you use the interior contour-cutting technique, you have to thread the blade through a hole and then reweld it.

through a hole, and rewelded. (See Illus. 141.) That's why it is usual for large metal-cutting band saws to have a welder on the column of the machine. (See Illus. 142 and 143.) This makes it easy to shear and reweld the blade quickly without removing the workpiece from the table.

Resistance Welding

The most commonly used welders used in industrial and professional shops are resistance-type welders. (See Illus. 144 and 145.) When a resistance-type welder is being used, first the blade ends are ground square. (See Illus. 146.) Then the ends are clamped together in the welder, and

heated until they fuse together to form the weld. (See Illus. 147.) Making a good weld takes skill, care, and practice, as there are a number of things that can go wrong during this process. (See Illus. 148.)

When the band is heated during welding, it is air-hardened and is, therefore, very brittle at the point where it has been welded. Before it can be used, you must anneal it to restore the weld joint to the same metallurgical hardness and strength as the rest of the band. This is done by reheating it to an annealling temperature and then cooling it slowly. The annealling temperature is detected by the color of the metal. For both carbon and high-speed-steel bands, the proper color is dull

Illus. 142 (above left). Large metal-cutting band saws have welders mounted on their columns. Illus. 143 (above right). A close-up of a resistance welder on a metal-cutting band saw. This welder expedites interior cutting.

Illus. 144 (below left). Two resistance welders. The large welder on the left is used for large blades. The small welder on the right is used for small blades. Illus. 145 (below right). Adjust the knobs and levers to get the proper band thickness.

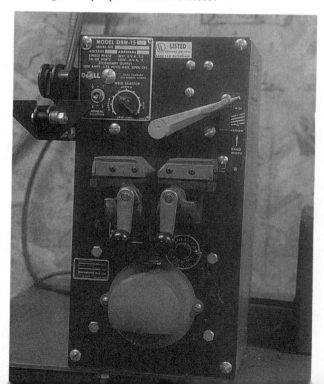

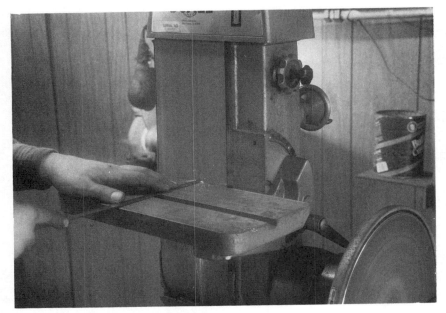

Illus. 146. Grind the blade ends flat before welding.

Illus. 147. Clamp the blade ends together in the welder.

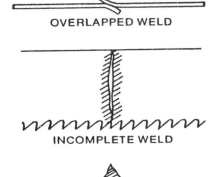

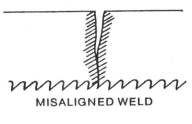

OVERLAPPED WELD

INCOMPLETE WELD

MISALIGNED WELD

EXCESS METAL AROUND WELD IN NARROW BLADE

"BURNED-OUT" WELD

Illus. 148. If the weld has any of these characteristics, it should be rewelded.

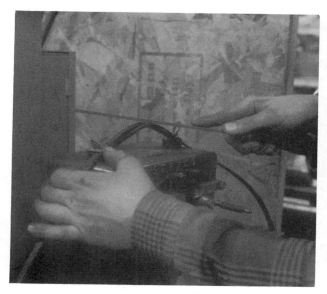

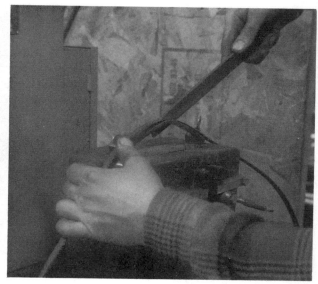

Illus. 149 (above left). When filing the blade back, it is important that the blade be straight and smooth. Check these features before installing a new blade. Illus. 150 (above right). File or grind the side of the weld smooth.

Illus. 151. This finished weld has a straight back. The tooth spacing could be better.

cherry red. Properly annealling the weld is as important as properly making the weld.

After the welding and annealling has been completed, file or grind the weld smooth. It is important that both the front and back of the blade are finished. (See Illus. 149 and 150.) A proper weld will be solid and smooth. (See Illus. 151.)

Silver Brazing

The alternative to resistance welding is brazing the joint together using a silver solder alloy between the two blade ends. Properly done, this joint is very strong and flexible. It also has the advantage of not requiring expensive or complicated machinery. (See Illus. 152.) The two blade ends are held in a vise and flux, and a small piece of the silver solder alloy is heated with a torch; this forms the joint. (See Illus. 153.) For a maximum surface area, the ends are first ground to 20 degrees. (See Illus. 154.) This technique takes some practice, but can be mastered and is a good way of salvaging blades that break but still are usable. It is especially useful if a professional resistance welder is not locally available.

The brazing kit shown in Illus. 152 is manufactured by New Milford Specialties Co. The kit comes in two sizes: one for blades ¼ to ¾ inch, and a smaller kit for blades from ⅛ to ⅜ inch. It is available from a number of the mail-order catalogues.

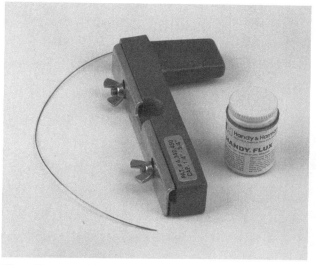

Illus. 152. A welding kit consists of silver solder wire, a blade holder, and flux.

Illus. 153. Use a propane torch to melt the silver solder alloy.

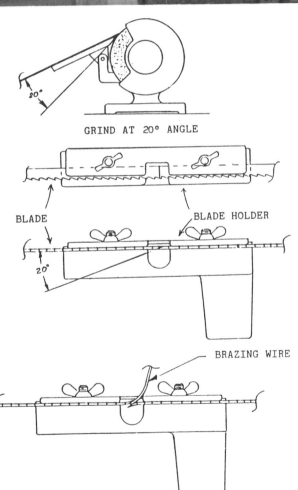

GRIND AT 20° ANGLE

BLADE — BLADE HOLDER

BRAZING WIRE

Illus. 154. Grind the blade ends at a 20-degree angle to increase the surface area of the weld.

Weld Problems

In order for the blade to cut and track properly, the weld must be straight and well aligned. Many band-saw problems can be traced to an irregularity in the weld. Following are some of the problems that can be encountered.

PREMATURE BREAKAGE
Experts feel that when a blade breaks, approximately half the time the break should be attributed to the weld, and half the time to the blade body. If it breaks consistently at the weld, the weld is bad. In this case, the blade should be rewelded. The local machine shop that I patronize will reweld a blade for nothing if it breaks at the weld. However, this may be too much to ask of a manufacturer.

BLADE DOES NOT FLEX PROPERLY
The blade should be flexible. Most band-saw users test the weld by flexing it. (See Illus. 155.) If it breaks, it needs to be rewelded. People often break a blade when they fold it for storage because they put undue pressure on the weld. The weld should withstand gentle flexing, but it shouldn't be expected to make a sharp bend.

BLADE IS OUT OF ALIGNMENT
There are three possible alignment situations. (See Illus. 156.) The one shown in C of Illus. 156 is very destructive because the sharp corner can damage the thrust bearing. When this weld is aligned as shown in B and C of Illus. 156, there

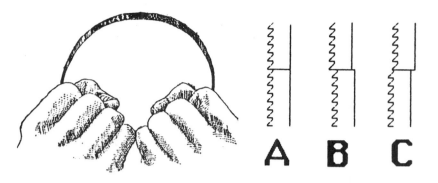

Illus. 155 (far left). The weld should be flexible so that it can withstand a fairly tight bend. Illus. 156 (left). The weld should be straight, as shown in A. If the weld is as shown in C, it will damage the thrust bearing.

will be a distinct ticking sound as the blade runs that's similar to that of a loud clock.

BLADE NOT WELDED STRAIGHT

The back of the weld should be straight. This is not as easy to do as it sounds. During the hardening of the teeth, the front of the blade shrinks. If a blade is rested on its back, it will often rock because the back is convex and the front (tooth) side is concave. Some blades rock worse than others.

Because of the arching of the blade, it is impossible to weld the blade perfectly straight. However, the blade should be welded as straight as possible. If the blade is not straight, it will pulsate back and forth on the saw. This can be very annoying. Sometimes it will make tracking the blade difficult. It may be hard to keep the blade on the saw because it will keep coming forward off the saw. This is because the back of the blade is longer than the front of the blade, and unequal pressure is being applied on the wheels.

Sharpening a Blade

When a blade becomes dull, its ability to cut is compromised. A dull blade should be replaced or resharpened. There are two means of sharpening: filing and grinding. Filing is the traditional method, and works with softer blades such as spring steel. Fine-pitch carbon blades with a standard tooth form can be refiled. Harder blades such as hardened spring steel and carbon blades are often too hard to file. These are usually ground. The only way to sharpen metal-cutting bi-metal blades is to grind them.

Filing

Many band-saw users feel that it isn't worth the effort to sharpen blades. It is not hard to sharpen them, but it is rather tedious. However, there are some advantages to sharpening blades. A properly filed blade is often sharper than a new one, and stays sharp for a longer period of time. This is especially true with a fine-pitch blade such as an ⅛-inch 14 TPI blade. A blade such as a ¹⁄₁₆-inch blade is impractical to sharpen.

Filing is usually done by hand, though some saw-sharpening shops use specialized automatic filing machines. A three-corner file is commonly used for filing band-saw blades. A file with a round corner is best.

Good light is important; natural daylight is best. Hold the blade securely in a vise. A saw-sharpening vise works best. (See Illus. 157.) A metal-working vise can also be used.

When filing, use the same number of strokes on each tooth, usually three. File the teeth straight across, 90 degrees to the body. (See Illus. 158.) File the teeth *after* the teeth are set. (See Illus. 159.) Set the teeth every 3 to 5 sharpenings.

You can use a handsaw set for the teeth. It is best to file the teeth that are set towards you first, and then reverse the blade and file the other teeth. When filing, stroke away from yourself. This leaves the burr on the inside. (See Illus. 160.) The rakers should be filed in a similar manner to the other teeth, with every other raker filed from the same side.

Some people like to file the blade on the saw. To do this, turn the saw blade "inside out" and remount it so that the teeth point up. Clamp blocks of wood together in a vise to prevent the

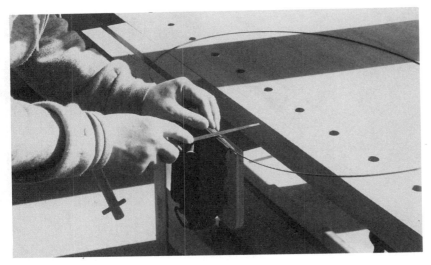

Illus. 157. A good vise and adequate light are needed when you file the saw blade.

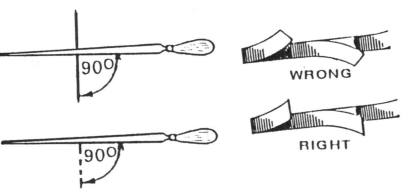

WRONG

RIGHT

Illus. 158 (far left). File the teeth 90 degrees to the blade body. Illus. 159 (far right). First set the tooth and then sharpen it.

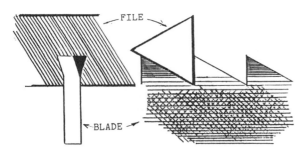

FILE

BLADE

Illus. 160. Filing from the outside inward leaves the burr on the inside.

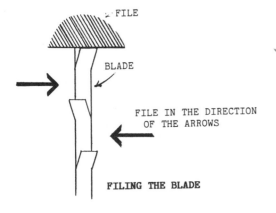

FILE

BLADE

FILE IN THE DIRECTION
OF THE ARROWS

FILING THE BLADE

Illus. 161. Here a 14-inch grinding wheel is being used to sharpen a band-saw mill blade.

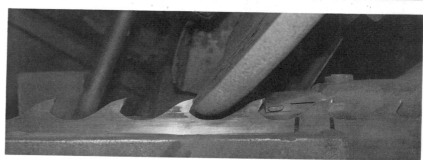

Illus. 162. The grinding wheel and the blade movement are synchronized so that the back and the face of the blade are ground.

Illus. 163. A look at the Kasco grinding motor and the blade support. The blade shown is 1¼ inches wide.

Illus. 164. A close-up of the Kasco grinder. An adjustable pin locates the blade in relationship to the grinding wheel.

wood from moving while the filing is being done. If you don't have a good saw vise, this may be the preferable approach.

Grinding

Grinding is done with a rotating grinding wheel. It is faster than filing, and can remove material that is too hard for a file. If a spacing jig is used, grinding is a very accurate process.

Illus. 161 and 162 show the huge automated grinding machine at Johnson Lumber Company in Charlotte, Michigan. The machine automatically synchronizes the movement of the blade and the wheel so that the front and back of the blade are touched by the stone. Illus. 163 shows the Kasco grinding jig used for sharpening the saw blade used on the mill saw. An adjustable pin is used to stop the movement of the blade, thus spacing each cut. (See Illus. 164.) This design is similar to that of a chain-saw filing machine.

The machines shown are fairly expensive. One option is to use one of the cheaper mitre saws that have a tilt mechanism. Such a model is available from either Black and Decker or Ryobi.

Blade Maintenance

The band-saw blade is a fragile tool that requires care both on and off the band saw. If the blade is properly cared for, it will last longer and give a better performance.

The condition of the band saw makes a difference. If the machine vibrates or has out-of-round wheels, the blade life will be shortened. Vibration is often decreased by good pulley and belt alignment. High-quality cast-iron pulleys and a high-quality belt often make a great improvement, especially on less-expensive saws.

Proper saw adjustment prolongs the life of the blade. Saw alignment and the tracking and adjustment of the guides and thrust bearing are very important. Poorly adjusted metal guides can damage the blade teeth. The new nonmetal guides such as Cool Blocks prevent tooth damage and also prolong blade life by decreasing the heat from friction between the blade and the blocks.

Overtensioning and undertensioning can shorten blade life. It is a good idea to decrease the tension after using the saw. This is also good for the wheels and the tires. When decreasing the tension, use the same number of turns on the knob each time. Then, when it comes time to increase the tension again, you can do it quickly and accurately.

How the operator uses the saw is also important. The movement should be smooth and slow. A quick turn can cause a kink, which is a sharp bend in the blade. A blade will usually break at the kink. Feeding too fast can shorten blade life. Forcing a wide blade around a tight curve twists the body of the blade, which often causes the blade to break. Running the saw for periods of time when the saw is not cutting also isn't good for the blade.

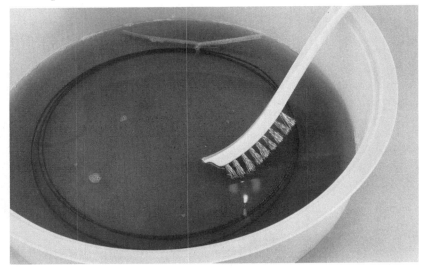

Illus. 165. The best way to clean a fine-pitch blade is to soak it in a cleaning solution. After the solution has softened the pitch and gum, remove it with a fine wire brush.

It is important that the blade is clean. With some woods such as pine and cherry, the residue can build up on the face of the tooth. The net effect is that the blade will cut like it is dull, when in reality is only packed with residue. This is especially true with fine-pitched saw blades. Cherry residue can actually become baked on the front of the tooth. This can also be a problem at times with some green woods.

To clean coarse-tooth blades, use a stiff bristle or fine wire brush. To clean fine-tooth blades, soak the blade in a solution first and then clean it with a very fine wire brush. (See Illus. 165.) A number of solutions work, such as cleaning ammonia, oven cleaner, or turpentine.

The blade should also be handled with care when it is off the saw. If the blade is to be stored in a humid place, it should be wiped with an oil rag. The oil will prevent it from rusting. If a blade has become rusty, wipe it with an oil rag to remove as much rust as is possible. If it is very rusty, steel wool will do a good job of removing the rust.

When being stored, blades are usually folded into three loops. You can hang a blade up in an unfolded position, but it will take up a lot of space on the wall. Some people find it difficult to fold a blade into three loops. It is not hard, especially if you master one of two basic techniques. The principle is the same for both: You hold the blade and make one twist; then you make another twist, which creates the three loops.

The easier technique is to hold the blade with your foot, which in this case functions like a third hand. (See Illus. 166.) It is a good idea not to apply too much weight to the blade so that you don't damage the teeth. Another option is to put a small piece of scrap wood under the blade. Hold the blade with one hand, and then twist it. (See Illus. 167.) After the first twist, use your free hand to hold the blade while you reposition your other hand. (See Illus. 168.)

Next, make another twist of the blade in the same direction as the first twist. (See Illus. 169.) This will create three loops. (See Illus. 170.) Open your hand so that all of the loops are captured. (See Illus. 171.)

If the blade is not too wide, you can easily fold it with your hands. Hold it so that your thumbs

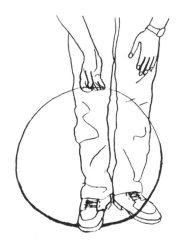

Illus. 166. Hold one end of the blade with your foot.

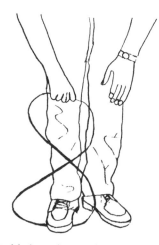

Illus. 167. Hold the other end with your hand and twist it.

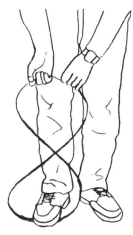

Illus. 168. Use your free hand to hold the blade while you reposition your other hand.

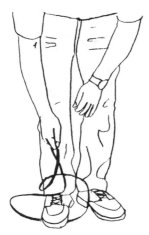

Illus. 169. Make another twist of the blade in the same direction of the first twist.

Illus. 170. This creates three loops.

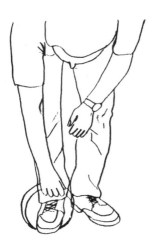

Illus. 171. Open your hand so that all of the loops are captured. (Illus. 166–171 courtesy of Chris Morris)

are pointed in opposite directions. (See Illus. 172.) Twist the blade by rotating your hands in opposite directions. (See Illus. 173.) This will create two loops. (See Illus. 174.) With a continuous twisting motion in the same direction (Illus. 175), complete the process by making another twist; this creates the three loops. (See Illus. 176.)

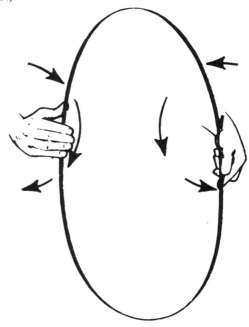

Illus. 172. Hold the blade so that your thumbs are pointed in the opposite directions.

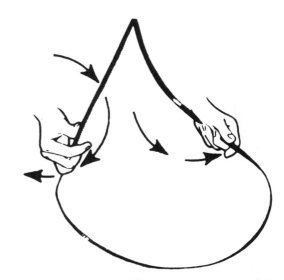

Illus. 173. To twist the blade, rotate your hands in opposite directions.

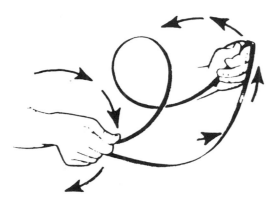

Illus. 174. Two loops are created.

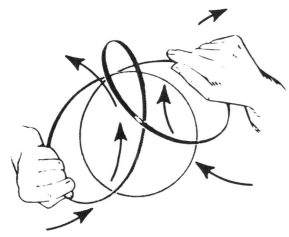

Illus. 175. Twist the blade again.

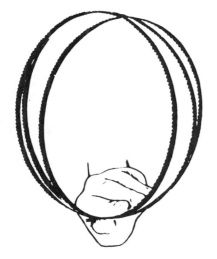

Illus. 176. The additional twist has created a third loop.

Illus. 177. This sharpened blade has been folded and tied with pipe cleaner. This photograph shows a good view of the board that the sharpening vise is attached to. The board fits into the bench vise.

You can use string, wire, etc., to hold the blade in the folded position. Pipe cleaners work very well, and are reusable. (See Illus. 177.)

When unfolding a blade, be careful—especially when using wide blades, because they have a lot of spring. Always hold the blade away from you; never try to catch or control it with your body. Hold one loop with one hand, and let the blade recoil at arm's length. If the blade is a coarse-toothed one, you may want to wear gloves. Always turn your face away from an uncoiling blade. After you unfold the blade, inspect it. Try to avoid using blades with cracks, bends, or kinks.

Determining Blade Length

Band-saw blades are selected by their length, width, pitch, tooth style, set, metal thickness, and type. Each of these characteristics will help you determine the best blade for the job. Band-saw blades are sold either in a single-blade length or rolls of 100, 250, and 500 feet. If you have a brazer or welder, it is more economical to purchase blades by the coil.

Band-saw length, as well as the machine's size, varies among the different manufacturers. The blade length may be found in the owner's manual, stamped on the machine, or stamped on the box the previous blade came in. If it isn't, or you want to double-check the length, calculate it from the following formula: $L = (3.14X) + (2 \times Y)$. L is the length (in inches) of the band-saw blade. X is the diameter (in inches) of either the upper or lower wheel. Y is the distance (in inches) between the wheel centerlines.

Before measuring the length, adjust the upper (tension) wheel so that it is located between the fully up and fully down positions. This midpoint will allow adjustment if the blade is made slightly long or short.

Ordering Blades

Blades can be bought locally at a hardware dealer. Some hardware dealers or sharpening shops sell blade stock and will make a blade to your required length. However, this may take some time and you may want to call them ahead of time. Many catalogues now sell band-saw blades in various lengths.

4
Selecting a Blade

Using the correct blade is important because it is the first step in attaining good band-saw performance. In fact, one of the most frequently asked questions about the band saw is "How do you decide which blade to use?" The answer depends on a number of interrelated factors. These factors will be explored in this chapter.

There is no ideal blade that does everything well. The blade that you choose determines the type of work that you can do. If you choose a very coarse blade, it will cut like a chain saw. In contrast, a very fine blade will allow you to do very intricate scroll work. The best choice you make will give you the most advantages for a particular application.

There is a huge selection of blades available that have various combinations of characteristics like width, thickness, pitch, tooth style, and set. This is an advantage. If you have ten different blades in your shop rather than a couple, you stand a better chance of finding the proper blade for the work that you are doing.

Blade life and tooth sharpness are prolonged if the proper blade is chosen for a particular application. Using a blade for the wrong application is the best way to abuse it. Blades can take a lot of wear, but they cannot take abuse. Using a blade for its intended purpose allows for maximum efficiency and is the best way to prolong its usable life.

Blade Groups

Band-saw blades are usually classified into three different groups: small, medium, and large. Width, tooth form and pitch figure in each classification, so each blade group has its own characteristics. Small blades usually have a standard (regular) tooth form and a fine pitch. Medium blades usually have a skip tooth with a raker set and a medium-to-coarse pitch. Large blades often have a hook tooth with a raker set and a coarse pitch. (See Illus. 178.) There are exceptions to the group classifications, an example being the ½-inch 14 TPI blade, which has a regular form and an alternate set. The teeth on this large blade are the kind that you would usually find on a blade classified as "small." Have at least one blade from each group. This way you will be prepared for most situations.

Following are the characteristics for each group of blades:

	SMALL	MEDIUM	LARGE
WIDTH	¹⁄₁₆–⅛ inch	³⁄₁₆–⅜ inch	½ inch and over
PITCH	14–32 TPI (fine)	4–12 TPI	2–4 TPI (coarse)
TOOTH FORM	standard skip	skip standard hook/skip hook	hook skip

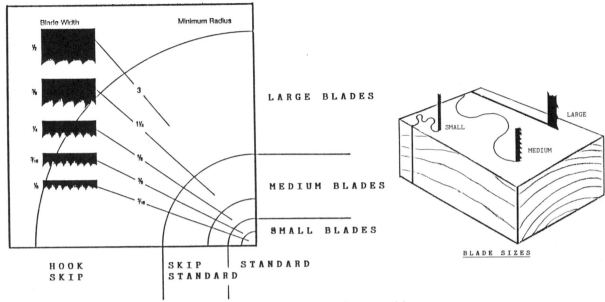

Illus. 178. Blades are usually divided into three groups: small, medium, and large.

Cutting Priorities

To define your cutting priorities, analyze the situation and select a blade according to your requirements. Depending on the situation, one or two of these factors will be more important than the others. The following is a list of possible requirements.

1. speed
2. smoothness
3. accuracy
4. straightness
5. depth (thick or thin stock)
6. tightness of curves
7. hardness or softness of material
8. orientation of grain
   A. Crosscutting (cutting across the grain)
   B. Ripping (cutting with the grain)
   C. Multigrain cutting (both ripping and crosscutting)

Some of these factors complement each other, and some do not. The three examples of cutting situations that follow will illustrate this point.

Example #1

In this situation, you require a blade to do the following: (1) cut thick stock; (2) cut straight; and (3) cut quickly. Smoothness *isn't* an important requirement. The blade that is the best choice when all these requirements are considered is probably a large blade—for example, a ½-inch-wide blade with a hook form and a 3 TPI pitch.

Example #2

In this situation, you require the blade to cut the following smoothly and accurately: (1) cross grain; (2) thin stock; and (3) hard material. It should also be able to make tight curves. The blade that will best meet all these requirements would be one with a ⅛-inch width, a standard tooth form, and a 12-14 TPI pitch.

Example #3

In this situation, you require the blade to do the following: (1) cut thick stock; (2) work tight curves (one-inch radius); (3) rip long and straight; and (4) make short cross-grain cuts smoothly. No blade can really meet all of these requirements. Some of these requirements contradict each other. For example, the best blade for cutting cross grain is not the best blade for cutting with the grain, and vice versa. You must reach a compromise here. A ¼-inch blade with a skip-tooth form and a 6 TPI pitch would be a good choice. It would meet all these requirements, even though it would not be the best blade to use to meet any single one of them.

For an idea of which blade to use that will

meet your cutting priorities, refer to the blade-selection chart. (See Table 1.) It is interesting to note that the medium-sized blade—the most popular blade for band-saw owners—is the best one to use only when you make gradual curves. However, it is popular because it is a good blade to use when you have to compromise.

Most band-saw owners are reluctant to change blades. Many see it as an inconvenience and would rather keep one blade on the saw all of the time. The medium-sized blade can cut all but the tightest curves and the thickest stock. However, if you are doing a lot of a particular type of work, it would be best to change to the most appropriate blade.

You should select a blade according to the following priorities:

1. **Width.** First decide on blade width. If all of the cuts in your work are straight, use a wide blade for added beam strength. If there are curves, you will determine blade width by how many and how large they are. (See Illus. 179.)

2. **Form.** The second most important choice is the tooth form. This is determined by the orientation of the grain. Choosing the tooth form also affects the pitch. The standard tooth form has twice as many teeth as the other forms.

3. **Pitch.** The tooth spacing (pitch) is the final consideration. After choosing the width and the form, you may not have much say about the blade pitch used unless you have a large selection of blades on hand. Following is an exploration of width, form, and pitch covered in detail.

Blade Width

The amount of detail and the size of the detail in your pattern determines the blade width you should use. Choose as wide a blade as possible, yet one that will make the tightest curves with ease. You will have to determine the smallest curve in the pattern and match the blade to that radius. An example is the elephant puzzle shown in Illus. 180. The small elephant's trunk is the smallest curve.

There are options to matching the blade to the smallest curve in the pattern. If there is only one very tight cut, it may be best to use a turning hole, a relief cut, successive passes, or to change the blade. If you have a lot of cutting to do, you can use a wider blade for the bigger curves and then switch to a narrower blade for the tighter curves. Changing blades can often save cutting and finishing time.

USING A RADIUS CHART

Radius charts can be found in many woodworking books, magazine articles, and on blade boxes. (See Illus. 181.) They differ slightly from one another, but are good as rough indicators of how tightly a curve can be cut with a particular blade. Each blade, saw, and operator is different, so it is impossible to make a truly accurate chart.

A blade can cut continuously without backtracking any curve that has a radius as much as or more than is shown on the chart. For example, a ³⁄₁₆-inch blade will cut a circle with a ⁵⁄₁₆-inch radius or a ⁵⁄₈-inch diameter. To test if a ³⁄₁₆-inch blade would work for a particular curve, place a dime, which is roughly ⁵⁄₈ inch, over the pattern. The ³⁄₁₆-inch blade can cut a curve bigger than the dime, but not smaller.

The dime test can also be used on the rabbit pattern shown in Illus. 182. By placing a dime on the tight curve, it is easy to determine that a ³⁄₁₆-inch blade is a good choice for this pattern. It should be noted that a different technique should be used to determine if a blade would work on the *tightest* curve.

On wide, gentle curves, the blade's width isn't critical.

As shown with the example of the dime, it is often easier to use an object rather than a radius chart to size a curve. It is more convenient to use a household object.

It is more difficult to use an object to size a curve for the smaller blades. The tightest curve that an ⅛-inch blade can cut is the size of a pencil eraser. The tightest curve that a ³⁄₁₆-inch blade can cut is the size of a dime. The tightest curve that a ¼-inch blade can cut is the size of a quarter. After a while, you won't even need an object to size the possible curve of a blade because you will have become familiar with this process.

CUTTING CURVES

Make a test cut with a piece of scrap wood if you are not sure that the blade and the curve match. Finding that the blade width is too big for a turn in the middle of a critical cut is the sort of problem that can easily be avoided by good planning.

TYPE OF CUT	TEETH	WIDTH	FORM	BLADE SPEED	FEED RATE
Resawing	Coarse	Wide	Hook	Medium or fast	Slow
Ripping (less than 2″)	Medium	Wide	Hook	Slow to Medium	Medium or fast
Ripping (more than 2″)	Corase	Wide	Hook	Medium or fast	Slow
Crosscutting (1″ or less)	Fine	Wide	Standard	Medium or fast	Slow
Crosscutting (1″ or more)	Medium or fine	Wide	Standard	Medium or fast	Slow
Mitre Cut	Medium or fine	Wide	Standard	Medium or fast	Slow
Tenons	Medium	Medium or wide	Standard	Medium or fast	Slow to medium
Round Stock Ripping	Medium	Medium or wide	Standard	Medium or fast	Slow
Round Stock Crosscut	Medium or fine	Medium or wide	Standard	Medium	Slow
Sharp Curves	Fine	Narrow	Standard	Slow	Slow
Gradual Curves	Medium or fine	Medium	Skip	Medium or slow	Slow to medium

TYPE OF MATERIAL	TEETH	WIDTH	BLADE SPEED	FEED RATE
Foam:				
Hard	Medium	Medium or wide	Medium or fast	Fast
Soft	Knife	—	Medium	Medium
Rubber:				
Hard	Fine or medium	Medium	Slow	Slow
Soft	Fine	Medium	Slow	Slow
Bone:	Fine or medium	Medium	Medium	Slow to medium
Plywood:				
3/4″	Medium	Medium	Medium	Slow to medium
Less than 1/2″	Fine	Medium	Medium	Slow to medium
Masonite:	Fine or medium	Medium	Medium	Medium
Plastic:				
Thick	Coarse	Medium	Slow	Slow
Thin	Fine or medium	Medium	Slow	Slow
Non-Ferrous Metal:	Fine	Medium or wide	Slow	Slow
Paper or Cardboard:	Fine	Medium or wide	Medium	Slow to medium

BLADE SPEED:

slow 800ft/min
medium 1800 ft/min
fast 2700 ft/min

FEED RATE OF STOCK:

slow 2 ft/min to 4 ft/min
medium 5 ft/min to 11 ft/min
fast above 11 ft/min

Table 1. Blade selection chart.

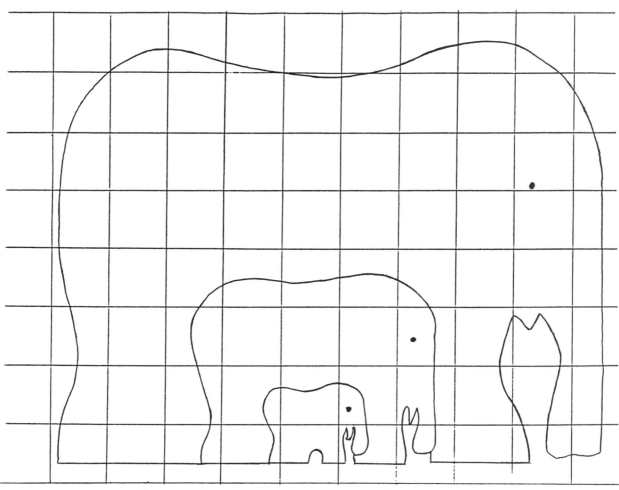

Illus. 179. The small elephant's trunk is the tightest curve in the pattern. The small elephant can be cut with a ⅛-inch blade. The medium-size elephant can be cut with a ³/₁₆-inch blade. The best blade for the largest elephant is a ¼-inch blade.

Illus. 180. These elephants are made out of thick oak.

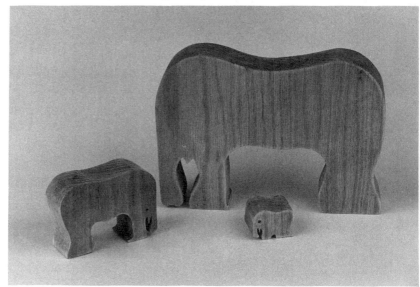

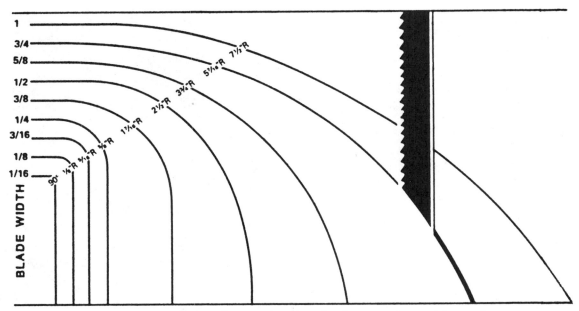

Illus. 181. Radius charts can be found in woodworking books, magazine articles, and on blade boxes.

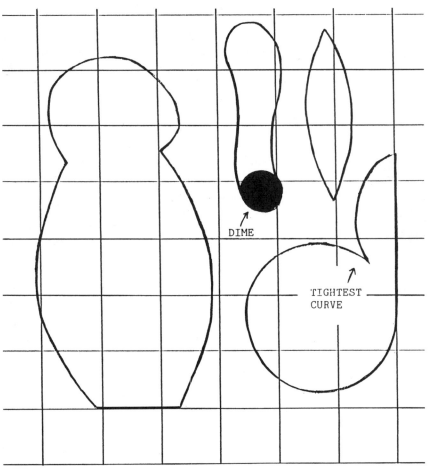

DIME

TIGHTEST CURVE

Illus. 182. To determine if a 3/16-inch blade can cut the tightest curve presented in the pattern, measure the turn with a dime. (Drawing courtesy of Chris Morris)

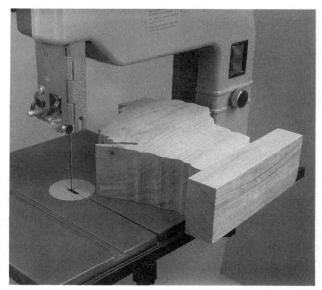

Illus. 183 (above left). This rabbit was made out of ¾-inch pine and then painted.
Illus. 184 (above right). Because of the detail, this pattern of the state of Wisconsin was cut with an ⅛-inch blade. (Photo courtesy of Rick Bechen)

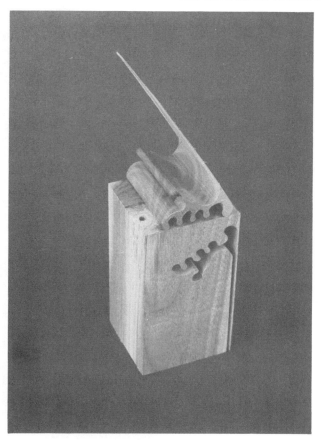

Illus. 185. The ⅛-inch blade is useful for tight curves, but it can also make an extremely straight cut even in thick stock.

On large curves, like a circle, try to use a blade that is close to the size indicated in Table I. For example, a ½-inch blade with a radius of 2½ inches is the best choice for a 6-inch circle because the tightest circle it can make is 5 inches. If the desired circle were 5 inches, it would be best to use a ⅜-inch blade to give yourself some leeway.

Use a smaller blade in a situation where there is a lot of detail. Illus. 186 shows a ⅛-inch blade with a raker set and a 14 TPI pitch being used to cut a butternut pattern depicting the state of Wisconsin. Butternut is a soft wood, and the blade gives a good finish. The ⅛-inch blade, which can be used to cut tight turns, can also be used for very straight cuts. (See Illus. 185.)

When you are making long, gentle curves, use as wide a blade as possible. In Illus. 186, a ½-inch blade with a 3 TPI pitch and hook-skip teeth with a raker set is used to give a good cut and a smooth finish. The wider the band, the less likelihood of blade deflection.

Tooth Form

Tooth form was discussed in detail in the previous chapter. This section concentrates on its practical applications.

There are two distinct classifications of material. Inorganic materials such as metal, plastic,

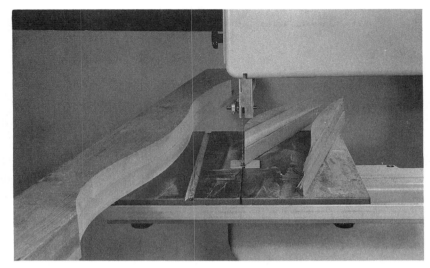

Illus. 186. Long, gentle curves can be made with a wide blade. Because smoothness was a consideration when this cut was being make, a ½-inch hook-skip blade was used.

and foam have a uniform consistency. With this type of material, you get the same results no matter which way the material is oriented into the saw blade. In contrast, organic material such as wood has grain (alternating hard and soft surfaces). This makes cutting wood more complex because the orientation of the grain affects the cut. Cutting along the grain (ripping) takes a different approach than cutting across the grain (crosscutting).

There are three basic types of sawing: ripping, crosscutting, and multigrain sawing. (See Illus. 187.) Ripping is cutting along the grain. Crosscutting, as its name implies, is cutting across the grain. Diagonal sawing (a mitre cut) is a type of crosscut. Multigrain sawing is when both ripping and crosscutting occur in the same cut, such as when cutting a circle.

Another type of cut that is not used often but has some advantages is called with-grain sawing. When you use with-grain sawing, you stand the wood on its end grain and saw it. Resawing is considered a rip cut.

Following is a discussion of these cuts and how they affect the tooth form you will choose.

CROSSCUTTING
When a band saw cuts across the grain (crosscutting), the teeth cut the hardest surface of the work, shearing thousands of tiny fibres.

It should be remembered that there is no cross cut band-saw blade per se. If the surface quality is important, it is best to use a blade with a 0-degree rake such as those with standard or skip teeth. Blades with standard or skip teeth will cleanly cut the small fibres rather than roughly tearing them. Blades with a standard form are better than those with a skip form if a fine finish is required because they have a finer pitch. For a fine finish, use a very slow feed rate. (See Illus. 188.) This is especially important in joinery such as dovetails. (See Illus. 189.)

Blades with hook teeth can be used for crosscutting, but the finish will be very rough—particularly on soft woods. (See Illus. 190.) If speed is *more* important than the finish, blades with hook teeth are a good choice.

RIPPING
When a band saw cuts along the line of the grain (ripping), the fibre that the tooth cuts is not as hard as those cut when crosscutting. The most efficient cutting approach is a chopping action such as that made by a hook tooth. (See Illus. 191.) The angled tooth can cut off the fibres more easily. It is good for ripping because it cuts straight without being deflected by the grain. Also, this type of sawing creates a lot of bulky sawdust, especially on thick stock that's being resawed. The large carrying capacity of the hook gullet is important in this situation.

Blades with standard and skip teeth can also be used for ripping if the wood isn't too thick and if a slow feed rate is used. A blade with standard teeth has a fine pitch, and will give the smoothest finish with a slow feed rate.

MULTIGRAIN SAWING
This term refers to a situation where you are doing both crosscutting and ripping in the same

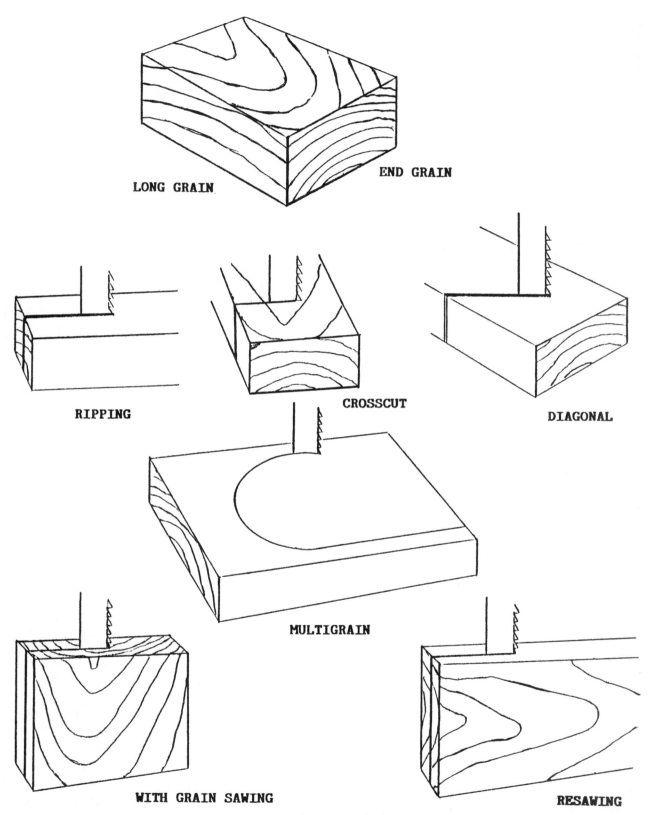

LONG GRAIN

END GRAIN

RIPPING

CROSSCUT

DIAGONAL

MULTIGRAIN

WITH GRAIN SAWING

RESAWING

Illus. 187. The basic cuts that can be made with a band saw.

 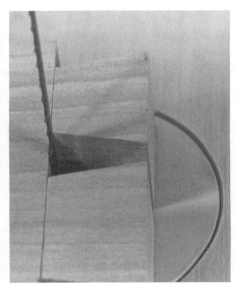

Illus. 188 (above left). The top piece was cut with a ½-inch, 14 TPI standard-tooth blade using a very slow feed. The bottom piece was cut with a 6 TPI skip-tooth blade. A slow feed was used on the first quarter of the cut, which is on the left side. The rate of feed was gradually increased, which created a rougher cut. Illus. 189 (above right). This ⅛-inch 14 TPI standard-tooth blade is being used to very accurately remove waste from a dovetail.

 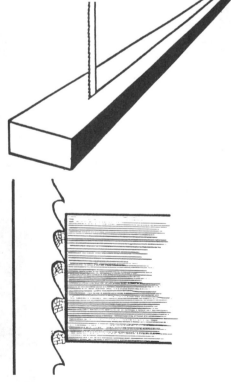

DANGER

ALLOW TOOL TO STOP BEFORE ADJUSTING

Illus. 190 (above left). A coarse, hook-tooth blade cuts quickly, but the results are rough when it is used to crosscut. This is a good blade to use when speed is more important than the smoothness of the cut. Illus. 191 (above right). A blade with hook teeth is the most efficient one to use for rip cuts.

cut. A good example of this is cutting a circle. About a quarter of the cutting is ripping, another quarter is crosscutting, and about half is diagonal sawing. (Saw Illus. 192.) The best blade for

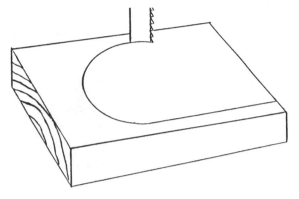

MULTIGRAIN SAWING

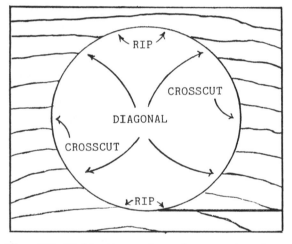

Illus. 192. Multigrain sawing refers to a situation where all three grain orientations are encountered.

Illus. 193. In a multigrain cutting situation, a fine-pitch standard-tooth blade gives the best finish. The red oak shown here has been cut with a 14 TPI standard-tooth blade. The pieces show the tightest turn a 1/8-inch blade can make.

diagonal and crosscut sawing has a standard-tooth form. The best blade for rough ripping has hook teeth. The best blade for smooth ripping has either skip or standard teeth.

Usually, the best solution is to compromise and use a blade between the hook and the standard-tooth form. The skip-tooth form shares some of the characteristics of the hook and the standard forms. Like the standard form, it has a 0-degree rake, which is important for diagonal cutting and crosscutting. It is similar to the hook form in that it has a coarse pitch, which makes it efficient at ripping.

Blades with skip teeth can both rip and crosscut. They are not as good at ripping as those with a hook form, or as good at crosscutting as those with a standard form. However, they are fairly good at both cuts, especially if a slow feed rate is used.

If you cut a circle with a blade with either hook or standard teeth, you will notice (if you pay attention) the difference when you change from ripping to crosscutting. The cuts sound and feel different. When you cut a circle with a blade that has skip teeth, you will feel and hear less of a change when you encounter different grain types.

One advantage of the standard-style teeth is that they cut well in all directions—with the grain (ripping), cross grain (crosscutting), or diagonally (mitre). This makes blades with this form the best choice for complex patterns where the blade must cut well in all directions (Illus. 193), and when a smooth finish is required. With a slow feed rate, a blade with a standard form is the choice for cutting multiple pieces. (See Illus.

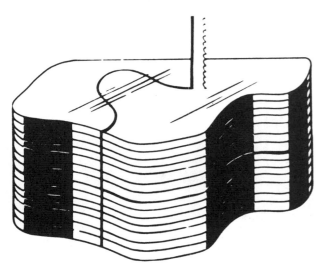

Illus. 194. When you are cutting multiple pieces, the finish is usually a priority. In such cases, use a fine-tooth standard blade like the one shown in Illus. 193 and make sure that you cut at a very slow rate.

Illus. 195. Resawing is cutting a board in half when the piece is on its edge. This technique is often used to make wide panels. When the piece is opened by resawing and then glued back together it is called book-matching. The grain pattern in this drawing is typical of a tangentially sawn board, and is called flat grain.

194.) It is also the blade of choice for plywood work. It would be the best choice for circle-cutting if the final finish were important.

CUTTING THICK STOCK

Resawing is a technique that is often used in cabinetmaking. (See Illus. 195.) When resawing, use a blade with a hook or hook-skip form. (See Illus. 196 and 197.) If one of these forms doesn't seem to work for a particular application, the other will. Blades with hook teeth do not cut curves well that have a lot of exposed end grain. In this situation, use those with hook-skip teeth. Also use a blade with hook-skip teeth for thick work requiring a fine finish, and when cutting oak and maple. For thick, rough green stock, use a blade with hook teeth. (See Illus. 199 and 200.) Walnut and cherry and softer woods can be cut well with either blade.

The 3 TPI hook-tooth blade is usually the best choice for very rough work. It isn't sensitive to grain direction, which can be a problem with a skip-tooth blade. If a blade is sensitive to grain direction, it follows the grain rather than the desired line.

Always be aware of the grain direction of the wood and the hardness of the wood. Illus. 201 shows a 2 × 4 that was eaten by ants. They ate everything but the winter wood (the hardest part of the growth ring) and the knot. This should give you an idea of how tough growth rings and knots can be.

Because a blade with hook teeth really bites into the wood, it takes more skill to cut smoothly than other blades. Illus. 202 and 203 show two boards cut one after the other with a blade with a 3 TPI pitch and hook teeth. The top piece was cut by an inexperienced person. The bottom piece was cut by me. The line on the left side of the photo occurred when I stopped the saw. The goal is to have a constant feed that keeps the teeth busy, but not too busy. The many lines on the top piece indicates that the operator stopped frequently.

WITH-GRAIN CUTTING

A blade with a standard form is a wonderful tool for cutting thick stock because with the appropriate slow feed it can give a very smooth cut in all types of grain. This is especially true if the cut is made with the grain. In this case, the piece is stood on edge with the end grain on top. (See

Illus. 196 (left). Resawing oak with a 3 TPI hook-tooth blade. Illus. 197 (above). Close-up of the 3 TPI hook-tooth blade cutting red oak.

Illus. 198. The finish on this hard maple was achieved with a 3 TPI skip-hook-tooth blade. It is smoother than one you would get if you used a hook-tooth blade.

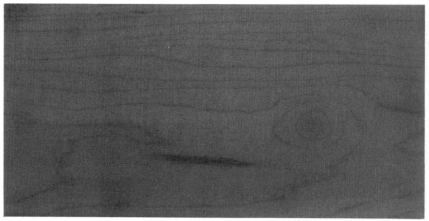

Illus. 199 and 200 (below). Where the finish is important, the hook-skip tooth blade is a good blade to use. It is particularly helpful when the piece will have to be finished by hand, in which case you want to cut the piece as smoothly as possible.

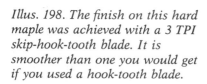

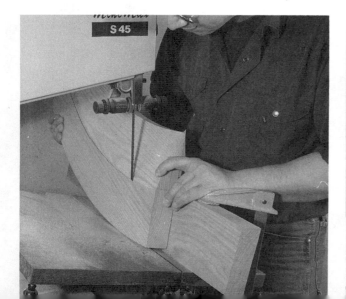

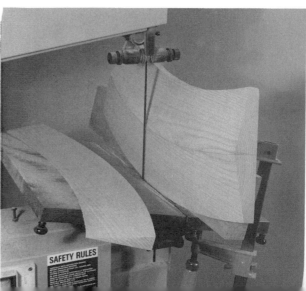

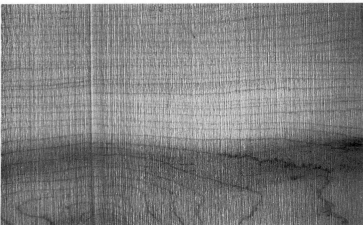

Illus. 201. The hardness of the knots and the direction of the grain are factors that you must be aware of. This ant-eaten piece of wood reveals the hardness of the winter wood and the knot. This can have an effect on the blade. Hook and skip-hook tooth blades are least affected by grain direction.

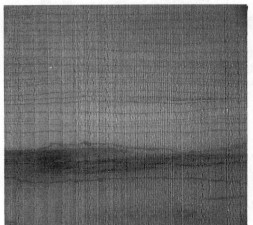

Illus. 202 and 203 (above). A smooth feed rate is important. These two pieces were cut at the same time by two different people. The difference in texture is due entirely to the feed rate.

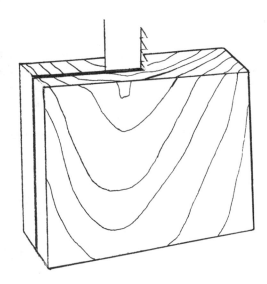

Illus. 204. A with-grain cut is a saw cut made with the grain rather than across (crosscutting) or along it (ripping).

 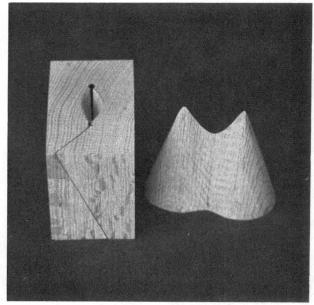

Illus. 205 (above left). This cone was cut with the grain. This technique gives a smooth finish. Not much sanding will have to be done. Illus. 206 (above right). Here is a double cone cut in red oak. Almost no sanding is required because the finish is so smooth.

Illus. 204.) Illus. 205 and 206 show two cones cut with the grain. Very little sanding is needed to finish the pieces. Cone puzzles are also cut with the same standard-form blade. The technique for making cones is covered in Chapter 13, Circular Work.

As the standard tooth dulls, the finish resulting from the cut becomes increasingly smoother. This can be used to advantage in some situations such as with-grain cutting. One must also be conscious of the fact that a dull blade will become hotter, thus increasing the likelihood of breakage. A dull blade will require more feed pressure than a sharp blade.

Pitch

The third consideration when choosing a blade is pitch. Pitch determines the speed and smoothness of a cut. Though it was discussed in detail in Chapter 3, here we will explore its practical application with specific species of wood. Wood hardness, moisture content, and resin content must be considered when choosing blade pitch.

Tooth form affects blade pitch. Blades with hook or skip teeth are coarser than those with standard teeth.

Larger blades usually have a coarse pitch. Smaller blades have a fine pitch. Medium-sized blades have a pitch between 4 TPI and 10 TPI, which represents extreme differences in the way medium-sized blades function. Be aware of this when selecting the pitch of a medium-sized blade.

The average skip-tooth blade has a pitch of 6 TPI. If it has a pitch of more than 6 TPI, it will start to function like a standard-tooth blade. If it has a pitch of less than 5 TPI, it will function more like a hook-tooth blade.

Speed and smoothness of cut should be the two priorities when deciding on blade pitch. At times, the top priority will be smoothness. As a general rule, the more teeth the blade has, the smoother the cut—especially when you are crosscutting. However, the set style also is a factor. A blade with standard tooth form, an alternate set and a fine pitch will give the smoothest cut because it has the most teeth contacting the surface, and thus provides the most cuts per inch of surface. (See Illus. 207.)

A blade with a fine pitch will generally give the smoothest finish. However, a lot also depends on the type of wood or metal being cut. Some material can be cut better with a coarser blade.

Illus. 207. You can make a smooth and accurate cut in hard maple with a ½-inch, 14 TPI standard-tooth blade.

Illus. 208. Multiple cuts in a two-inch red-oak puzzle. The cuts were made to test the accuracy and longevity of the ¹/₁₆-inch blade.

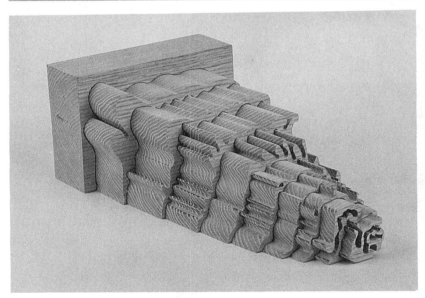

Illus. 209 (above left). The ¹/₁₆-inch blade gives a smooth finish in a multigrain cut. Illus. 210 (above right). The darkening on the tight turns shows a slight "burning." As the blade dulls, the finish becomes smoother. Fine blades last for a fairly long time in oak.

Illus. 208 shows a piece of two-inch oak. The numerous cuts shown on it were made with a ¹⁄₁₆-inch, 24 TPI saw blade. As Illus. 209 reveals, the cut is very smooth on all the surfaces. Illus. 210, a closeup of the oak, shows a very slight burning (darkening of the wood) on the sharp corners. This burning was made by an old blade, and some burning can be expected. A blade with a pitch of 24 TPI can cut oak for a long time because oak cuts cleanly without either packing the gullet full with sawdust or baking a deposit on the tooth face.

Try to match blade pitch to the wood that you are using. Oak, walnut, and maple are woods than can be cut well with blades with a fine pitch. Illus. 211 shows two pieces of walnut end grain. The top piece was cut with a 40-tooth For-rest combination circular blade. The bottom piece was cut with a 14 TPI metal-cutting blade. The finishes are equally smooth. A blade with 14 TPI is a good choice for walnut. Using a blade with a finer pitch doesn't seem to improve the cut. Use as coarse a pitch as possible that will still give good results. For curves, a standard-form blade with an alternate set and 14 TPI is a good choice when cutting walnut.

Illus. 212 shows a 24 TPI, ¹⁄₁₆-inch blade cutting 2-inch maple. The pitch of 24 TPI allows the blade to give the smoothest cut possible in maple. The blade is narrow and flexes rearward in a straight line during the cut, thus creating a straight cut. A very fine blade can cut maple extremely well because the wood is hard and doesn't seem to clog the teeth.

Illus. 211. The top piece of walnut was cut with a high-quality table-saw blade. The bottom piece was cut with a 14 TPI standard-tooth band-saw blade with a slow feed. The finish on both pieces is about the same.

Illus. 212. This hard maple was cut with a 24 TPI, ¹⁄₁₆-inch blade. The surface of the cut is exceptionally smooth. Safety note: The straight cut is best made with the top bearing about an inch above the blade. This technique exposes about an inch of blade, and the operator should pay special attention to avoid contact with the blade.

Illus. 213 shows a 14 TPI, ½-inch blade. This blade also gives an excellent cut, and would be a good choice if only straight cuts were going to be made in maple.

Woods that are soft or have a lot of resin tend to "load" or clog the gullet on a saw with a fine-pitch blade. Pine and cherry are the two best examples of this. Illus. 214 shows a fine-toothed blade clogged with a resinous pine sawdust.

The orientation of the sawcut also makes a difference. Crosscutting usually clogs the teeth the least. Cutting "with the grain"—that is, standing a piece on edge so that it rests on the end grain—clogs the teeth the most.

Illus. 215–216 show a small piece of cherry that "loaded" the blade in only a couple of inches of cutting. As the blade loaded up, it became quite hot. The black discoloration in the illustrations shows that burning occurred. Burning occurs when the resins in the wood discolor from heat. Cherry probably discolors the easiest because it will discolor at a fairly low temperature. It also easily discolors with router bits. For cherry and pine, it is best to use a coarser blade.

Softer wood such as butternut and mahogany can be cut easily with a very fine-pitch blade and not show signs of burning. The finish will be very smooth, and very little sanding will be needed. Illus. 219 shows a butternut pattern being sawed with a ¹⁄₁₆-inch blade. The finish is very smooth.

Harder wood such as ebony requires a finer pitch than woods of average density. (See Illus. 220.) A blade with 14 TPI pitch is the best choice. The finish is quite good. A blade with 24 TPI is just too fine. The teeth dull quickly because of the hardness of the wood and because of the heat.

A ¹⁄₁₆-inch blade becomes too hot very quickly with wood as hard as ebony. The 14 TPI, ½-inch blade has the advantage here because the large blade's body draws heat off the tooth tip. The wide body is also useful when you want a long, straight cut with a fine finish. (See Illus. 221.)

Most metals require a blade with a fine pitch. This is particularly true of thin metal such as sheet metal. (See Illus. 222 and 223.)

CUTTING THICK STOCK

A coarse blade should be used to cut thick stock. The biggest blade that should be used on consumer-grade band saws is one ½-inch wide. One with a hook- or hook-skip tooth form and a pitch of 3 TPI is the best choice. (See Illus. 224.)

A finer blade can be expected to give a fine cut when being used to crosscut, but not always when being used to rip or resaw. Illus. 225 and 226 show two hard maple boards that were resawed. The top board was resawed with a blade with a hooktooth form and a pitch of 6 TPI. The bottom one was cut with a blade with a hook-

Illus. 213 (above left). This hard maple was cut with a 14 TPI, ½-inch blade. Illus. 214 (above right). The blade on the left is clogged with pine resin.

Illus. 215–218 (above and below). Cherry wood clogs a fine-tooth blade after only a couple of inches of with-grain cutting.

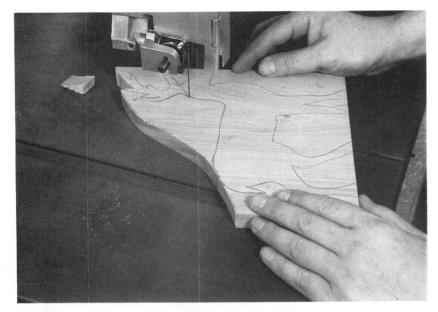

Illus. 219. This deer pattern is being cut out of butternut. The blade shown here is good for cutting fine detail in woods without pitch or resin.

Illus. 220. When cutting extremely hard wood such as ebony, you'll discover that a blade with a fine pitch works best. The wide blade body helps to dissipate the heat. Shown here is a ½-inch, 14 TPI standard-tooth blade.

Illus. 221. These are replacement toy pieces made out of pine. The holes were drilled first, and then the pieces were resawed with a ½-inch, 14 TPI standard-tooth blade. The width of the blade helps it to maintain a straight cut, and the pine pitch gives a smooth finish.

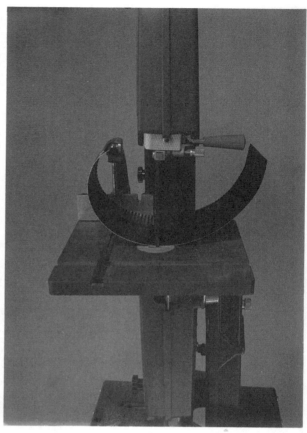

Illus. 222 and 223 (above). A ¼-inch, 14 TPI blade can be used for straight cuts if the stock isn't too thick. Here it is shown cutting metal stove pipe. A fine pitch is required for cutting metal, especially thin metal. A Shopsmith band saw was used to make these cuts. This band saw has two speeds; the slower speed was used.

Illus. 224. A blade with a 3 TPI pitch is best for cutting thick stock. Shown here is a 3 TPI hook-tooth blade cutting red oak.

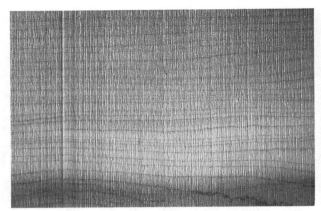
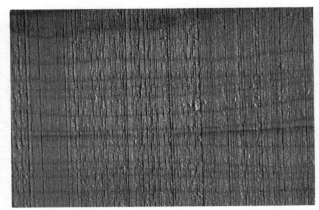

Illus. 225 and 226 (above). Shown here is an exception to the woodworking rule that the finer the pitch the smoother the cut. These cuts were made in hard maple with the same saw. The cut on the left was made with a 3 TPI hook-tooth blade. It is smoother than the cut shown on the right, which was made with a 6 TPI hook-tooth blade.

tooth form and a pitch of 3 TPI. The bottom board has the smoother cut. A blade with a hook-skip form and a pitch of 3 TPI would leave an even smoother cut. This situation, in which the "coarse" blade gives a finer cut than the "fine" blade, illustrates why it is important to experiment when choosing a blade. There are other factors that may determine the type of blade pitch that should be used. If your saw is underpowered or runs at a slow speed, a blade with a 6 TPI pitch may be the better choice because a blade with coarse teeth requires more power.

GREEN WOOD

Moisture has an effect on the cut of a fine-pitch blade. The drier the wood, the smoother the cut and the slimmer the chances that the gullet will be clogged. Green pine can instantly clog a fine-toothed blade. It should be noted that blades with standard teeth or hook-teeth tend to clog more than those with skip-teeth.

When resawing green wood, remember that the coarser the blade pitch the better the cut. There are two reasons for this. First, green wood expands as it is cut, so blades with larger gullets are better. The second reason is heat. Green wood generates a lot of heat when it is cut. A blade with a coarser pitch is more efficient, and does not generate as much heat. Illus. 227 shows a Ryobi being used to resaw green walnut burl. The Stelite-tipped teeth on the Ryobi band saw are the more durable teeth to use during hours of battle with an awesome opponent like green wood.

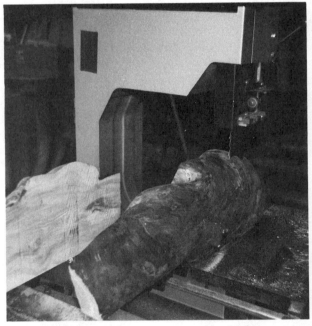

Illus. 227. This Ryobi resaw is cutting thick green wood. A very coarse hook-tooth blade is being used.

SPEED AND POWER

Pitch (tooth spacing) is also affected by the speed of the machine. As the speed is increased, so should the pitch of the blade. Therefore, high-speed machines can be operated efficiently with saw blades coarser than those that would normally be used.

The faster the speed of the saw, the coarser the blade that you can use. Conversely, if the saw is being run at a slow speed or is underpowered, you should use a blade with a finer pitch.

Consider, for example, the popular 14-inch saws sold by Delta or the Taiwanese. When used with a riser block, they will accept a 12-inch piece of stock. These saws are grossly underpowered for resawing with the standard ½ horsepower motor. To adequately resaw thick stock, you should either slow down the speed to get more torque, use a finer pitch, or do both. However, it may be best to use a more powerful motor.

CUTTING METAL

When selecting the tooth pitch, always ensure that with the blade you are selecting at least two consecutive teeth are in contact with the workpiece. A blade with a fine-tooth pitch is advisable for harder metals, thin sections, or work that will be interrupted. A blade with a relatively coarse pitch should be used for large, solid sections or softer materials.

Thin-walled workpieces like tubes, pipes, shapes, sheet, etc., require blades with fine teeth. If the teeth aren't fine, they will get stuck and break off. To prevent this, make sure that three teeth on whichever blade you use are in contact with the workpiece simultaneously.

Soft metals such as aluminum and bronze require blades with a large chip space. A coarse-pitched blade prevents the chips from building up in the gullets, which can impair sawing and damage the blade. Aluminum is gummy and requires so much chip clearance that if many more than three teeth engage the metal they may load up with chips too fast.

Testing a Blade

It is extremely difficult to positively predict what a blade will do in a specific situation. As one gains experience, foreseeing what a blade will do becomes easier. But, there can still be surprises occasionally. The best approach to take when determining which blade to use in a specific situation is to make a sample block and test the blade on it.

Each species of wood, depending on its hardness and consistency, will cut differently and provide different results. As a rule, the harder the wood, the finer the blade that is required. A blade with a hook-tooth form and a 4 TPI pitch, for example, will give a rougher cut in maple than in pine. It is useful to make a sample block for each blade and each species that you use.

Sample blocks can be made out of a scrap piece. Start your sample cuts by cutting a piece off the end and side of the block. (See Illus. 228 and 229.) This will give you a sample of a crosscut and ripcut. Illus. 230 shows a sample block on which crosscuts and ripcuts have been made.

Next, cut pieces off the broad sides of the block; make one a resaw cut and the other a with-grain cut. (See Illus. 231 and 232.) This will give you a comparison of those surface cuts. (See Illus. 233.)

After you have cut the surfaces, make a cut while turning the workpiece; this reveals how tightly a curve can be cut. (See Illus. 234.) It also reveals how well a blade will perform in a multi-grain cutting situation.

Blade Suggestions

The type of blades you choose depends on the type of work that you are doing. For general woodworking, a blade from each group would be a good choice. Three good choices would be the following:

1. A ¼-inch, 6 TPI skip-tooth blade. This is a good general blade for curves and straight cuts.
2. A ⅛-inch, 14 TPI standard-tooth blade. This blade is good for tight scroll work, gives a good finish, and is good for crosscutting and joinery.
3. A ½-inch, 3 TPI hook-tooth or hook-skip tooth blade, if you have a band saw with a ½ horsepower motor. This blade is good for thick stock and straight cuts.

These blades would take care of about 90 percent of the average band-saw owner's needs.

If you do a particular type of work, you would need a blade suited for that purpose. If you want a group of blades that fall in between the cutting ranges offered by the first group, consider the following additions:

4. A ³⁄₁₆-inch, 10 TPI standard-tooth blade. This

is coarser than the ⅛-inch blade, but finer than the ¼-inch blade.

5. A ¼-inch or ⅜-inch 4 TPI hook- or hook-skip-tooth blade. This blade is more aggressive than the ¼-inch-tooth blade.

6. A ¹⁄₁₆-inch, 24 TPI standard-tooth blade. This is best for tight scroll work or very smooth cuts.

7. A ½-inch, 14 TPI standard-tooth blade. This blade is useful for making fine cuts when it is helpful to have a blade with a wide body, such as when making straight crosscuts or straight short rip cuts.

With these seven blades, you will cover each cutting extreme and will have good options for all but the most specialized work.

Illus. 228. This piece has been crosscut off the end of the block.

Illus. 229. The second piece has been ripped off the side of the block.

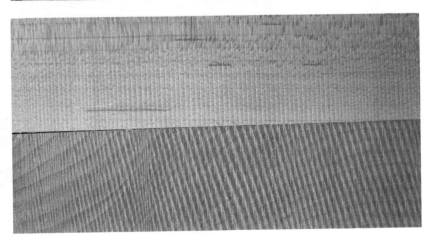

Illus. 230. Shown here is the surface of each cut. The rip cut is on top and the crosscut is on the bottom.

Illus. 231. With-grain cutting.

Illus. 232. The piece on the right has been cut with the grain. The piece on the left has been ripped.

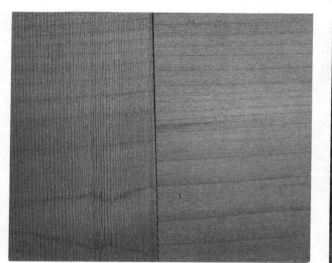

Illus. 233 (above left). A close-up look at the two cut surfaces. The with-grain cut on the right is smoother. Illus. 234 (above right). The last cut in a sample piece is a curve. This cut will give you an idea of how tight a curve you can make and the quality of the surface.

PRE-USE PROCEDURES

5
Alignment and Tracking Procedures

Aligning the Wheels

The band saw can be the most useful tool in the shop. It can resaw thick stock or slice off thin veneer, cut curves, circles, tenons, and dovetails, etc. However, to do all these things well, it has to be very accurately adjusted. Do not assume that the band saw comes from the factory already adjusted and ready for serious work.

The more you expect from your saw, the more aligning and adjusting you will have to do. These techniques do not need special tools, just a little time and patience. Here I will present some straightforward suggestions for improving band-saw performance by focusing on alignment of the wheels, a critical but often overlooked adjustment.

The goal of good alignment is to allow the blade to run as straight as possible. With poor wheel alignment, the blade travels over the wheels with a twist or a bend. This abuses the band and shortens blade life. A blade that is running straight has a better chance of cutting straight and lasting longer. With good alignment, it takes less tension to maintain good cutting accuracy.

The woodworker of today expects more from the band saw than his predecessors did years ago. With the European band saws that have cropped up in the past 10 or 15 years, we now expect to be able to accurately resaw and rip with the band saw. When we attempt these things with the average American or Taiwanese band saws, it often leads to frustration. This is because American band saws come from the factory best suited for cutting curves with medium to narrow blades. Because of the factory setup, or lack of setup, wider blades which are ideal for resawing often give disappointing performances when used with American band saws. When wheels are aligned to blade size and tension, the larger blades can be used successfully on these machines.

Band-saw wheels are either crowned or flat. The flat wheels are slightly crowned, but for our purposes, they will be referred to as flat. Both designs have advantages and disadvantages, Each design affects the blade differently, thus there are two completely different tracking systems. "Tracking" is a term that refers to the positioning of the blade on the wheels.

The crowned wheel is popular in America for use on consumer-grade band saws, and is used on the Sears, Delta, and Taiwanese models. The flat-wheel design is often used on larger industrial saws and some European machines. One flat-wheeled band saw sold in the United States is the Inca from Switzerland.

The crowned wheel is used because it makes

tracking very easy. The crown exerts a controlling force on the band, pulling the blade towards the top of the crown. (See Illus. 235.) This tracks the blade close to but not necessarily in the middle of the wheel.

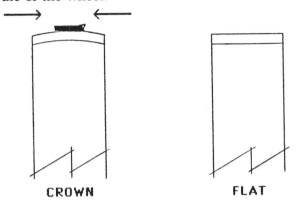

Illus. 235. The crown exerts a controlling force on the band, which helps track the blade near the center of the wheel.

The flat wheel takes a little practice, but it allows the operator more control and flexibility. It allows free movement of the blade without any controlling force such as the crown. Blades are usually tracked in the middle of the wheel, and large blades are sometimes tracked with the teeth off the tire. (See Illus. 236.) With both systems, the top wheel angle exerts final control on the blade.

One of the big differences between the flat- and crowned-wheel designs is the amount of contact area between the tire and the blade. The flat-wheel design supports the blade body no matter what the size of the blade. The top of the

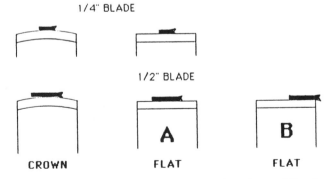

Illus. 236. Blades are usually tracked in the middle of the wheel. Some flat-wheel manufacturers recommend that you track wide blades with their teeth off the tire, as shown in B.

crowned wheel only contacts about ¼ inch of the blade. Thus, the largest blade that maintains full contact with the crowned wheel is the ¼-inch blade. This is perhaps the justification for using the ¼-inch blade for resawing. However, the ¼-inch blade is not very stiff. To maintain stiffness on the blade, excessive tension is needed; this, in some cases, can damage the band saw, and in severe cases can lead to breakage of the wheel shaft.

The larger blades best suited for resawing are ½-inch wide. This means that only half of the ½-inch blade is supported by the ¼-inch surface of the crown wheel. (See Illus. 237.) Larger blades such as the ½-inch blade can sway on the crowned wheel and increase the likelihood of vibration and harmonic flutter. Under heavy sawing stress, the blade can rock on the crown, causing the loss of tension, and causing lead and wander. Lead is when the blade pulls in one direction. Wander is when the blade pulls to one side and then the other. Lead is usually (often incorrectly) blamed on the blade; it is assumed that one side of the blade is dull. This can happen, but the most likely cause of lead is wheel misalignment. All of the problems associated with the crowned wheel are magnified when the wheels are poorly aligned.

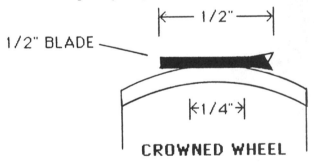

Illus. 237. Crowned wheels provide about ¼-inch of contact between the blade and the tire. The lack of support for wide blades can lead to problems.

A band saw that has coplanar wheels—wheels that are lying in the same plane—will cut best. (See Illus. 238.) This applies less to band saws with flat wheels than with crown wheels because the crown exerts a controlling force on the blade. If the two crowns are not in the same plane, each crown vies with the other for control of the blade. The more the crown wheels are out of alignment, the more important it is to angle the

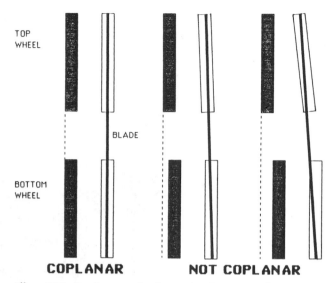

Illus. 238. Coplanar wheels are in the same plane.

top wheel so that the blade can be tracked near the center of both tires. (See Illus. 239.) This misalignment puts an unwanted and unpredictable stress on the blade. One or more of the band-saw wheels will bind.

Narrow blades are more flexible than larger blades and withstand misalignment better. Misalignment increases vibration, flutter, heat, and shortens blade life. If the wheels are misaligned, more tension is needed to stabilize the blade and maintain accuracy.

Coplanar wheels greatly improve band-saw performance by improving its efficiency. The wheels work together rather than competing with each other. The blade can track itself without any unneeded interference. Thus, when wheels are coplanar, there is less vibration, more accuracy, more power, and less lead and wandering. It will be easier to get good results without having to overtension the blade. There is better performance from blades larger than ¼ inch. You will notice this when you are resawing and making straight cuts.

If wheel alignment is so critical, why isn't it done at the factory? Unfortunately, the proper alignment is more complicated than simply lining up the wheels with a straightedge at the factory. As the tension on the blade is increased, the wheel alignment may change. Wheels that are coplanar with no tension can be thrust out of plane or out of parallel when the tension is increased a certain amount. Wheels that are

coplanar at normal tension can become out of parallel as tension is increased. (See Illus. 239–243.) This should not necessarily be considered a deficiency of the saw.

The coplanar adjustment of wheels is most critical when you are tracking wide blades that are well tensioned. For this reason, the wheels should be aligned when a wide, tensioned blade is on the saw. This will ensure that they are coplanar when this is most critical.

When you align the wheels when the wide, tensioned blade is on the saw, you are aligning them to the proper blade and blade tension. You are conforming the band saw to the blade rather than the usual method of conforming the blade to the saw. This realignment is very important for crown-wheel machines, and less important for flat-wheel machines.

If your saw has historically performed poorly at cutting straight and resawing and no amount of tracking adjustment seems to help, improving the performance may simply be a matter of aligning the wheels for a correctly tensioned ½-inch blade.

It is important to always keep in mind that tension and alignment are interrelated. If you

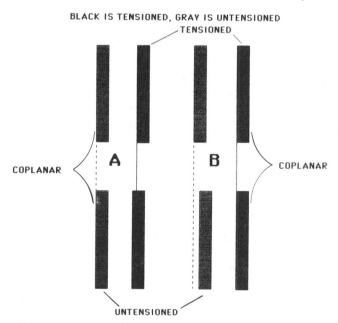

Illus. 239. Wheels that are coplanar at no tension can become out of plane when the tension is increased, as shown in A. The coplanar relationship is most important after the tension has been applied to the blade, as shown in B.

Illus. 240 (above left). These wheels are coplanar when there is no blade on the saw.
Illus. 241 (above right). The wheels remain coplanar with moderate blade tension.

Illus. 242 (below left). When adequate tension is applied to the blade, the wheels are no longer coplanar. Illus. 243 (below right). A close-up of Illus. 242. The top wheel is ⅛-inch out of plane. More tension would increase the misalignment.

change one, it may affect the other. A saw that is aligned at normal tension may be pulled out of alignment as tension is greatly increased. Rather than being an advantage, increased tension can actually become a problem that will reveal itself in a number of different scenarios. Under high tension, the wheels can twist out of alignment with each other. (See Illus. 244.) The wheels can be pulled out of plane (Illus. 245) or pulled out of

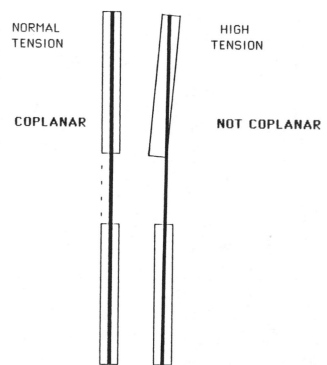

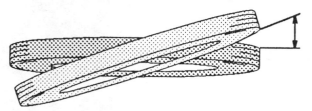

Illus. 244. A great deal of tension can cause the wheels to twist out of alignment with each other.

Illus. 246. Wheels that are coplanar at normal tension can become unparallel at high tension.

parallel (Illus. 246) with each other. With the proper blade and alignment and adequate tension you will get a good blade-cutting performance, and not be tempted to overtension the saw.

The wheels on some saws can be twisted out of line, as shown in Illus. 244. Unfortunately, most saws do not have an adjustment for this. You can check for this problem with a straightedge by checking the outer edges of the wheels, not just the middle. If your saw has top and bottom castings that are bolted together, you can unbolt and readjust them.

It is interesting to note that some old saws have top wheels that rotate from side to side; this allows the wheel to find equilibrium. This technique is still used on some European saws.

Alignment Procedure

Aligning band-saw wheels is a very simple procedure that should take only a couple of minutes to accomplish. They may or may not be already aligned. The first thing to do is to check. Use the following steps to check, and then to align the band-saw wheels.

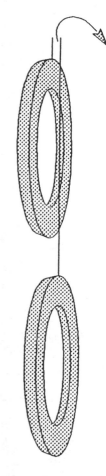

Illus. 245. Excessive tension can aggravate wheels that are not coplanar, causing them to move further apart.

1. *Tension the saw*. Tension the widest blade that you can use on your saw. The ½-inch blade is the largest practical size to use on a consumer band saw. Use the tension scale on your band saw. (See Illus. 247.) If your saw is old or if you don't release the tension after using the saw the spring may be compressed. If the spring is compressed, you will not get a true tension reading, so you should use more tension than the amount indicated on the scale. (When the spring is compressed completely, it loses its ability to function as a shock absorber—which is its secondary purpose.) The best solution is to go to the next setting. However, if you are using a wide blade, the scale may not have another setting mark. Increase the tension slightly past the highest setting, but not to the point where you are at the end of the adjustment. Tension will be discussed at length in the chapter on blade tension.

Illus. 247. The first step in making the wheels coplanar is to tension the blade. Tension the widest blade that you use. Here a Sears saw is being tensioned with a ½-inch blade.

2. *Make sure that the wheels are parallel to each other*. With a straightedge, check to determine if wheels are parallel with each other. (See Illus. 248.) You may have to angle the top wheel to get them parallel. Use the straightedge in the middle of the wheels. If it touches the tops and bottoms of both wheels, then the wheels are parallel and in line—they are coplanar. (See Illus. 249.) If this is the case, you do not have to align them. If you are going

to use coplanar tracking, use the saw just as it is without adjusting the top wheel.

If the wheels are not in alignment, the straightedge will not touch the tops and bottoms of both wheel points. Instead it will either touch the top and bottom of the top wheel or the top and bottom of the lower wheel. In either case, you will have to move one of the wheels to make both wheels coplanar.

3. *Measure the misalignment*. It is important to know how far one of the wheels has to be moved to achieve coplanar alignment. This is essential if you are going to achieve coplanar alignment by adding or removing washers from behind the wheel. Make the measurement at two points: the top and bottom of the

Illus. 248. Use a straightedge to check wheel alignment. You may have to angle the top wheels. The top-wheel angle adjustment on the Sears band saw is made with a screwdriver in the middle of the top wheel.

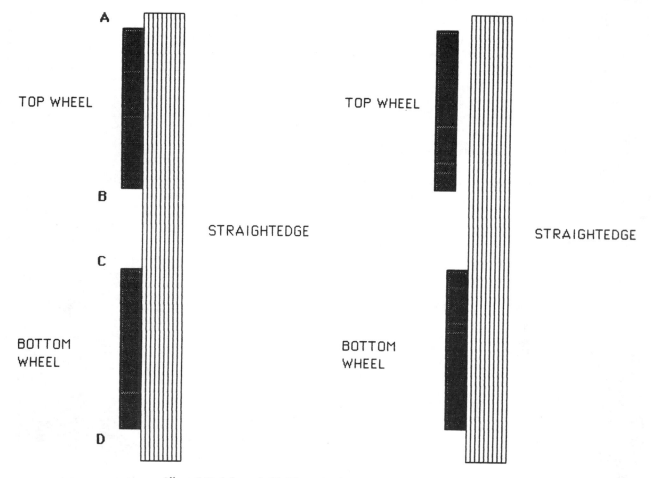

Illus. 249 (above left). The wheels are coplanar if the straightedge touches the tops and bottoms of both wheels. These positions are designated in the drawing as A, B, C, and D. Illus. 250 (above right). If the wheels are not coplanar, the straightedge will only touch one wheel.

wheel that is not touching the straightedge. (See Illus. 251–453.) The measurements at both points should be the same. If they are not exactly the same, angle the top wheel until they are. (See Illus. 254 and 255.) Once they are the same, that amount (X) is the distance needed to align the wheel. In the situation shown in Illus. 251–253, move the top wheel forward X amount to achieve alignment.

4. *Make the adjustment.* Each manufacturer uses a different mechanism for making the alignment adjustment. On Sears and Inca models, the adjustment is made with a moveable bottom wheel. (See Illus. 256.) This is the easiest and most convenient way. The bottom wheel is mounted on a shaft with a key way (a

groove on the shaft that prevents the wheel from spinning on the shaft), and the wheel is locked in place with a setscrew. When making the adjustment, loosen the screw and move the wheel to the desired amount.

On the Delta and Taiwanese band saws, the adjustment is made on the top wheel, which is mounted on a threaded shaft and held secure with a nut. (See Illus. 257.) To make the adjustment, unscrew the nut and then remove the wheels; this will expose the washers. Make the alignment by either adding or removing washers. The Delta band saw has a ⅝-inch hole, and standard hardware dealers washers will fit. (See Illus. 258–260.)

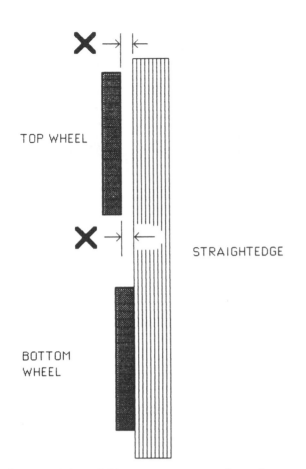

TOP WHEEL

STRAIGHTEDGE

BOTTOM
WHEEL

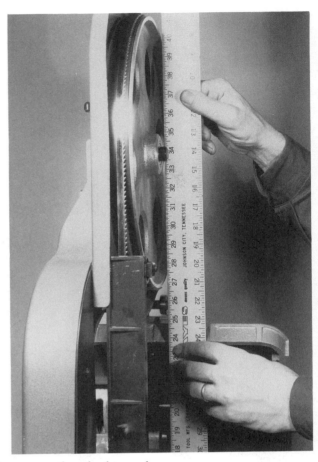

*Illus. 251 (above left). It is important to know how much to move the wheel to make
the wheels coplanar. This amount is measured from the top and bottom of the wheel.
Illus. 252 (above right). Hold the straightedge against the bottom wheel.*

*Illus. 253. With a straightedge against the bottom
wheel, use a ruler to measure the distance between the
top wheel and the straightedge. You may have to hold
the straightedge against the bottom wheel with your
knee.*

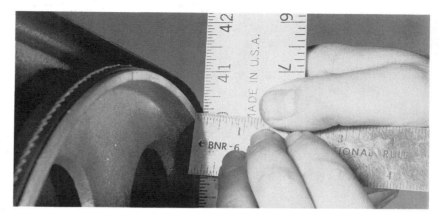

Illus. 254. With a fine ruler, make the final measurement.

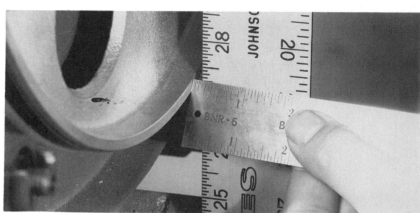

Illus. 255. The bottom measurement should be exactly the same as the top. If it isn't, the top wheel should be tilted until it is the same on the top and the bottom.

Illus. 256 (above left). You can adjust a Sears band saw by moving the bottom wheel. A screw holds the wheel on the shaft. Illus. 257 (above right). You can adjust the Delta and Taiwanese band saws by moving the top wheel, which is held in place with a nut. First, remove the nut, and then the wheel. Add or subtract the washer behind the wheel to make the adjustment.

Illus. 258 (left). When you remove the wheel, you expose the washers used to align the saw when it was assembled. Illus. 259 (above). Most often, the saw will need more washers for proper alignment. The washer on the right is a standard hardware store washer with a ⅝-inch hole.

Illus. 260. Shown here is the hardware store washer behind one of the original washers. The hardware store washer is about twice as thick as the original washer.

After the first alignment, always rotate the wheels several times to make sure that the blade is tracking; then recheck the alignment. It is a good idea to mark the original wheel positions in relationship to the straightedge. Use a pencil, magic marker, or file to mark the wheels. If the wheels are warped, you will get a different reading against the straightedge each time that you check the alignment. This can be very confusing unless you mark the wheels.

Align your saw for the biggest blade that you use. Do not use a blade larger than ½ inch unless you have a very large saw. If the largest blade you use is ¼ inch, align the saw with that blade. If you plan on doing a lot of work with one particular blade, it is not a bad idea to align the saw for that blade. You can still use the top wheel angle for any final adjustment, but don't depend on it too much.

Don't be afraid to realign your saw often. Think of the procedure as just another adjustment that should be made. After you have aligned your saw a couple of times, it will become very simple and easy to do. And you'll

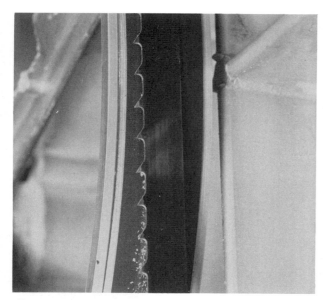

Illus. 261. The blade may track towards the front of the saw when the wheels are coplanar.

notice how useful it is—the minute that it takes for alignment is a small price to pay for good performance.

If you have a crowned-wheel saw and you realign the wheels using a ½-inch blade, you may notice that the blade doesn't track exactly in the middle of the crown when the wheels are coplanar. The blade may track so that it is closer to the front of the saw. (See Illus. 261.) The blade is balancing on the crown. When the wheels are coplanar, the large blade finds it own equilibrium and runs truer, thus cutting straighter. This is called coplanar tracking.

There are a number of reasons why the blade may track towards the front of the wheel when coplanar tracking is used. One reason is because the teeth don't carry as much weight in this balancing equation. Another reason is the fact that the front of the blade is often shorter than the back. During the manufacturing of the blade, especially the hardening of the teeth, the front of the blade shrinks. This would explain why the blade balances on the front of the crown.

The lack of support for blades over ¼ inch wide is the biggest weakness of the crowned wheel. Proper alignment of the wheels helps stabilize the blade, but it cannot make up completely for the lack of support by the tire.

Coplanar tracking is preferable to the usual approach of tracking the blade exactly in the middle of the top wheel, especially when ½-inch blades are used. This is also true of smaller blades, but it is not as important with them because they are more flexible. However, if the work that you are doing requires straight cuts with a small blade, you may find that coplanar tracking gives a straighter cut, particularly if you are using a fence or a mitre gauge.

The advantage of the flat-wheel system is the amount of blade support, especially for blades wider than ¼ inch. (See Illus. 262.) The flat wheel is less sensitive to misalignment than the crowned wheel, although it is a good idea to use coplanar tracking.

Illus. 262. The ½-inch blade shown here is being tracked on a flat wheel. Its teeth are just off the edge.

It takes a little practice to track small blades on a band saw with flat wheels. Blades smaller than a ¼ inch should be tracked very lightly against the trust bearing because there is no crown to hold them in place. If the tire is concave because of wear or compression (from having the tension left on), it will be harder to track small blades. The opposite is true of a crown wheel which maintains the blade close to the middle of the wheel. In this case, the surface of the tire should be sanded so that there is a very slight crown; this would make tracking small blades easier. This procedure is often required on old saws that have flat tires.

The flat wheel tends to be much better at

straight cuts with larger blades because the blades have less lead and wander. This means that you can use a rip fence for ripping an resawing. The rip fence gives much better support than the single point. The flat wheel is ideal for resawing because the blade is so well supported. (See Illus. 263.)

The flat- and the crown-wheel systems each have advantages. The flat-wheel system is best for wide blades. The crown-wheel system is probably best for narrow blades. If you have two saws, it would be handy to have one of each design.

There is a way of combining the two systems so that the advantage of each can be utilized. The idea is to have one wheel of each type—that is, one flat wheel and one with a crown. The crown-flat wheel system was popular at the turn of the century and is similar to the designs of many belt sanders. The one flat wheel helps to support the blade, and the crowned wheel helps to maintain a stable position. This decreases the need for perfect alignment, which is so necessary when there are two crowns.

Though either wheel can be crowned or flat, the system seems to work best if the top wheel is the one with the crown and the bottom wheel is flat or less crowned. (See Illus. 264.) You can alter the wheel design by changing the shape of the tire. The procedure for doing this is covered in Chapter 8. It is a good idea to use coplanar tracking with the crown-flat wheel design to get the most benefits.

Tracking the Blade

The term "tracking" refers to the act of positioning or balancing the blade on the band-saw wheels. There is no external force which holds the blade on the saw, so it must be positioned by the operator. To position it properly, tilt the top wheel. The angle of the top wheel steers the blade in the direction of the tilt. The top wheel is hinged, and you adjust the tilt with a knob. (See Illus. 265 and 266.) Track the blade when it is under full tension. When it is properly tracked, the blade will run in a straight line. Proper tracking makes a difference in band-saw performance, particularly when you are cutting a straight line or thick stock.

Illus. 263 (above left). The flat wheel gives maximum blade support. This is important when you are cutting straight or thick material. The 1/2-inch, 3 TPI hook-tooth blade shown here is cutting red oak. The slice is a uniform .015 inch, or a 64th of an inch. Illus. 264 (above right). The crown on the bottom wheel has been decreased, giving it more surface contact with the tire. This adds to blade stability and increases accuracy and performance. The white material on the tire is chalk.

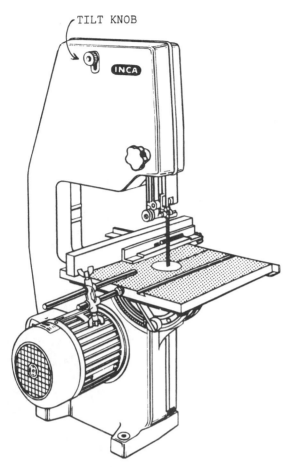

Illus. 265. The tilt knob adjusts the angle of the top wheel.

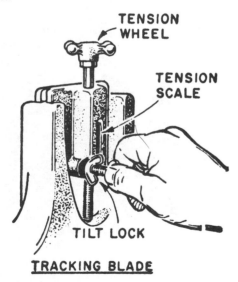

Illus. 266. On some saws, the tilt mechanism is on the back of the saw. The tilt knob often has a tilt lock, which is a stop nut that locks the adjustment.

Most owner's manuals give very simple instructions for tracking the blade in the middle of a crowned wheel. These instructions are an oversimplification, and are one of the reasons some woodworkers rarely get really good performances out of their band saws.

Each blade that you use will track slightly differently—that is, it will settle in a slightly different place on the wheels. There are a number of factors that affect the tracking of a blade. They include the following: (1) top-wheel angle; (2) wheel design; (3) the straightness of the blade; (4) wheel alignment; and (5) blade tension

All of these factors are interrelated, and will be discussed separately in the sections that follow.

Top-Wheel Angle

The top wheel of the band saw is designed to tilt either forward or rearward. The blade on a crowned-wheel band saw usually tracks close to

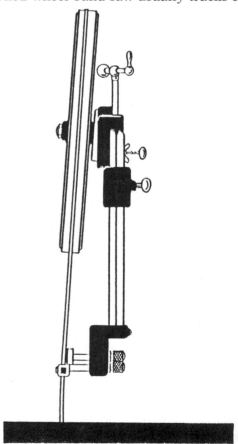

Illus. 267. The rearward angle of the top wheel causes the blade to ride against the thrust bearing.

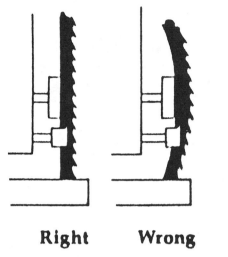

Right   **Wrong**

Illus. 268. An excessive top-wheel angle causes the blade to ride hard against the thrust bearing. This causes the blade to flex, which decreases performance and shortens blade life.

the middle of the top wheel. If the top wheel is angled too far forward, the blade will easily come off the wheels, especially when backing out of a cut. When the blade is angled too far rearward, it is likely to ride too hard against the thrust bearing, which prevents it from running off the back of the wheels. (See Illus. 267 and 268.) The friction between the bearing and the blade will shorten the life of both.

Wheel Design

The design of the wheels has an effect on the way the blade tracks. The crown on the crowned wheel attracts the blade towards, but not exactly to, the middle of the wheel. So does the crown on a band saw with a crown-flat wheel design. The blade on a band saw with flat wheels can be tracked anywhere on the wheel.

Blade Straightness

The straightness of the blade has an effect on tracking. A straight blade will track by maintaining a constant position on the wheels. A blade that is not straight will appear to change position on the wheels, giving the impression that it is weaving back and forth.

Each blade will track differently. This is due to the straightness of the weld and also to whether or not the blade is straight; this latter charac-

teristic occurs during the manufacturing process. When you heat-treat the front of the blade to harden the teeth, the front often contracts. Thus, the back of the blade is often longer than the front, making a perfectly straight weld impossible. This may also explain why the blade will find its equilibrium slightly towards the front of the wheels when coplanar tracking is used.

Wheel Alignment

The closer the wheels are aligned to each other, the less the top wheel will have to be angled to track the blade. This was discussed at length on pages 112–166, under the heading Aligning the Wheels.

Blade Tension

Wheel angle is affected by blade tension. This was also explored at length on pages 112–116, under the heading Aligning the Wheels. Flat wheels are more sensitive to misalignment caused by changes in tension. This is because there is no crown to stabilize the blade in one spot.

Tracking Systems

There are two ways to track the blade. The usual way that the owner's manual suggests is called center tracking. The blade is tracked in the center of the wheel. This is accomplished by angling the top wheel until the blade is in the center of the top wheel. Coplanar tracking is a technique by which you make the wheels coplanar and let the blade find its own equilibrium, which may or may not be in the center of the wheels.

Each method is discussed below.

Center Tracking

With this method, the top wheel is angled so that the blade tracks in the middle of the top wheel. This is fairly easy to do and can be done even if the wheels are not well-aligned. When you use this method, you assume that the blade will find its equilibrium in the middle of the wheel. Some blades—especially some narrow blades—do. However, the biggest drawback to this system is the fact that many blades, particularly wider blades, are not balanced or in the state of equilibrium when tracked in the middle of the wheels. To track these blades in the center of the wheels, you have to angle the top wheel out of plane with the bottom wheel. In some cases the angle required is extreme, which causes problems such as binding, lead, and wander.

Coplanar Tracking

In this method, you track the blade and keep the wheels coplanar. This simply means that after you have tracked the blade you check the wheel alignment with a straightedge. (See Illus 269.)

With this method, you allow the blade to find its own equilibrium. It may or may not track in the center of the wheels. If the blade is wide or crooked, it may track towards the front of the wheels.

Because the wheels are aligned with each other, the blade exerts the same amount of pressure on both wheels. One wheel is not exerting

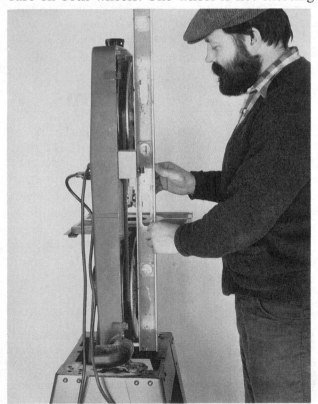

Illus. 269. Coplanar tracking is achieved when the blade is tensioned and the wheels are coplanar. Check for coplanar tracking with a straightedge.

more force on the blade than the other. The blade runs truer and lasts longer because there is no binding or twisting. When there is no binding or twisting, the blade cuts straighter without the tendency to lead or wander. This is noticeable when cutting thick stock or making straight cuts.

If you want your band saw to cut accurately, coplanar tracking is the best approach. If you want to change the relationship of the blade with the thrust bearing, angle the top wheel very slightly.

With both tracking systems, it is important to pay constant attention to the performance of the saw. New blades often stretch, and blades expand as they get warm from sawing. This may affect the tracking of the blade.

Tracking Procedure

You will have to track the blade each time you put a new or different blade on the saw. If you use a consistent step-by-step method, it should take only a minute or two. A lot of people do not like to change saw blades, and go to great lengths to avoid doing it. However, to use the band saw to its greatest advantage, you will have to use the appropriate blade and quickly change and track it, a habit that can be quickly developed if you are so inclined.

Be careful when using blades, especially wide and sharp ones. Some people prefer to use gloves when handling large blades. Safety glasses are always a good idea. Following are the step-by-step procedures for tracking a blade.

Removing the Blade

1. Unplug the saw.
2. Remove the mechanism for aligning the table halves. It will either be a pin, bolt, or a front rail.
3. Unscrew the blade guard. (See Illus. 270.)
4. Remove the throat plate.
5. Release the tension, thus lowering the top wheel.
6. Expose the wheels by opening or removing the cover(s). (See Illus. 271.)
7. Take the blade off the wheels with both hands, and carefully slide it out of the table slot.

Illus. 270 (above left). Remove the blade guard. Illus. 271 (above right). To expose the wheels and the blade, open the cover.

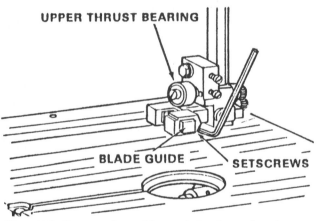

Illus. 272. Retract the guides and the thrust bearing above and below the table so that nothing interferes with the tracking of the blade.

8. Fold the blade.
9. Retract the thrust bearings above and below the table.
10. Loosen the guides on the side of the blade and then retract them too. This way, you can easily install the next blade without having any obstructions. (See Illus. 272.)

Installing the Blade

1. Uncoil the blade. If it is a new blade, it may have oil or dirt on it. The blade may have been oiled to prevent rust. You do not want the oil or dirt touching the workpiece, so remove it before installing the blade. Wipe it off with a rag or a paper towel. Pull the blade through the rag rearwards so that the teeth don't hook. (See Illus. 273.)
2. Hold the blade up to the saw. Inspect the teeth. If the teeth are pointed in the wrong direction, you will have to turn the blade inside out. To do this, hold the blade with both hands and rotate it. (See Illus. 274.)
3. Hold the blade with both hands with the teeth edges towards you. Slide it through the table slot and place it on the wheels. (See Illus. 275.) Some people like to hang it from the top wheel.
4. Position the blade where you want it on the wheels. Slowly raise the top wheel with the tension knob. Start to rotate the wheels by hand in the normal direction while the blade is still fairly slack. As you do this, watch to determine where the blade wants to track. If the blade is tracking too far forward or rearwards, make an adjustment with the tilt mechanism. As you rotate the blade with one hand, increase the tension with the other. Continue to do this until you have adequate tension. A blade can not be correctly tracked until the tensioning is completed. *Never track the blade with the saw running.*

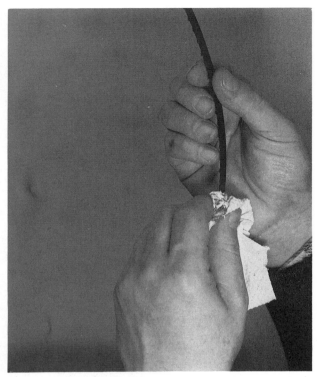

Illus. 273. To clean the blade, pull it rearwards so that the teeth don't hook on the cloth.

Illus. 274. If the teeth are pointed in the wrong direction, turn the blade inside out. Grasp it with both hands and rotate it inward.

Illus. 275. Hold the blade with both hands and carefully guide it through the table slot.

5. After the blade has been tracked, replace the cover and the blade guard. Plug in the electrical cord. Turn the saw on for a second, and then turn it off again. Observe to see how the saw runs. If the blade seems to track well, run it under full power. With the tracking of the blade completed, you are ready to adjust the guides and the thrust bearings, which will be covered in the next chapter.

Tracking the Blade

If you are using *center tracking*, rotate the wheel by hand and angle the top wheel until the blade is tracking in the middle of the top wheel. Make several revolutions of the blade to make sure that the blade stays in the same place on the wheels. Lock the tilt knob.

If you are using *coplanar tracking*, align the wheels with a straightedge. Make several revolutions of the blade to make sure that it stays in the same place on the wheels. The blade may or may not track in the center of the top wheel. Lock the tilt knob.

Having a well-tuned band saw in your shop has many benefits. It will greatly increase your confidence and your cutting options. It makes the work more efficient and enjoyable.

It also has another important benefit: safety. When your band saw is accurate, you can use it to rip small pieces that are dangerous to cut on table or radial arm saws. There is no dangerous kickback with a band saw. If a well-tuned band saw can help prevent an accident, all the attention you gave it is certainly worth the effort.

128

6

Adjusting the Thrust Bearings and Guides

Band-saw performance is directly related to how it is adjusted. Poor adjustment fosters poor performance, and, a well-tuned and adjusted saw encourages good performance. Working with a well-adjusted saw is a real pleasure. All you have to do to adjust your saw correctly is pay strict attention to detail.

When you adjust the band saw, you want the blade to run as straight as possible. This sounds very simple, but it takes effort to accomplish. Anything that will cause or allow the blade to deflect or twist will have a negative effect on band-saw performance.

Correct blade alignment is controlled by the thrust bearings at the back of the blade. Sideways deflection or twisting is prevented by the side guides. If the thrust bearings and guides are not accurately set, many problems will crop up. In some cases, blade lead and wander can be traced directly to poor bearing and guide adjustment.

Blade life and performance can be affected by how the thrust bearings and guides are adjusted. Poor adjustment increases twisting, wear, stress, and heat, which decreases blade life. It can also increase vibration and noise.

Terms

The blade is suspended around the two wheels. As the workpiece is moved into the blade, a mechanism is needed to prevent the blade from being shoved off the wheels. On most saws, a round wheel bearing called the thrust bearing is used to stop the rearward movement of the blade. (See Illus. 276.) A bearing is used because it decreases the friction at the back of the blade.

There are usually two thrust bearings, one above and one below the table. The thrust bearing is called a number of other names, including the blade support, roller guide, bearing, support, etc. In this book it will be called a thrust bearing.

"Guides" are paired with each thrust bearing on each side of the blade. The guides prevent the sideways movement or deflection of the blade. They also prevent excessive twisting of the blade when it is being used to cut curves. There are usually four guides, one on each side of the blade above and below the table. The guides are also called "blocks," "pins," or "guide blocks." (See Illus. 277.)

The sideways movement of the blade is controlled by the guides. The rearward movement of

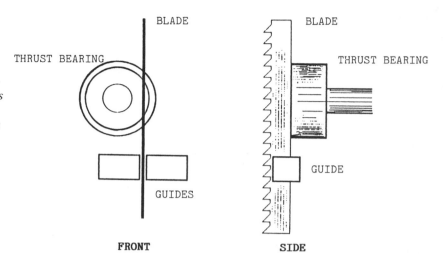

Illus. 276. The thrust bearing is located behind the blade and prevents the blades from being shoved rearwards by the workpiece. The guides are located on each side of the blade, and prevent twisting and deflecting.

Illus. 277. The bearings and guides are located above and below the table.

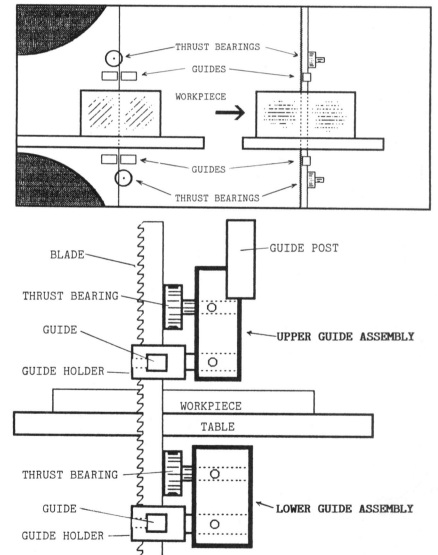

Illus. 278. The guide assembly is a casting that holds the bearings and the guide holder.

the blade is controlled by the thrust bearing. The forward (towards the operator) movement is controlled by "tracking" or balancing the blade on the wheels. If one is not careful and doesn't plan ahead, the blade can be pulled forward off the wheels. This is especially true when "backing out" of a long, curved cut.

The guides and bearing are held in place by a metal casting called the "guide assembly." There are two guide assemblies: one above and one below the table. (See Illus. 278.) The top guide assembly is attached to the guide post, which is movable up and down and is thus adjustable to the thickness of the workpiece. Each guide assembly has a mechanism for the independent forward-and-rearward movement of the guides and thrust bearing. This guide-assembly design accommodates different blade widths.

The guides are held secure in a unit called the guide holder. Both guides are held in line with each other so that both move forward and rearward in unison. Each guide is locked in place with a setscrew. (See Illus. 279.)

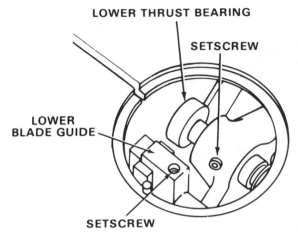

Illus. 280. On some saws, the bottom guides and thrust bearings are adjusted through the table top.

Illus. 281. This is the bottom guide on a Taiwanese saw. The long distance between the table and the guide assembly decreases the blade's beam strength and increases blade deflection.

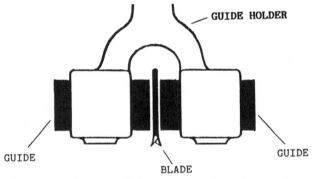

Illus. 279. The guide holder secures the guides and maintains their alignment with each other.

The guide assembly below the table is fixed (not movable). On some saws, the setscrew adjustments for the guide holder and thrust bearing are made through the hole in the table. (See Illus. 280.) On other saws, all of the adjustments are made from underneath the table. (See Illus. 281.) The setscrews are tightened after the guides and bearings are correctly positioned.

As mentioned, the top guide assembly is connected to the bottom of the guide post, which is adjustable up and down to accommodate different thicknesses of work. A lock screw locks the post in position. (See Illus. 282.) The post is usually locked, so that there is about ¼-inch clear-

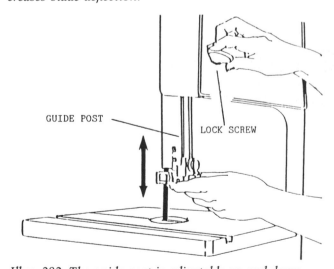

Illus. 282. The guide post is adjustable up and down.

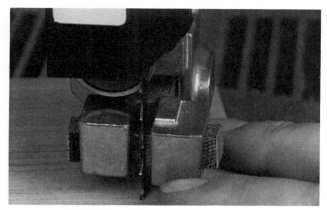

Illus. 283. Set the top-guide assembly about ¼ inch above the work to prevent your fingers from contacting the blade.

ance between the top guide assembly and the workpiece. This prevents the operator's finger from coming into contact with the blade. (See Illus. 283.)

There is another benefit to the lowest possible post position. The lower the post, the less the blade span between thrust bearings. This gives the band saw blade greater beam strength and thus decreases the likelihood of blade deflection.

Thrust Bearings

The thrust bearing is located behind the blade. As the workpiece is moved during the cut, the blade is shoved rearward into the thrust bearing. If the thrust bearings weren't in place, the blade would be shoved rearward off the wheels.

The bearings should be positioned about ¹⁄₆₄ (.015) inch behind the blade. This means that the blade doesn't touch the bearings when the saw is not cutting. (See Illus. 284.) If the blade and bearings are always in contact. it causes both to wear prematurely.

When you begin the cut, the blade moves rearward ¹⁄₆₄ inch and contacts the bearings, causing them to rotate. (See Illus. 284.) When properly adjusted, the bearings don't rotate unless the blade is cutting. After the cut, the blade should return to its position ¹⁄₆₄ inch from the bearings, and the rotation will stop.

When properly aligned, the thrust bearings support the back of the blade and keep it in a straight line. (See Illus. 285.) If both of the thrust bearings are not accurately aligned, the back of the blade will contact one bearing before the other. The back of the blade will not be equally supported by both bearings. Under sawing pressure, the blade will twist or deflect sideways until the back contacts both bearings. This twist causes the blade to cut at a slight angle. (See Illus. 286.) This decreases the likelihood of a straight cut. The better the bearing alignment, the straighter the cut and the longer the blade body will last.

Adjusting the Bearings

Track and tension the blade before adjusting the thrust bearings. Position the weld opposite the bearings. This is done because the weld is the least straight part of the blade.

Illus. 284. The blade should not touch the thrust bearings unless the saw is cutting.

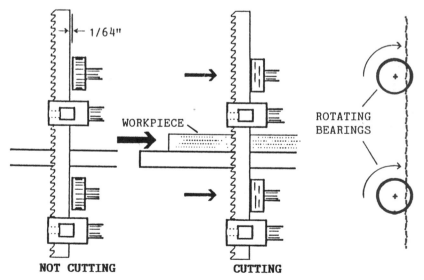

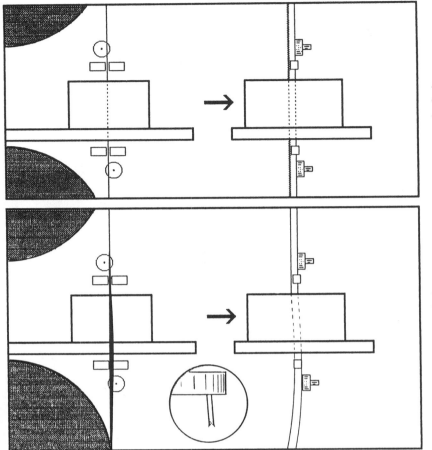

Illus. 285. If the bearings are well aligned, the back of the blade will stay straight during the cut.

Illus. 286. In this case, the bottom bearing is too far back, which causes unequal support. This allows the blade to deflect and rotate.

Both thrust bearings are attached to the end of a shaft. The shaft is locked in place with a screw. Some bearings are moved manually (Illus. 287), and others are moved by rotating a knob. (Illus. 288.)

The thrust bearings should be positioned ¹⁄₆₄ inch behind the blade. You can use a number of means to accurately make this measurement, including a feeler gauge or paper. (See Illus. 289 and 290.) A feeler gauge is a tool used to measure the thickness of the space between two machine parts. It consists of small sheets of metal, each of a different thickness.

After you have adjusted the bearings, rotate the wheels by hand and listen for any noise. If you hear a noise, retract the bearing back another ¹⁄₆₄ inch until the noise stops.

Thrust-Bearing Damage

Ideally, the back of the weld should be straight. (See Illus. 291A.) If the weld is not straight, it can damage the thrust bearing. If this is the case, you will hear a distinct ticking sound like a clock when the saw runs. The worst damage to the thrust bearing can occur if the weld is as shown in 291C. The sharp corner will quickly scar and

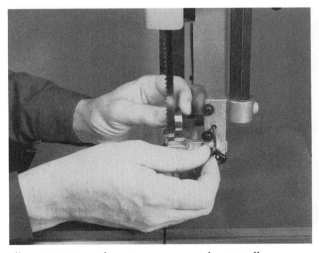

Illus. 287. Some bearings are moved manually.

Illus. 288 (above left). When you rotate a knob, you can move this bearing forward or rearward. Illus. 289 (above right). A .015- or .016-inch feeler gauge blade can be used to determine the distance between the back of the blade and the bearing.

Illus. 290. A dollar bill folded twice will be about .016 inch thick, which is equal to the correct distance between the blade and the bearing.

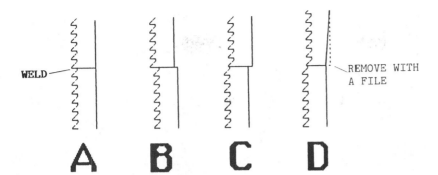

WELD

REMOVE WITH
A FILE

A B C D

Illus. 291. A. The back of the blade should be straight. B. This weld is not good, but it will not damage the bearing. C. This is the worst possible situation for the weld. It will damage the thrust bearing. D. The sharp corner should be filed off.

ruin the bearing. The best approach is to file off the sharp corner, as shown in Illus. 291D.

If the blade has a rough spot or a bad weld, it can scar the thrust bearing. The bearing will rotate, but stop at the scar. As the saw runs, the scar becomes deeper. Illus. 292 shows thrust bearings that have been scarred by the blade. Eventually, the bearing stops rotating and the blade runs in the scar. The metal-to-metal contact between the blade and the bearing heats up the blade. Heat destroys blades. The blade will either undergo metal fatigue and break or it will lose its ability to stay sharp. Either way, the blade is destroyed by the heat.

One problem with band-saw blades now being manufactured is that the corners on the back of the blades are square and become very sharp with use. A square blade back is very hard on the thrust bearing. As the back of the blade contacts the thrust bearing, the back wears and the corners become increasingly sharp. Under heavy use, the back can actually form a burr like that on a cabinet scraper. This type of "cold forming" causes the blade to become brittle, and adds to potential blade breakage. Years ago, some manufacturers rounded the backs of the blade to avoid this problem.

Observe the thrust bearing often during the sawing process to make sure that *both* bearings (above and below the table) are rotating. It is not unusual for a band-saw owner to realize after many blades have been broken that one of the bearings is damaged or frozen. It is often the thrust bearing that is below the table that is the culprit.

The surface of the thrust bearing should be smooth and show no signs of scarring. If it appears to be damaged, it should either be replaced or reversed. Some bearings can be easily pressed off their shafts and then pressed back on in a reversed position. Other bearings are attached to the machine with a screw; these bearings can be unscrewed and reversed. (See Illus. 293 and 294.)

If the bearing itself is not functional, change it. Keep one or two spare thrust bearings on hand.

To prevent bearings from being damaged, round the back of the blade. The round back cannot dig into the thrust bearing the way that a sharp, square corner can. (See Illus. 295.) This is especially true if the blade gets twisted, which is often the case when sharp curves are being made. (See Illus. 296.)

Use either a file, a diamond hone, or a sharpen-

Illus. 292. The bearing on the left is new. The bearing in the middle has a scar on the top of it. The bearing on the right is completely destroyed. This bearing was under the table and was covered with pine pitch, which prevented it from rotating efficiently.

135

Illus. 293 (above left). Some bearings are attached to the saw with a screw. Illus. 294 (above right). Reversing the bearing exposes a new surface.

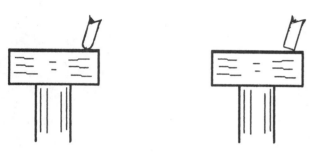

Illus. 295. A square blade has a sharp corner, which can damage the thrust bearing.

Illus. 296. Potential damage to the thrust bearing is not a problem if the corner is rounded.

Illus. 297. Round the back of the blade with a file, stone, or diamond hone while the saw is running. Be sure that you wear safety glasses. Before rounding the back of the blade, clean the sawdust from the inside of the saw to prevent potential fire hazards from the sparks.

ing stone to round the back of the blade. I like the hone for small blades, but use the file for blades over ¼ inches.

After tracking the blade in the usual way, tilt the top wheel rearward so that the blade engages the thrust bearing. This rearward pressure of the blade will help to keep it from coming forward off the wheels when you apply pressure to the back of the blade with the file or hone. (See Illus. 297.)

Wear safety glasses. Start the saw and file the corners first by gently moving the file back and forth. You should do this for a minute or two on each corner. Then slowly rotate the file so that the back and the corners are filed in one slow circular movement. (See Illus. 298.) Stop the saw and feel the back of the blade. You shouldn't feel any sharp corners. If you are going to make a lot of tight, curved cuts, it may be worthwhile to file the corners a while longer. After you have

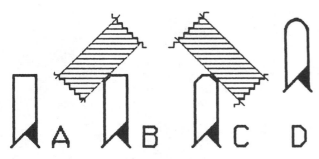

Illus. 298. To round the back of the blade, first file the corner as shown at B and C. Then slowly rotate the file around the back, as shown in D. This takes about two or three minutes.

rounded the corners, remember to angle the top wheel forward again, taking pressure off the thrust bearings.

After the filing, the saw will run quieter and the blade will be less likely to damage the thrust bearings. It will also cut more smoothly on curves, especially tight curves where the back of the blade is in close contact with the fresh kerf. The cut will be smoother because the smooth back of the blade will not get caught on each imperfection in the cut. The front of the blade will stay more stable because it will not be jostled as much as the front of a blade with a square back. It is important to remember that any rough movement at the back of the blade is transferred to the front, and affects the smoothness of the cut.

Guides

Band saws are usually equipped with two sets of guides. One set is located above the table, and the other is located below the table. The top set is held by the top guide assembly, which is attached to the guide post and is adjustable up and down. The guides hold the blade secure during a straight cut and prevent the blade from twisting or deflecting during a curved cut. (See Illus. 299.)

The most common guides are metal blocks or round metal rods. On more expensive machines, bearings are used as guides. (See Illus. 300.) The bearing rotates with the blade, which decreases the friction between the blade and the guide. Bearings are used for guides on metal-cutting saws because of the decreased friction but also

Illus. 299. The guides prevent the blade from deflecting or twisting during a curved cut. The guides shown here are Cool Blocks, which are a new nonmetal replacement for the standard metal blocks.

Illus. 300. The larger Inca saw has bearing guides that accommodate small blades.

because of the fact that the blade is twisted. (See Illus. 301 and 302.) Inca of Switzerland makes an optional bearing guide that is used for small blades such as ⅛-inch or 1/16-inch blades. (See Illus. 303.)

Though the bearing guide is better than solid metal blocks, the new nonmetal blocks available such as Cool Blocks provide a better performance than bearing kits at about a fourth of the cost.

When a band saw is used to cut curves, especially tight curves, the blade rubs against and

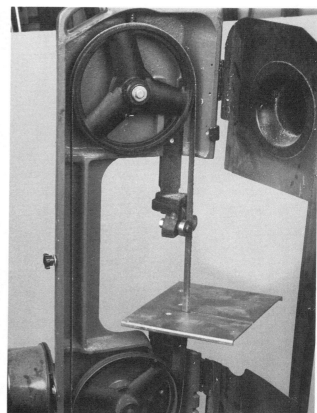

Illus. 301 (above left). Horizontal metal saws have roller bearing guides. Illus. 302 (above right). Roller bearings are used on vertical-horizontal saws because the blade is twisted outward.

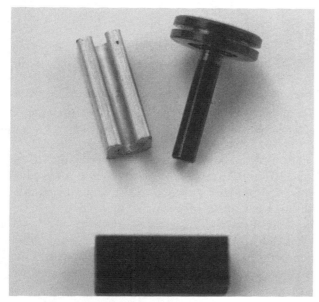

Illus. 303. Inca sells an optional roller system for small blades. This system replaces the rectangular block shown at the bottom of this photograph.

wears the front of the guides. Small blades are the worst offenders. For this reason, the guides should be checked often for wear. When the end of guide does wear, it can be resurfaced with a file. The guides can also be reversed, which exposes a new surface. Square blocks such as the ones on the Sears and Delta band saws can be rotated 90 degrees, which also exposes a new corner.

Band-saw wheels are seldom perfectly round. There are two buffer systems that function to neutralize the effects of eccentric wheels, which cause a change in blade tension as the wheel rotates. The primary buffer is the tension spring. The spring neutralizes the extremes in tension, maintaining an average tension. The guides are a secondary buffer. They neutralize the side-to-side movement of the blade caused by eccentric wheels.

You can test the eccentricity of your wheels in a number of different ways. The most sophisti-

Illus. 304. A dial indicator is the most sophisticated way of measuring wheel eccentricity.

cated way is to use a dial indicator. (See Illus. 304.) Another way is to pinch both guides against the blade and slowly rotate the wheels a couple of times. The blade will shove the blocks outward if the wheels are eccentric. You can make the wheels round by truing the tires. This is covered in Chapter 8.

The wheels are never exactly the same size, so they are always changing in proximity to each other. At times, your saw may vibrate more than usual because the wheels are out of synchronization.

Adjusting the Guides

Adjust the guides after you have tensioned and tracked the blade correctly and set the thrust bearing. There are actually two adjustments for the blocks. One adjustment is the distance between the blocks and the blade. The other adjustment is the distance between the front edge of the block and the tooth.

Setting the Tooth Guide Distance

It is very important that the blade teeth do not accidentally touch the guide. If there is contact between the teeth and the metal guide, the teeth will be damaged and the blade ruined. The metal guide will also suffer damage and will have to be resurfaced.

Set the guide so that the front edge of the guide is even with or just behind the back of the blade gullet when the saw is cutting. (See Illus. 305.) Because the blade moves rearward during the cut, the distance between the back of the blade and the thrust bearing (.015 inch) must be allowed for. This means that the guide should be positioned about .015″ (¹⁄₆₄) inch behind the blade gullet. (See Illus. 306.)

Setting the Guide-Blade Distance

The distance between the guide and the blade is usually about .003 to .005 inch. (See Illus. 307.) This is the thickness of a piece of paper. Paper is a good measuring device to use until you have developed an eye for this small distance. Paper money is usually .004 inch and is a good choice because it is generally right at hand. (See Illus. 308.)

It is important that you do not deflect the blade when the guides are locked in place. (See Illus. 309 and 310.) After you have locked the guides with the setscrew, rotate the wheels to study the travel of the blade. Ideally, the blade will run down the middle of the guides, but if the wheels are eccentric it may touch one guide and then the other. It should not touch just one guide.

If the guides are too close, especially metal guides, there will be too much friction between the blade and the guides. If they are not close enough, the blade will be unsupported when it makes turns.

For the last 100 years, guide blocks have been made out of metal. This was an appropriate choice of materials a hundred years ago when band saws ran at very slow speeds. However, band saws can now run at much higher speeds. The average wood-cutting band saw now runs at about 2,800 feet per minute. At this high speed, metal is no longer the appropriate material for use as band-saw guides. Friction is created between metal guides and the metal blade. The friction creates heat, which causes premature blade failure and/or the loss of tooth hardness. This is especially true with narrow blades mak-

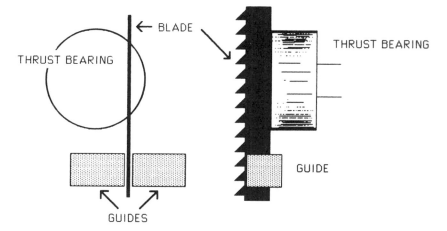

Illus. 305. When the saw is cutting, the front of the guide should be close to the back of the tooth gullet.

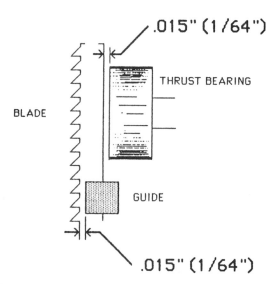

Illus. 306. When the saw is not cutting, the blade will spring back to its original position. When you are adjusting the guides, make sure that the distance between the gullet back and the guide is the same as the distance between the blade and the thrust bearing.

Illus. 308. A piece of paper on each side of the blade will maintain the desired distance as you lock the blocks in place. Paper money, which is about .004 inch thick, works well here.

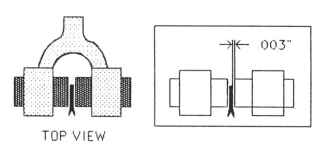

Illus. 307. The distance between the blade and the guide should be from .003 to .005 inch.

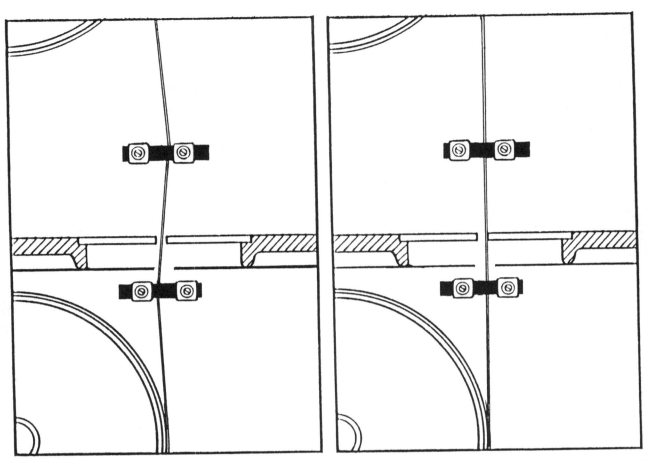

Illus. 309 (above left). Make sure that you do not deflect the blade as you tighten the guides. Illus. 310 (above right). The blade should be as straight as possible.

ing tight curves. They don't have the mass to absorb and dissipate heat well.

Aside from creating friction and shortening blade life, metal guide blocks are very noisy. If they are not set perfectly, they can accidentally touch the teeth, destroying the set and thus the blade. Because of friction, the guides cannot be set close to accurately hold the blade secure for very accurate work. To adequately hold small blades, you have to replace metal guides with a roller bearing, which is expensive.

Metal guide blocks should be replaced with just about any other material. A lot of oldtimer woodworkers in Wisconsin use green sugar maple. Some European manufacturers still use hard wood. Tropical hard wood has been tried, but doesn't seem to work as well because most of the hard tropical woods initially leave an oil film that coats the blade. Rather than lubricating the blade, the film can dry and create a crust on the blade that can actually cause a heat buildup. For this reason, hard tropical or exotic woods are not the best choice.

In the last year, two manufacturers have started to make nonmetallic replacement guide blocks for band saws. One guide block, which is made in Idaho, is a black plastic that melts when a match is held to it. The other one, manufactured in Kentucky and called Cool Blocks, is made from a specially formulated phenolic laminate material that doesn't melt. A phenolic laminate material is a plastic with layers of linen cloth compressed into it. It was developed during the 1930s as an insulation material in the electronics industry. It is strong, nonconductive, and dissipates heat. Cool Blocks have three synthetic dry lubricants that are designed to lubricate the blade, but not make it oily. (See Illus. 311.)

After experimenting with various materials—

Illus. 311 (above left). The metal guide blocks on this saw have been replaced with Cool Blocks. Cool Blocks are a high-tech, non-metallic material that has a dry lubricant. Shown here are a Cool Block on the left, a metal block in the middle, and a plastic replacement block on the right. Illus. 312 (above right). Because Cool Blocks contain a dry lubricant, they can be adjusted so that they are right near the blade, with the result that they offer extra support with no increase in noise or heat.

including wood, plastic, and other material—for the last six months in an attempt to replace metal guides, I've discovered that Cool Blocks work the best. After I replaced the standard metal guides with Cool Blocks, the saw ran smoother and quieter. The blades seem to last and stay sharp longer, especially the small blades. Cool Blocks can be set right up to the blade, making the saw extremely accurate. (See Illus. 312.) This tight fit gives the operator great control, which is unusual when a band saw is used. Because the blocks are very close to the blade, they wear a bit faster, but can be easily resurfaced with a file. Cool Blocks are slightly less expensive than the standard replacement metal guides.

A friend of mine who does a great deal of band-saw work with a ⅛-inch blade says that with Cool Blocks small blades last from two to three times as long. The blades often get too dull to use, which is a contrast to the way they would break when they were still fairly sharp. When Cool Blocks are used, the problem of premature blade breakage has greatly decreased.

I used a sound meter to determine whether Cool Blocks are quieter than metal guides. This produced some very interesting results. Cool Blocks were quieter, especially when the guides were set fairly close (.003 inch) to the blade. At this distance, they made roughly half the noise.

They were even more effective on less-expensive band saws, perhaps because these saws have wheels that are less round, and which cause more contact between the blade and the guides.

Perhaps the most surprising aspect to Cool Blocks is that when they are used the saw actually becomes quieter the longer it runs. They somehow polish the blade and make it more slippery and quieter. After the saw has run for approximately an hour, you can tell by touching the blade that its body is smoother (don't touch it when the machine is running!). Even after the metal guide blocks were replaced for test purposes, the saw remained quiet for awhile, though it did get progressively louder. This indicates that Cool Blocks have a direct effect on the surface of the blade, making it run smoother and quieter.

It appears that Cool Blocks will soon become standard equipment on one of the major brands of band saws now sold in America. It would not be surprising if they became standard equipment on all band saws within the next couple of years. This would go a long way towards modernizing the band saw.

Cool Blocks are now made in six sizes. They are made to fit the following band saws: the 14-inch Delta saw, the 14-inch Taiwanese saw, the 12-inch Sears saw, the old Sears (round ¼-inch) saw, and the 340 Inca and Shopsmith models.

Adjusting the Guide Post

Manufacturers are under pressure to produce inexpensive tools. This has been particularly true in the last couple of years, with new competition constantly entering the market. As a consequence, the alignment and adjustment features on some of the less-expensive machines are not as well made as they could be. This means that the band-saw owner will have to assume more and more responsibility for alignment and adjustment. He will have to double-check some adjustments to ensure good performance, and assume less and less that the adjustments are correct.

You have to align the two thrust bearings perfectly with each other to support the back of the blade. When the saw is not cutting, the blade should not touch the thrust bearing. When the workpiece is shoved into the blade, the blade is shoved rearward about ¹⁄₆₄ inch and touches both thrust bearings. When the cutting stops, the blade should spring back to its original position and the thrust bearings will stop rotating. The force applied to the workpiece should be evenly distributed between the two thrust bearings.

If the two thrust bearings are not perfectly aligned with each other, the blade will touch one first and bend or deflect until it touches the other bearing. This deflection or twisting of the blade has a negative effect on the ability of the blade to cut straight. Needless to say, the rearward twisting doesn't do the blade any good either. Thus, thrust-bearing misalignment is a very subtle but serious problem with band saws.

Part of the problem with bearing misalignment is with the guide post, which holds the top assembly and thus the top thrust bearing. You cannot assume that the guide post will go straight up and down and stay square to the table. (See Illus. 313 and 314.) If it is out of square, and most are, it may be correct at one height and not correct at another. If it is out of square front to back, it will affect the alignment of the thrust bearings. If it is out of square from side to side, it will affect the accuracy of the top guide blocks.

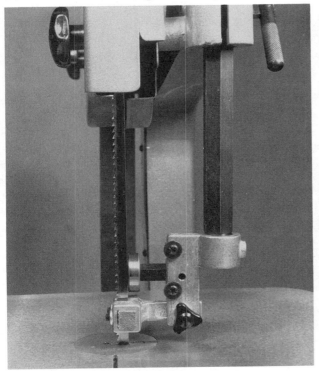 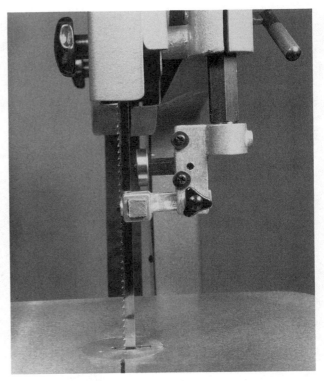

Illus. 313 (above left). This guide post is not square to the table. It is properly adjusted in its low position. Illus. 314 (above right). When the post is raised, the guide assembly is grossly misaligned. When a guide assembly is misaligned this severely, the thrust bearing and the guide holder have to be reset each time the post is moved.

On most saws, the top guide assembly is a separate casting. (See Illus. 315.) It is very important that the guide assembly is accurately aligned so that the thrust bearing is at a 90-degree angle to the blade and locked very securely to the guide post. (See Illus. 316.) Next, adjust the top guide assembly to the correct position. This should be about a ¼ inch above the thickness of the workpiece. For example, if the workpiece is ¾ inch thick, adjust the bottom of the top guide assembly for 1 inch to give you the correct height allowance for a ¼-inch clearance.

Next, track the blade and set the thrust bearings with the blade weld on the opposite side of the saw. The weld is the least straight part of the blade and should be avoided when you set the thrust bearings. Remember, you will have to check and possibly readjust the top guides and thrust bearing every time you change the position of the post. If the space between the blade and each thrust bearing is not exactly the same, the performance of the band saw will be compromised.

Adjusting the Table for Squareness

After you have tensioned and tracked the blade, it is time to adjust the table so that it is square to the blade. This is best done by using a high-quality square. Use a combination square because of the broad surface on the table. (See Illus. 317.) If you are using a small square, it is best to have the longest arm referencing against the table. The table has an adjustable stop, which will allow repeated squaring of the table. The stop on a Sears band saw is adjustable through the tabletop. (See Illus. 318.) Other saws have an adjustment screw under the table, which will take some trial and error to adjust correctly. A similar approach can be used if you are setting the table to a specific angle. (See Illus. 319.)

TABLE INSERT

The table insert surrounds the blade. It is removable, which allows for access and adjustments to areas close to the blade. If the blade is twisted too much, it can damage the table insert. (See Illus. 320.) On some saws, the table insert should be filed so that it isn't too close to the blade. (See Illus. 321.)

American band saws usually have metal inserts, which can damage the blade if there is contact between the blade and the insert. (See Illus. 322.) A friend of mine by the name of Ed Hinsa likes wood inserts, which he makes himself. (See Illus. 323.) Whichever type of insert you use, its front should be very slightly lower than

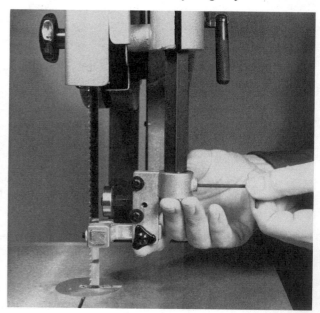

Illus. 315 (above left). The guide assembly is usually a separate casting. Illus. 316 (above right). The guide assembly should be adjusted so that the thrust bearing is at 90 degrees to the blade. Check this alignment often.

Illus. 317. A combination square provides a broad base.

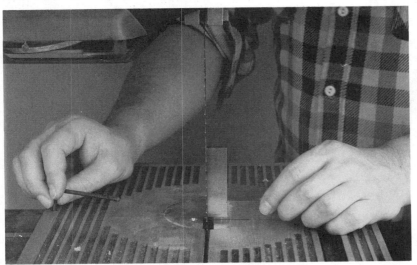

Illus. 318. The table is adjusted with a bolt or screw. The Sears band saw is adjustable through the top. If you are using a small square, use the broadest surface on the table.

Illus. 319. You can use a bevel gauge to set the table angle.

the table. File the bottom to remove excess material. The back of the insert should be slightly higher than the table. If it is low, increase its height by adding a layer of tape to the bottom of the insert. By having the front a little low and the back a little high, you will not have to worry about the workpiece binding on either the table or the insert. (See Illus. 324.)

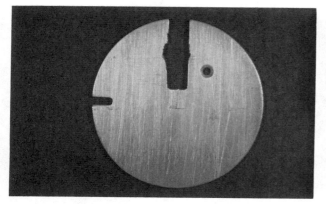

Illus. 320 (above left). If the blade touches the metal insert, both will be damaged. Illus. 321 (above right). File the insert if it is too close to the blade.

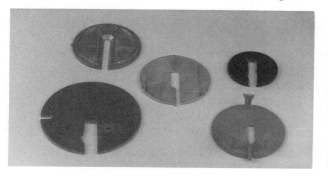

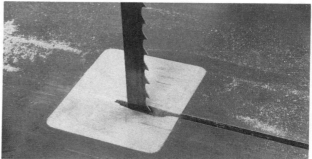

Illus. 322 (above left). The European inserts on the right are plastic and cannot damage the blade. Illus. 323 (above right). Wood inserts are good to use; you can fit them very close to the blade without damaging it.

Illus. 324. Use your finger to feel the level of the insert. If the front is slightly low and the back slightly high, it will prevent binding.

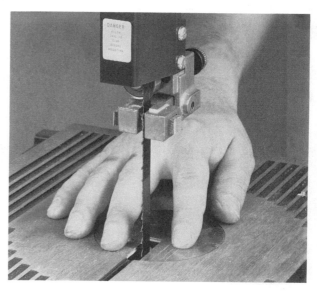

7
Tensioning the Blade

The band-saw blade must do two things: it must bend around the wheels, yet stay straight between them, and it must be stiff enough so that it doesn't flex or deflect during the cut. Blade tension keeps the blade straight. The blade is stretched taut between the wheels. One of the wheels is adjustable and it can be moved away from the other wheel, which applies the tension. The tension acts like a weight hanging from a rope. The greater the weight (tension), the greater the resistance to side pressure or blade deflection.

One of the most important single factors affecting band-saw performance—and the easiest one to change—is the tension of the blade. A poor-quality saw that is well-tensioned will perform better than a quality tool that is poorly tensioned.

For an understanding of blade tension, it is necessary to look at the frame and the coping saw—the ancestors of the band saw. The concept that all three share is a simple one. The blade is narrow, and therefore flexible. A frame is used to support and tension the blade and keep it straight and stiff.

As the frame-saw blade cuts, the tension at the back of the blade increases. (See Illus. 325A.) The wood applies a drag effect to the blade, which actually tensions the blade, and in effect causes a self-tensioning mechanism. If the frame isn't applying enough tension to the blade, it will buckle and flex in the area of least tension. (See Illus. 325B.) In this case, the saw blade will be difficult to control. It will wander when cutting, with little regard for the position of the frame.

The proper amount of blade tension balances the tension of each side of the cut during sawing. This will keep the blade straight. It will also make the blade more controllable because the frame and the saw blade will maintain a direct relationship to each other. A note of caution is appropriate here: You only need enough tension on the blade to equalize the forces on each side of the workpiece. If you tension the blade beyond this point, you risk damaging the frame of the saw. This same principle applies to the band saw.

The coping saw is also a frame saw. The blade is pulled through the wood rather than pushed. Because the blade is cutting on the pull stroke, the blade tensions itself. The light tension the frame applies to the back of the blade prevents buckling or flexing.

The coping saw and Japanese saws share similarities in that both cut on the pull stroke. Toshio Ōdate, a Japanese craftsman and writer, compares these saws to a string. It is hard to push a string straight, but it is easy to pull straight. The combination of the pull stroke and the spring frame help the coping saw always maintain proper blade tension. Pulling the saw tensions the first half of the blade. (See Illus. 326A.) The spring frame acts as a buffer and maintains tension on the back half. (See Illus. 327B.) The band saw is similar to the coping saw in that both blades are pulled through the wood, and both have a spring mechanism to help maintain tension.

The band saw is a motorized frame saw. Its narrow blade obeys the same laws of physics that govern the blades on frame and coping

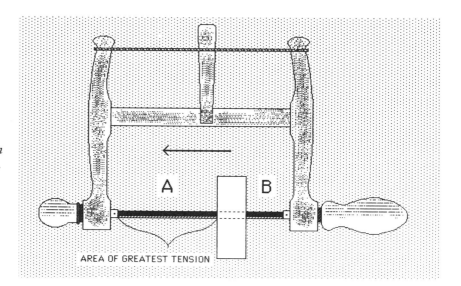

Illus. 325. As the frame saw cuts, the tension on each side of the workpiece changes and the tension on the back of the blade increases.

A B

AREA OF GREATEST TENSION

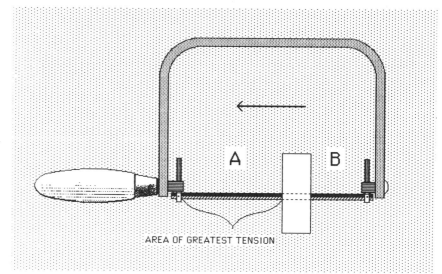

Illus. 326. Pulling the coping saw increases the tension on the first half of the blade (A). The spring frame acts as a buffer and maintains tension on the back of the blade (B).

A B

AREA OF GREATEST TENSION

saws. However, because the blade is endless, band-saw adjustment and tensioning is more complex. Wheels suspend the blade. The top wheel rotates freely. The bottom wheel rotates under power and drives the blade. The top wheel is adjustable up and down by means of a threaded rod. Upward wheel movement tightens the blade in a similar fashion to blade tensioning on a frame saw. (See Illus. 327.) The threaded rod compresses a spring as the tension is increased. The spring serves the same purpose as the spring frame on the coping saw. It is a buffer and shock absorber.

The tension on each side of the blade is roughly even. (See Illus. 328A and B.) When the blade starts to cut, the blade tension changes, which is similar to how blade tensioning works on the traditional frame saw or coping saw. The blade is pulled through the wood like the blade on a coping saw, by the bottom wheel rotation. The act of cutting creates a dragging effect on the blade. During the sawing process, the tension becomes greatest between the bottom wheel and the workpiece. (See Illus. 329.)

The harder and thicker the workpiece or the faster the material is fed into work, the greater the drag effect, and the greater the tension between the bottom wheel and the workpiece.

It is important to have enough tension on the blade so that it is fairly equal above and below the table. If the tension on both sides of the workpiece is not similar, the blade will be harder

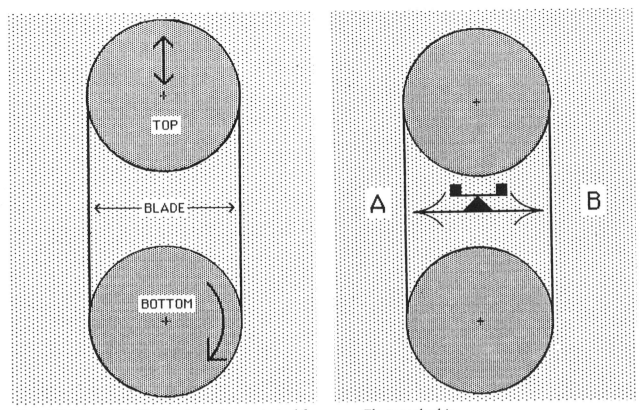

Illus. 327 (above left). The band saw is a motorized frame saw. The top wheel is adjustable up and down. Upward adjustment tightens the blade and increases the tension. Illus. 328 (above right). When the band saw is not cutting, the blade tension is equal on either side of the wheels (A and B).

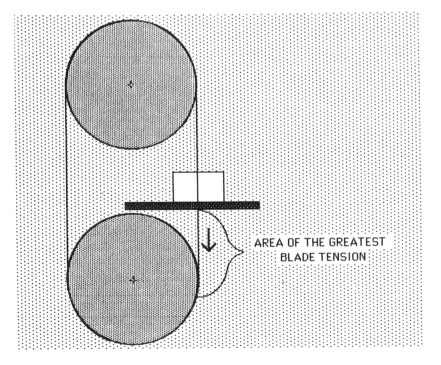

Illus. 329. As the saw cuts, the workpiece produces a dragging effect on the blade. This dragging effect increases the tension between the workpiece and the bottom wheel.

to control. Decreasing the feed rate decreases the drag on the blade, thus lessening the need for tension.

When there is trouble with the machine setup, you will notice problems when cutting. The first thing that you may note is a condition known generally as the "wandering cut." A well-adjusted band saw will cut fairly straight. If a blade isn't sufficiently tensioned, it will flex as it cuts. The cut on thin wood (less than one inch) won't stay straight and will be hard to control. (See Illus. 330.) This is more of a problem when you intend to cut straight.

When you are cutting curves, it isn't difficult to compensate for a wandering blade or for blade lead, which occurs when a blade pulls to one side. Lead can be caused by a number of things other than insufficient tension, including poor wheel alignment, poor tracking, uneven teeth or uneven sharpening.

When thicker stock is cut with an undertensioned blade, another phenomenon called a "barrel cut" occurs. (See Illus. 331.) The blade will flex sideways in the work, making a curved cut. This is very frustrating and wasteful. During the cut, the blade will maintain a fairly straight course, progressively straying from the desired line. As the cut progresses you will start to feel the blade pulling the wood to one side, which signals that something is wrong with the cut. If

this happens, make sure that your fingers are not on the side of the workpiece nearest the blade! The blade can flex enough to come out of the side of the board.

When a barrel cut has been made, you will notice two things. (See Illus. 332.) The first is that the cut will not be straight from front to back. Secondly, the final cut is curved through the thickness of the workpiece from top to bottom. By the end of the cut, the blade will be very hot because it has flexed enough to rub hard against the guides, causing friction and heat. This all adds up to blade breakage.

If the band-saw blade doesn't have enough tension, it will flex during the cut (especially the barrel cut) until it tensions itself. The blade will follow the path of least resistance and deflect at the point of greatest stress, which is the saw cut. As the blade deflects, the tension on the blade increases until it reaches a more appropriate tension. This means that the band saw—like the frame and coping saw blades—literally tensions itself.

This self-tensioning phenomenon is evident in experiments. A slightly undertensioned blade will make a slightly barrelled cut. A grossly undertensioned blade will make an extremely barrelled cut. If you stop the saw before the very end of a barrel cut and check the blade tension, it will be close to correct.

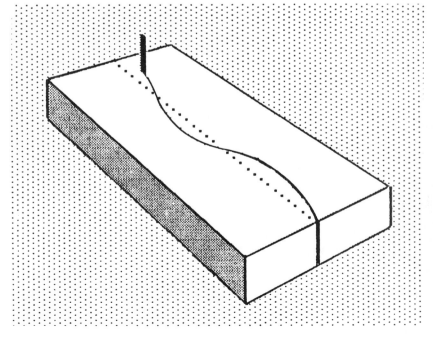

Illus. 330. If the blade is not sufficiently tensioned, the effect on narrow wood will be a "wandering" cut.

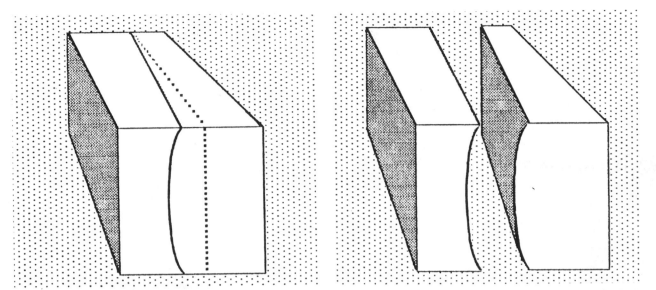

Illus. 331 (above left). An insufficiently tensioned blade causes a "barrel" cut in thick stock. Illus. 332 (above right). A barrel cut will be curved from top to bottom and crooked from front to back.

It is extremely important to have enough tension on the blade to keep it from flexing during the cut. Once the blade starts to flex, it is very difficult to reverse. The blade follows its wayward path. But how much tension is needed? It has to be enough to equalize the tension on the blade both above and below the table. Simply put, it should be enough to keep the blade straight on each side of the workpiece.

If you note that you are making wandering or barrel cuts, how do you know for sure if indeed it is a lack of tension that is causing them? Try increasing the tension. If this doesn't work, there may be one or more factors responsible. It is hard to pinpoint one direct factor because they are all interrelated. Other factors that may be contributing to this type of cut include the following:

1. Dull blade.
2. Poorly set guides and/or thrust bearings.
3. Poor wheel alignment and tracking.
4. Wrong blade selection. If the blade is too narrow, it will flex and more easily decrease the quality of the cut. The blade should also have the correct pitch and width.
5. The tooth pitch is too fine (too many teeth per inch).
6. There is not enough of a tooth set. This will give the same slow, labored cut as a dull blade.
7. Uneven set or uneven sharpening. This will cause the blade to "lead," which means that the blade will cut faster on one side and pull in that direction.
8. Blade speed is too slow. Correct this by feeding the material more slowly or increasing the blade speed.
9. Poor operator technique. If this is the case, experiment with different feed speeds. A slower feed will often improve performance because it requires less tension.

You can correct these problems by readjusting the machine, changing the way you operate it, or by changing the blade. Try only one change at a time.

Tensioning Procedures

To tension the blade, adjust the upper wheel assembly up or down by turning the knob or hand wheel. Because the upper wheel assembly is adjustable, it allows for slight variations in blade length.

It is important that constant tension be applied to the blade and that there is something to absorb the shock generated by this tension. This is accomplished by using a spring or, on old saws, a weight. After the blade becomes tight, further tension compresses the spring. This spring applies a constant tension to the blade, which is important if the saw has eccentric wheels. (See Illus. 333 and 334.)

New industrial saws often used hydraulic pressure, which maintains a uniform tension. Old

Illus. 333 (above left). The spring on the 14-inch Delta band saw is visible through a slot in the casting. Illus. 334 (above right). This shows the tension spring on the inside of the Sears band saw.

Illus. 335. Old saws did not have springs. The blade was tensioned by a weight on an arm. The tension was increased when the weight was moved away from the saw.

saws used a fulcrum with the upper wheel assembly on one end and a movable weight on the other. As the weight was moved away from the fulcrum, the tension on the blade increased. (See Illus. 335.)

The correct amount of tension is needed for efficient sawing. Ideally, you want enough tension to get a good cutting performance, but not so much that you will damage the saw or the blade. Consideration must be given to a whole range of factors. For example, more tension is needed when wide blades are being used, hard, thick stock is being cut, or if you are cutting material with a dull blade and a fast feed rate.

There is no foolproof technique for measuring tension. With experience, you will learn how much tension is required for a particular situation. Following is information on how to measure tension.

Tension Scales

Most machines have a tension scale. (See Illus. 336 and 337.) Tension scales are designed to indicate the compression of the spring. As a rule, the greater the spring compression the greater the blade tension. These scales don't register until the saw blade is relatively taut, so variations in blade length do not make any difference. Tension

scales are adequate for average work—that is work that is less than two inches thick.

Over a period of time, the spring will lose its stiffness, particularly if it is under constant tension. This is one of the reasons why the tension should be released when the saw is not in use. If the spring loses its stiffness, the scale will be off. To adequately tension a blade, you may have to use a higher setting.

For example, you will adjust a ¼-inch blade to the ⅜-inch setting on the scale to ensure adequate tension.

Strain Gauges

As mentioned, most band saws are fitted with a tension scale. These scales give only a rough approximation of proper tension, and their readings should not be taken verbatim. There are more accurate blade tension indicators that clamp at two different positions on the blade. These gauges measure the tension between two fixed points on the blade.

They are more appropriate to metal sawing, where high tension is commonly used. Tension on these gauges is measured in Pounds Per Square Inch (PSI).

Some blade manufacturers list these gauges, which are expensive, in their catalogues. Be-

Illus. 336 (above left). The tension gauge on the Sears band saw is an arm (visible to the left of the top wheel) that swings upward as the blade tension is increased. Illus. 337 (above right). The spring on a 14-inch Delta band saw can be seen through a slot in the casting. The scale indicates the compression of the spring as the blade tension is increased. The larger the blade, the greater the spring compression required to tension it.

cause they are expensive, these devices are impractical for the homeowner or small professional shop user. It is, therefore, important for the individual craftsperson to be able to determine blade tension through other, less expensive means. These means are examined below.

Adjusting Tension by Sound

The easiest way to adjust the tension is to use sound. Slowly increase the tension while plucking the back of the blade (opposite the teeth). To pluck the blade, hook your finger over the blade, pull it sideways, and then let go. You will hear a musical note like one that would be given by a guitar string. Pluck on the coasting side opposite the blade guides. The narrower the blade, the higher the sound. Conversely, the wider the blade, the more base-like the sound.

The sound heard is caused by the blade vibrating under tension. As the tension is increased, the sound becomes less flat and more clear, which is what you are aiming for. When you overtension the blade, the sound will decrease because the blade will vibrate less. With a little practice, this can become a viable way of checking the tension. Try for the clearest musical sound.

Blade Deflection

Some people determine tension by *how much* the blade deflects when side pressure is applied to it. To use this method, raise the top guide assembly all the way up. This will expose at least six inches of blade. Then push on the side of the blade with moderate force. The more tension used, the stiffer the blade. The stiffer the blade, the less the amount of deflection. With moderate force, the blade should flex about ¼ inch. "Moderate force" is different for each person. The actual deflection of ¼ inch isn't the indicator, it is how much force it takes to deflect it that far.

Measuring blade tension by how much it deflects is a method that, like the use of sound, can be developed with practice.

Testing the Blade

The only real way to be sure that the saw will run correctly is to test it. Check the quality of the cut on a practice piece of scrap that is the same wood and the same size as your project. Don't be afraid to experiment, particularly if you are not confident. This is when you should experiment with the saw.

Don't be too goal-oriented at first because that only leads to frustration. Figure out what the saw can do before you start planning what you can do with it. To use the band saw efficiently, you must be able to tension it correctly. As with developing most types of skill, this takes time, patience, and concentration.

Always pay attention to the performance of the blade. A well-adjusted blade will often change. As it heats up from hard use, it will expand. As it expands in length, it decreases in tension. When doing thick sawing for long periods of time—especially when cutting thick and dense wood such as hard maple—you may have to retension the blade to compensate for this expansion. If you do increase the tension to maintain performance, it is important that after you have finished sawing, you release the tension and allow the blade to cool and, consequently, to decrease to its original length. If you don't release the tension, you will have an overtensioned blade by the time the blade cools down.

Overtensioning the Blade

Though having enough tension on the blade is important, resist the temptation to put too much tension on it. The blade should never be so tight that the spring is compressed completely. When this happens, the spring no longer functions as a shock absorber and cannot cushion the blade and the machine from sudden shock—especially if the wheels are not perfectly round. Maximum tension places tremendous strain on the blade, bearings, wheels, tires, and shafts, risking damage to these parts.

The band-saw wheel shaft is designed to tolerate a certain force. This endurance level is more than is needed for a normally tensioned blade—that is, a blade tensioned according to the saw's scale. When the blade is tensioned at this level, the shaft will last forever. However, when the blade is overtensioned and the metal on the band-saw shaft is stressed beyond a certain limit, the shaft will eventually fail.

The revolving band-saw shaft is one place on the band saw where the flexing cycles that cause metal fatigue are inadvertently applied. The greater the excessive force, the fewer the number of cycles it takes to cause the failure. Therefore, it is important not to use too much tension for too long a period of time.

Excessive tension can cause other problems. A saw that is well-aligned at normal tension can be pulled out of alignment as the tension is increased. Also, blade life is shortened by increased tension.

Adequate tension is important for good band-saw performance. However, it is equally important that you use the correct blade, proper tracking, and good wheel alignment. There is a problem with your band saw if you have to greatly exceed the tension-scale setting on your saw to get an acceptable performance. If you do not correct the problem and continue to use excessive tension, you risk the chance of damaging your band saw.

An Examination of the Band-Saw Blade as a Structural Beam, Contributed by Jack Turley

While writing this book, I did as much research and experimentation as possible and talked to quite a number of experts. One of the people who I talked to a great deal is Jack Turley—a friend of mine who is an architect and also a woodworker. I found his perceptions using engineering principles to be very interesting and quite useful. The following are his thoughts on the problems of determining and choosing the correct tension, which I'd like to share with you.

Why Band-Saw Cuts Drift

Band saws drift in their cuts for basically two reasons. First, the band-saw's basic geometry may have been compromised because it was badly made or designed or because it has been damaged. Secondly—and this is what we will focus on here—it can drift because the various factors that affect straight cutting are not understood and the saw is not properly set up. Of all the factors we consider when setting up a saw, we tend to focus on tensioning the blade as crucial; although this is partly justified, it is far from being the whole story. Following is an examination of the interrelationship between the various influences on straight cutting, and the central role occupied by blade tension.

Why Pre-Tension Blades?

Why do we pre-tension band-saw blades in the first place? If the blade were slack when we began the cut, it would simply twist to one side and begin cutting off at a tangent as soon as it felt the pressure of the wood being fed into it. When the blade is stretched taut, it takes a far greater force to cause it to twist, or, to use the technical term, buckle. We pre-tension the blade by turning a knob that moves the wheels farther apart, and stretches the blade.

The most often asked (and most badly answered) question in woodworking is how much should one pretension blades. An answer can only be reached in context to the other factors that influence how a blade cuts.

Beam Strength

In order to understand the effects of pre-tension on the behavior of band-saw blades, one should understand some basic information about structural beams. A beam is a horizontal structural member that carries a load while spanning over some distance. If a beam is supported at its ends and a load is applied to it, it will sag under the load; the degree it sags is proportional to the size of the load. What many people do not consider, however, is that the fibres on the underside of the beam are being stretched by that sag and that the fibres on the top surface are being compressed. You have seen this many times. When you break a piece of wood over your knee, the outside fibres break under the tension. The piece of wood against your knee is also being compressed, and if you were to examine it you would see wrinkles that indicate a compression failure.

When the force that is stretching or compressing these fibres is expressed as an x-amount-of-force-per-unit area, such as pounds per square inch, it is called stress.

My professor of engineering used to demonstrate compressive and tensile stress with a huge pink eraser. On the sides of the eraser he had drawn closely spaced vertical lines. When he bent the eraser the way a beam would bend, you could clearly see the lines were now spaced further apart at the bottom of the eraser where there was tension and closer together at the top where the compressive forces were. The only place the spacing of the lines remained unchanged was right down the center of the eraser. This is the neutral axis, which even in the most heavily laden beam remains unstressed. So the compressive forces, which are greatest at the top surface of the beam, diminish to zero at the center, the neutral axis, and then increase as tensile forces which reach a maximum at the bottom surface.

The amount of stress induced on a beam depends upon the size of the load, the span, the material, and the cross-sectional dimensions of the beam. This seems obvious. For example, you know that for a given load the more you move the supports for the beam apart, the more it will sag, and therefore, the higher the stress. You also realize that if you double the load, you double the stress. Another obvious point is that if you make the beam twice as wide, it will carry twice the load with the same sag. What isn't so obvious to some, however, is the fact that if you make the beam twice as deep, it will carry *eight* times the load with the same amount of deflection.

In other words, for any given amount of cross-sectional area, a beam will carry a great deal more load if you make it deeper rather than wider. That is why 4 × 5's are never used for floor joists even though they have the same amount of lumber as 2 × 10's. This is an important concept, which we will come back to shortly.

Think of the band-saw blade as a vertical beam spanning between the two thrust bearings that are above and below the table, the upper one being adjustable vertically. Force P—the force exerted when we push the wood into the teeth of the blade—induces a compressive stress in the front (toothed) edge of the blade and a tensile stress in the back edge. The magnitude of those stresses are proportional to the force applied, a principle illustrated in the example of the beam.

But—and this a crucial point—there is already stress in the "beam!" When we mounted the blade, we deliberately pre-tensioned the band-saw blade and induced a uniform tensile stress in it so that it wouldn't buckle. The stress in the back of the blade, while it is cutting, is simply the sum of the original tensile stress from the pre-tensioning and the tension force induced by feeding the wood. Stress on front edge of the blade is also the sum of these two forces, but the tensile stress of the pre-tensioning is added to the *compressive* stress induced by the feeding force. Since the stress from pre-tension and that from compression are counter forces, the original pre-tensioning stress in the front edge is reduced by the compressive stress caused by feeding force. If these forces become equal, the resultant stress would be zero and the front edge of the blade would drift, which is precisely what we are trying to avoid.

To prevent the blade from buckling, you would obviously have to increase the pre-tension forces or decrease the feeding force, but both methods are limited. These methods and a third—minimizing the stress the feed force produces—are discussed below.

LIMITING THE FEEDING FORCE

There are some things one can do to limit the feeding force. Obviously, this force will be determined by the thickness of the wood and how hard and resinous it is. You may not have much control over these factors, but you can control the set, size, and sharpness of the blade teeth and the feeding rate of the material.

Blade Sharpness As the blade loses it's initial sharpness, it takes more force to keep it cutting at the same speed. How can you determine if a blade is sharp? Sharpness is relative. A given blade may cut ½-inch mahogany perfectly well, but when you resaw 10 inches of maple, the blade requires so much force that it begins to wander. So determining whether a blade is sharp enough depends on what the task requires.

Heat plays a critical role in the dulling of edges. As an edge gets duller, it generates more heat, which dulls it faster. Sometimes one starts a job with a blade that is barely sharp enough, and that in a few minutes is hopelessly dull. As one pushes harder, the blade which had been cutting straight, begins to drift. This is due not to some problem with the band saw, but because of the blade. An extremely slow feed helps for a short while, but the heat eventually takes its toll and shortly the cut simply stops or drifting begins. Remember, if this happens when you are resawing 10 inches of maple, it is likely that there is still useful life in the blade if you use it to cut thin materials.

Tooth Spacing and Set Another factor of importance is the shape, spacing, and set of the teeth. A blade that has more teeth per inch produces a smoother cut, but also requires a great increase in feeding force. This is not a problem with thin material where fine teeth are required, but it is a very real problem with thicker stock. When resawing, use a blade with approximately three teeth per inch.

It is often said that the cuts that a band-saw blade can make are limited because all the sawdust has to be carried out of the cut in the gullets between the teeth. This is somewhat true for a blade with a very fine set, but if one is observant he will note that because of the set of the teeth there is room for the sawdust to slip back into the kerf past the body of the blade. This can be determined by looking at the blade directly from the front, which will show how the dust gets past, and examining the kerf part way through a cut which shows that it is packed with dust. Reserve your finely set blades for thin stock, where the feeding force is extremely low anyway.

A blade with hook teeth is a self-feeder. This may be some of advantage since the blade's hook shape may reduce the feeding force you need to supply. It resists being fed very slowly, however, and as the blade dulls this may become a disadvantage.

The Rate of Feed One of the interesting differences I've noticed between those very skilled in using the band saw and those who are not is the rate of feed. Beginners invariably feed much faster than the pros. It is foolish to feed any slower than one needs to get the desired result, but bear in mind that a slower feed requires less

force and lessens the chances that the blade will buckle. The cut surface is also smoother.

In summary, learn to feed slowly and steadily. Use the coarsest blade possible. Learn to switch blades quickly. You can save money by keeping blades that are reaching the end of their lives to cut thin stock and reserve the newest blades for the resawing of thick stock.

INCREASING THE PRE-TENSION
Since some of the factors that govern the amount of force used for feeding are beyond your control, what about increasing the pre-tension of the blade? After all, the greater the stress preloaded into the beam, the greater force it would take to overwhelm it. Use all the tension that the manufacturer's instructions permit. You might even exceed this amount for a few minutes to make an important cut, but don't leave these very high loads on the saw overnight. Get into the habit of noting how many turns of the knob you use to tension the blade, so you can quickly switch from high tension to low.

Should you apply all the force the blade can take when mounting it? This is not very feasible. The force can be determined by calculating the force required to stress blades to maximum values. For example, an 1/8-inch blade which is .025 thick and .125 deep might have an effective cross section of .0025 square inches. So stressing it to the sometimes recommended 25,000 psi (pounds per square inch) requires a force of 62.5 pounds times two (for both sides of the blade), or 125 pounds. That's like having a 156-pound weight resting on top of your saw. A 1/4-inch blade might require 250 pounds, and a 1/2-inch blade might need 500 pounds! A one-inch blade would probably need about a half a ton!

A small shop band saw or even a small professional saw simply cannot sustain a load this great, so the best thing to do is to work to the limits imposed by the manufacturer. For example, Inca puts a limit on its big saw of 2½ turns of the knob after an initial setting. This is more than enough to stress a 1/4-inch blade to 25,000 psi, though the stress will be far less on the bigger blades.

Those who recklessly ignore the limits imposed by the manufacturer can pull the saw out of alignment (temporarily or permanently, depending on the force), break axles, or peel off tires. You would do well to take advantage of your knowledge and reduce the tension when the wood is thin and the blade is a fresh one. Reserve the maximum stress for when you really need it.

MINIMIZING THE STRESS PRODUCED BY A GIVEN FORCE

The exact amount of stress a given feeding force will produce is not fixed. It is a function of the cross-section dimensions of the blade and the distance between the thrust bearings. These factors are discussed below.

Blade Thickness You will recall from the beam analogy given earlier that doubling the width of the beam halved the stress produced by a given load. This same principle is applicable to the blade used on a band saw. If you use a thicker blade, the stress is reduced in proportion and you can use a greater force before buckling occurs. Blades come in only a few thicknesses, and the one chosen must be flexible enough to bend easily to the radius required by the wheels on your saw. If the manufacturer of your saw offers a choice of blades, the thicker one offers some advantage. If you are at at the limit of tension for your saw, you will be able to increase the tension again.

Depth of Blade The advantage of the thicker blade is a modest one compared to that which you receive when you increase the depth of the blade. If you double the depth of blade, pre-tension is reduced to one half, but the stress produced by the feeding force is reduced to *one eighth* the previous amount. So always use the deepest blade you can for a cut. This is especially true when resawing, because blade tracking is very important and there is no advantage to using a small blade anyway. Even though the pre-tension is low (because you've reached the maximum for your machine), the resistance to blade buckling will be very high because of the inherent stiffness of the deeper blade. If a ¼-inch blade were used to resaw, it would start to drift before it began to dull. For stable resawing, use the deepest blades with the highest pre-tension capacity the saw manufacturer will permit.

Location of Thrust Bearings The location of the thrust bearings is very important because an increase in buckling resistance that can be made here has no offsetting effect. Remember that the stress produced by a given force is directly increased by the span, which is the distance of the length of the beam. So if you always keep the thrust bearings at their highest positions, you can increase the blade's resistance to buckling by lowering the top one as low as you can get it and still see well.

Side Bearings (Bowed Cut) What type of role do the side blocks or bearings play in minimizing the stress produced by a given force? They will not keep a blade from drifting. If you have them down close to the work, they restrain the blade there, but the blade drifts anyway within the wood and you get the familiar bowed cut. The bowed cut is not a separate phenomenon, it is merely the manifestation of a drifting but partially restrained blade. The main use of the side bearing seems to be to resist the blade's momentary tendency to drift caused by a sudden variation in the grain such as a knot.

Conclusion

A well set up saw should be able to cut a slice of veneer ¹⁄₆₄ inch thick or thinner off a 10-inch piece of maple that's several feet long. To do this, use your sharpest deep blade with fewest teeth and biggest set. Set the blade's pre-tension to the highest level the manufacturer recommends, and the thrust being as low as the wood permits. Feed slowly and watch and listen to cut.

It must be understood that even when a perfectly set up band saw is used, sooner or later the cut will begin to drift. This indicates that the blade has reached the end of its life. If you apply the principles explored in this chapter, you will put off that moment for as long possible.

MAINTENANCE AND CUTTING TECHNIQUES

8

Maintenance and Troubleshooting

All tools and machines require maintenance. The band saw in particular requires constant attention. It requires attention to operate the saw because the blade and thus the cutting operation can change. The blade can become warm from heat and stretch. As the blade becomes dull, it will cut differently than when it was sharp. These are just some of the subtleties to consider when using the band saw.

The major variables that affect band-saw performance have been discussed in detail in earlier chapters. These include blade choice, wheel alignment, and guides and tension adjustment. There is, however, another group of factors that may not be as basic as the major variables, but can be equally important. These factors will be discussed at length in this chapter.

Cleanliness

One of the major factors is cleanliness—in particular, how clean the tires are. As the saw cuts and the sawdust falls down, some sawdust lands between the blade and the bottom wheel. As the blade rotates, the sawdust becomes compressed on the bottom wheel. (See Illus. 338.) This is especially true of woods such as pine. The compressed sawdust can have a number of negative

Illus. 338. As the blade rotates, sawdust becomes compressed onto the bottom wheel. This can cause problems such as vibration and shorter blade life.

effects. It can cause vibration, shorten blade life, and cause the blade to lead.

Some manufacturers such as INCA mount a small brush that contacts the bottom wheel and helps to prevent dust buildup. (See Illus. 339.) This is a good idea, and is something that you should consider doing yourself. A wire or hard bristle brush works well.

Illus. 339. Some manufacturers such as INCA mount a stiff brush on the band saw so that it cleans the bottom wheel. This is advantageous, and should be done on other models.

It is a good idea to keep the wheels clean, especially the bottom wheel because that is the one that has the greatest problem with dust buildup. The best way to clean the wheel is to sand it with sandpaper. Ideally, this is done with the wheel rotating. This will also take off a little of the rubber from the tire and expose a new tire surface, which is desirable. The old tire surface often hardens or glazes over and should be redressed occasionally. (See Illus. 340.)

Obviously, you have to be careful when touching a rotating wheel with sandpaper. You may feel more comfortable if you first attach the sandpaper to a stick. (See Illus. 341.) Some sandpaper comes with a back that has adhesive, or it can be attached with glue or rubber cement.

The top wheel should also be sanded occasionally. This presents a problem because the top wheel is not powered as is the bottom wheel. The best approach is to use an outside power source

Illus. 340. Sanding removes the thin layer of the old tire, and creates a new smooth and uniform surface.

Illus. 341. You may feel more comfortable sanding the band-saw wheel if the sandpaper is mounted on a stick.

such as an electric drill to power the wheel. (See Illus. 342.) Attach a small sanding drum such as a 1¼-inch drum. You can also use the electric drill to power the bottom wheel rather than use the saw motor. The drill can be used at a slower speed.

Vibration

Band saws have a tendency to vibrate more than other machines. The vibration can be very frustrating because it is difficult and fatiguing to try to do a good job on such a machine. Vibration also affects the quality of the cut. Illus. 343 shows two pieces of wood cut with the same saw. The piece on the left was cut after the vibration

problem was corrected. There is a significant difference in the qualities of the cut.

Vibration can come from a number of different elements. It could be the motor, pulley, belt, saw shaft, eccentric wheel, bad tires, or a bad blade. It can also be a combination of several of these elements.

It is best to try to isolate the vibration with a systematic approach. Check one element at a time. First take the blade off the saw, and then take the belt off the motor. Run the motor. Does it vibrate? If it does, take the pulley off and check how the motor runs without it. If it vibrates without the pulley, you need to determine if it is the motor or the setup on the saw. Take the motor off the saw. If it vibrates off the saw, start looking for a new motor.

Illus. 342. The top wheel does not have a source of power, so an outside source such as a drill should be used to rotate the wheel. Here a drill is being used with a 1¼-inch sanding drum to rotate the wheel.

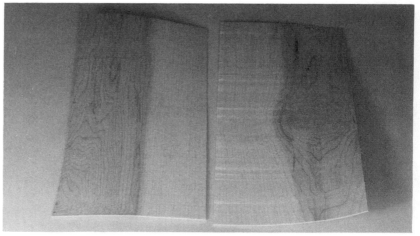

Illus. 343. This photograph demonstrates the effect vibration can have on the saw cut. These two cuts were made on the same saw with the same blade. The cut on the right has the ripples associated with vibration. The cut on the left was made after new tires were mounted and trued on the band saw.

If the motor doesn't vibrate off the saw, but does on the saw stand, your stand may need some work. Consider building a new wood stand or reinforcing your metal stand with plywood.

If the motor and stand do not vibrate until the pulley is attached, you need a new pulley. The average band saw comes with a cheap cast pulley. For a good performance, it should be replaced with a new machined steel pulley.

There may still be some slight vibration. This can often be controlled by mounting a rubber pad under the motor or the saw. Recently, a British company patented a Visc-Elastic polymer, which is a black rubbery material designed to absorb shock and dampen vibration. The material is used to form a sandwich. A layer of the material is used on top of and underneath the machine and/or motor. If you use this material on the saw and the motor, you can control a significant amount of vibration.

The next step in testing for vibration is to attach the belt and try the machine. This will tell you if the saw pulley, the belt, or the saw shaft is causing the vibration. If there is vibration, it may be hard to detect the cause of it.

Start by replacing the belt because this is cheaper than buying a new, large machined pulley. Next, check the pulley by holding a piece of wood against it and rotating the pulley by hand. If the machine still vibrates, the shaft may be causing the vibration. Take off the bottom saw wheel and run the machine. Determine if the shaft is moving in an eccentric fashion by turning the saw off and watching the shaft when it is slowing down. Rotate the shaft and measure it by holding a piece of wood against it; this procedure—called checking the "middle" of the machine—often doesn't work if the shaft has a keyway slot. Another option is to use a dial indication if you have one.

After you have checked both the bottom and the middle of the machine, check the "top" of the machine. This consists of checking the machine with the bottom wheel attached but without a blade. Turn the machine on and observe the bottom wheel. Is there more vibration? Does the wheel appear to run eccentrically as the saw slows down?

You can test the roundness of the wheel with a dial indicator if you have one. Another method is

to hold a piece of wood against the wheel and feel if the wood moves as you rotate the wheel by hand. (See Illus. 344.) You can get a rough indication of how much the wheel is out of round if you place the stick on the support and rest it against the wheel. Slowly turn the wheel by hand. Watch and you will see a gap between the stick and the wheel as it rotates. The bigger the gap, the more eccentric the wheel.

The next step is to check the eccentricity of the top wheel. This can also be done with a support piece and a stick if you don't have a dial indicator. Finally, run the saw with the blade on. If the vibration increases when you run the saw with the blade on, there is a good chance that your wheels are either eccentric or unbalanced. The solutions to these problems will be discussed in the next section.

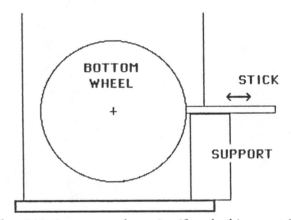

Illus. 344. One way to determine if a wheel is eccentric is to rest a stick on a support and rotate the wheel by hand. Watch the gap between the stick and the wheel as the wheel rotates.

Eccentric Wheels

The term "eccentric" when used to describe band-saw wheels means that the wheel is not perfectly round. This may be caused by one of two factors: The wheel itself may not be round or the tire, which acts as a cushion on the wheel, is not of a uniform thickness. The tire and the wheel have to work together to form a true circle. If you were to leave the tension on the saw all of the time, the wheels would be under constant strain; this can warp the casting of the wheel and compress the tire.

The best time to check for wheel eccentricity is when the blade is on the saw. The metal blade is a better surface to test than the rubber wheel. With the blade installed, you are testing the actual effect of the eccentricity. The best approach is to use a dial indicator. (See Illus. 345.) A simple method without any instrument is to use the guides as a gauge. To do this, loosen the guides so that they move freely. Hold the guides against the blade. Slowly rotate the wheels. If the wheels are ecentric, the blade will move back and forth as the wheels rotate and push the guide away from the blade. After rotating the wheels slowly for four or five revolutions, check the space between the guides and the blade. The more eccentrically the wheel revolves, the farther the guides will be pushed away from the blade.

Illus. 345. The best way to check for wheel eccentricity is to use a dial indicator on the saw blade.

Truing the Wheels

If the wheels on a band saw are eccentric, the band saw will vibrate as the wheels rotate. Wheels are never exactly the same size, so they change in proximity to each other. The various wheel combinations have different vibration characteristics.

As a rule, the truer your wheels are the less vibration you will have. The wheels and tires can be trued by a motorcycle or auto tire store. The process is similar to truing the tire on a car. They could also balance the wheels for you.

You can also true the tire on your saw yourself. This technique should only be used by those who know what they are doing. It consists of truing the wheel down with a very sharp gouge. This is similar to truing the outside of a plate on a lathe. In Illus. 346–349, the table is used as the tool rest for the lathe tool. The power can come either from the motor or from a hand-held drill with a sanding drum mounted on it. This technique was shown earlier in this chapter.

You will have to use the drill to power the rotation of the top wheel. Clamp a piece of wood to the frame to use as a tool rest. You can also use a piece of wood as a tool rest for the bottom wheel if you choose.

Before starting to turn the wheel, put chalk on the wheel so that you can see what is a fresh surface and what isn't. It doesn't make any sense to remove more material than you need to true the wheel. Stop turning the wheel when the outside surface of the rubber has been completely removed.

It is imperative that the cutting tool does not "dig in" and remove a lot of material. There still should be at least $\frac{1}{16}$ inch of material left on the tire after it is trued. If $\frac{3}{32}$ inch of material were left, it would be better yet. Check the amount of material by sticking a pin into the tire up to the metal wheel. If there is less than $\frac{1}{16}$ inch of rubber, replace the old tires. This is discussed later in this chapter.

After truing the wheels, you can make their surfaces smoother by sanding them. Sanding either freehand and by using a sanding stick are both discussed on pages 161 and 162.

Before attempting to turn the tires true, make sure that you assess the shape of the tires first. If a tire is torn or damaged, it should be replaced. If the tire is loose on the wheel, it should be glued at no less than eight points around the wheel. Gluing the tire will prevent slippage.

When you true the wheel, it is best to follow the profile of the original wheel shape. The tires can wear and their original shapes may be hard to determine. In this situation, lift up the tire so that you can see the shape of the wheel underneath. New tires are flat and are designed to conform to the shape of the wheels that are underneath them.

Illus. 346 (above left). You can true the wheels on a band saw with a small, super-sharp gouge. Be careful. This technique can be potentially dangerous. Illus. 347 (above right). Cover the wheel with chalk. Here you can see the remains of a black line on the top of the wheel that was removed with a gouge.

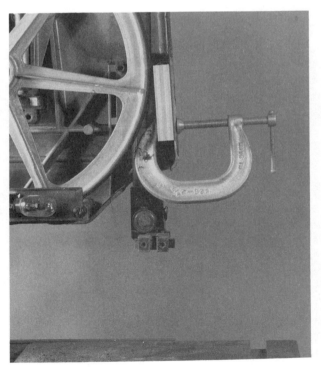

Illus. 348 (above left). When you have removed all of the chalked area, the wheel has been trued. Illus. 349 (above right). A piece of wood clamped to the saw frame functions as a tool rest for the top wheel. Since turning is a two-hand job, you should have someone else spin the wheel with a drill, as shown in Illus. 342.

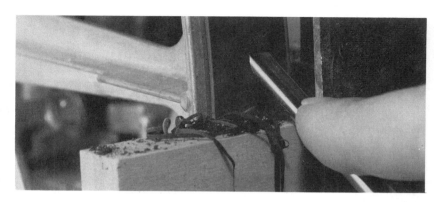

Illus. 350. Carefully remove material with the gouge. Try to maintain the shape of the wheel. To ensure this, check by lifting the tire up and observing the shape.

When large industrial saws need tires, the wheels are often sent back to the manufacturer for the job. A new tire is put on the rim and is turned true. The tire is mounted and rotated like a lathe. A sharp rotating cutting tool cuts off the excess rubber until it is turned true. At this point, the tire has had some material removed from the whole surface. No attempt is made to change the wheel; all of the correction is done with the tire.

Balancing the Wheels

After you have made the wheels true, the next step is to balance them. If your wheels are true and you still get a vibration out of the top half of the machine, it is because the wheels are not balanced. The wheels are unbalanced when one side of the wheel is heavier than the opposite side.

To test for wheel balance, remove the blade and belt. Spin the wheel and let it come to a stop on its own. Mark the bottom of the wheel with a magic marker. Spin the wheel several more times and mark the bottom spots with different colored markers. If all or most of the marks are in one spot, that side of the wheel is the heavy side.

To lighten the heavy side of the wheel, remove material. The best way to do this is with a drill bit. Use a ¼-inch drill bit and slowly drill a hole, removing small amounts of material at a time. Drill the hole in the web of the outside wheel casting rather than the outside rim. After you have removed a small amount of material, spin the wheel again to see if it stops in the same place. If the wheel is badly out of balance, you may have to drill more than one hole or several holes if it is a large wheel.

An alternative to the technique just mentioned is to take the wheels to an electric motor repair shop. These shops often have the facilities to balance things like band-saw wheels.

You may find that the wheel was balanced by the manufacturer, who either used drill holes or weights on the light side of the wheel, the way that car wheels are balanced. If holes were used to balance the wheel, just rebalance the wheel with holes again. If the manufacturer used weights to balance the wheels, balancing the wheels will be a little more complicated. The weights often slip or come loose. The best approach is to take the weights off completely and start from scratch using the testing and drilling method. Although it may sound very tiresome, this method only takes about half an hour and the benefits are well worth the time spent.

The Rubber Tires

The rubber tire is used as a cushion between the blade and the wheels. It acts as a buffer, particularly when the wheels are not truly round. As the tire ages, it will have a tendency to stretch. (See Illus. 351.) The stretching will allow the blade to slip or slide on the wheels. This has a negative effect on blade tracking and will often cause the blade to slide off the wheel. When you have tracking problems, a loose tire may be the cause.

With a lot of use, the tire will become thin in the middle. When this happens, the blade will not track in the middle of the wheel. The reason for this is fairly simple. When a wheel is convex or "crowned," the blade will automatically be pulled towards the crown. It usually will not track exactly in the middle of the crown, but will

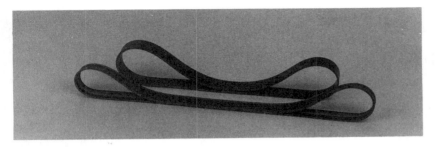

Illus. 351. As rubber tires get older, they stretch and wear thinner. The old tire shown here is longer and thinner than the new tire behind it.

balance towards the front of the crown. As the tire wears, the crown is worn down, which creates a concavity. The blade will not track in the concavity but on either side of it. In other words, it will track on the front half or the back half of the wheel, but not in the middle.

For this reason, it is important to occasionally restore the original shape of the wheels by sanding the outer edges off so that the middle forms the crowns again. This can also be done by "turning" the corners off with a sharp gouge. Both of these techniques are discussed on page 165.

Installing New Tires

Eventually the tires on your band saw will wear out and new tires will have to be installed. New tires should also be installed when they have cracked, stretched or worn thin. This is not a particularly hard task. The new tire should be at the very least 1/16 inch thick. You can check the thickness by pressing a pin into the tire until it touches the metal wheel.

Replacing the tires often solves some of the problems that a particular band saw might have, such as the blade falling off frequently. New tires will improve track and may even improve the life of the blade.

New tires can be ordered through machine dealers and specialty supply houses. If there is a Sears dealer near you, you can order the tires through the parts department. Local tool dealers may have the tires on hand. It's at times like this that having an offbrand band saw may be a problem, particularly if the manufacturer has gone out of business. The best thing to do in this case is to order a set of tires from a company that sells a saw that's about the size of your saw. This may take some research on your part.

If your old tires were cemented in place, buy some cement. Use it with the new tires.

When you get the tire, check it for defects. Al-low the tire to reach room temperature. Never put a cold tire on a saw; it does not stretch as much and is more likely to be brittle and snap.

Take the wheel off the saw and remove the old tire. First, check the bearings for play. (See Illus. 352.) Then clean the wheel as best you can with mineral spirits and a wire brush.

Clamp the tire onto one side of the rim. Place a dowel through the wheel hole and place the dowel in a vise. (See Illus. 353 and 354.) This will give you access to all sides of the tire and wheel.

Next, stretch the tire over half of the wheel. (See Illus. 355.) Then, using a screwdriver or a

Illus. 352. A good time to check the shaft for any play is when you have the wheel off.

167

flat object between the tire and the wheel, stretch the tire until it is on the outside of the wheel. (See Illus. 356–358.) After the tire is in place, remove the clamp and make sure that the tire is straight. (See Illus. 359.) Some tires are held in place with an adhesive. Remember, if the old tire were held on with an adhesive, the new tire should also be glued in place.

Illus. 353. Clamp the tire on one side of the rim. Then place a dowel through the saw hole. A tapered dowel will work best.

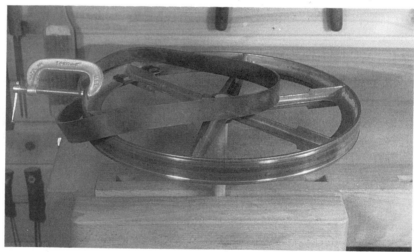

Illus. 354. Place the dowel in a vise. Press the wheel securely into the dowel.

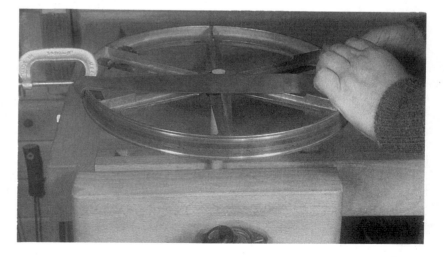

Illus. 355. Stretch the tire as far as you can by hand.

Illus. 356. Insert a screwdriver or another object without sharp corners between the wheel and the tire.

Illus. 357 (above left). Advance the screwdriver with one hand and secure the tire on the wheel with the other hand. Illus. 358 (above right). After the tire is in place around the wheel, remove the screwdriver.

Illus. 359. Straighten the tire on the wheel.

Troubleshooting Techniques

Following is a list of problems you may encounter when using a band saw, and ways to solve them:

1. Machine will not start

REASON	SOLUTION
A. Machine not plugged in	Plug the machine in.
B. Fuse blown or circuit breaker is tripped	Replace fuse or reset breaker.
C. Cord is damaged	Replace the cord.
D. Overload relay is not set	Push reset button on the motor.
E. Motor is defective	Replace or rebuild the motor.
F. Motor capacitor is defective	Replace the capacitor.
G. Machine is stiff from the cold	Warm shop up to at least 55°F.

2. Motor is overloaded and kicks out frequently

REASON	SOLUTION
A. Low current	Put your saw on a higher circuit or contact your electrician.
B. Feeding material too fast	Feed material more slowly.
C. Extension cord is too light or too long	Replace with a cord of an adequate size.

3. Machine does not come up to full speed

REASON	SOLUTION
A. Low circuit current	Use higher circuit or consult with electrician.
B. Extension cord too light or too long	Replace with adequate size cord.
C. Motor not wired for correct voltage	Refer to motor nameplate for correct wiring. Refer to wiring diagram, which is usually on the motor.
D. Motor wired incorrectly	Rewire according to diagram.

4. Motor runs in the wrong direction

REASON	SOLUTION
A. Motor wired incorrectly	Rewire motor following wire diagram.

5. Blade slows and/or stops

REASON	SOLUTION
A. Blade binding in stock	Keep kerf open. Do not squeeze workpiece so as to close kerf.
B. Blade turning in too tight a radius	Select smaller blades.
C. Blade twisting or pressing against guides	Use light forward pressure.
D. Upper blade guide too tight	Readjust upper blade guide.
E. Oil level low	Check oil if your machine has oil. Add oil if needed.
F. Feed rate too fast	Feed stock more slowly.
G. If band saw is driven by V-belt, belt may be slipping	Increase tension on V-belt.
H. Pulleys slipping on shafts	Secure pulleys or drive shaft.

6. Excessive machine vibration

REASON	SOLUTION
A. Stand or bench on uneven floor	Reposition on flat surface. Support low end with a wedge. Fasten to the floor if necessary.
B. Machine not mounted securely to stand	Tighten all mounting bolts using lock washers.
C. Poor-quality drive belt	Replace belt.
D. Belt not tensioned correctly	Readjust tension.
E. Bent or poor-quality pulley	Replace with high-quality cast and machined pulley.
F. Motor not fastened securely	Tighten all bolts.

G. Eccentric wheels — True wheels as discussed earlier on pages 164–166. Isolate motor and saw with rubber pads, preferably shock-absorbing pads.

7. Upper wheel is noisy or does not turn easily

REASON	SOLUTION
A. Needle bearing is dry	Regrease the needle bearing.
B. Bearing is worn or damaged	Replace bearings. You may want a factory-authorized service center to do this.

8. Lower wheel is noisy or does not turn easily

REASON	SOLUTION
A. Pulley is slipping on the shaft	Secure pulley. If the pulley is worn, replace it.
B. V-belt may be too tight	Relax the tension on the V-belt.
C. Pulleys not aligned	Align the pulley(s) with a straightedge.
D. Shaft bearings are worn or damaged	Replace bearings. You may want a factory-authorized service center to do this.

9. Upper guide post is hard to adjust

REASON	SOLUTION
A. Post needs to be cleaned	Clean post and lubricate with graphite.

10. Guides are not parallel to the blade

REASON	SOLUTION
A. Guides are worn or damaged	Resurface guides with sandpaper or file. One option is to replace old metal blocks with the newer style non-metallic blocks.
B. Guides not aligned properly	Resurface and realign guide blocks.

C. Blade is twisting in guides	Guides are set too far apart. When turning a corner use light forward pressure. Do not twist the blade without simultaneously moving the workpiece forward.

11. Thrust bearing is damaged or scarred

REASON	SOLUTION
A. Thrust bearing surface has scars and ridges	Reverse the bearing by pressing off the shaft. If the bearing is not reversible, replace the whole unit.
B. Thrust bearing makes a squealing noise	Bearing is damaged and should be replaced. Replace only the bearing unit if possible.

Note: You can extend the life of a thrust bearing if you round the back of the blade as described in Chapter 5.

12. Table is not properly aligned

REASON	SOLUTION
A. Table is not secure	Secure tilt lock. Secure trunnion bolt.

13. Table is not tilted as indicated by the pointer

REASON	SOLUTION
A. Scale is out of alignment	Square table at 90 degrees to the blade and then readjust the scale.

14. Table is not flat

REASON	SOLUTION
A. Warped table	Shim the table from underneath. The trunnion may have pulled the table out of alignment. If this doesn't work, replace the table.

15. Table is hard to tilt

REASON	SOLUTION
A. Sawdust buildup between the base and the trunnion	Clean trunnion and table slot in the base. You may have to remove the table. Lubricate the table trunnion with a dry-type lubricant such as graphite. Oil and grease are bad choices because they attract dust.
B. Metal burrs on the trunnion or in the table slot	Remove burrs with file or sandpaper. You may have to remove the table from the machine.

16. Table insert contacts the blade

REASON	SOLUTION
A. Poor alignment from the factory	File the table insert.
B. Table insert is turned around	Turn insert around.

17. Workpiece does not slide easily on the table

REASON	SOLUTION
A. Dirt or pitch on the table	Clean and wax table. If pitch is the problem, remove it with mineral spirits.
B. Table insert is too high	If the table insert is bent, try to straighten it or replace it. Sand or file the back down.
C. Dirt under the insert	Clean the area under the table insert.

18. Blades break

REASON	SOLUTION
A. Bad weld	Reweld or replace blade.
B. Worn tires	Redress or replace tires. This is discussed in detail on pages 166–168.
C. Dull blade	Blade is at the end of its life cycle and breakage should be expected.

REASON	SOLUTION
D. Blade has become overheated	Poor blade choice; try a coarser blade. (See Chapter 3.)
E. Poor wheel alignment	Align the wheels. (See Chapter 4.)
F. Improperly adjusted guides or thrust bearings	Readjust guides and bearings. (See Chapter 5.)
G. Blade tension is too high	Decrease blade tension. Use only as much tension as you need to perform an operation. Thick or hard wood will require more tension.
H. Poor operator technique	Slow the feed rate and avoid twisting the blade.

19. Blade noise

REASON	SOLUTION
A. Ticking sound as the saw is running caused by poor weld or poor weld alignment	File the back of the blade when the saw is not running, and then file the back round when the saw is running. Wear safety glasses for this operation.
B. Blade is twisted or bent and hits the guides	Remove blade and straighten the kink if possible. Replace the blade if that doesn't work.
C. Blade runs quietly and then starts to make a ticking sound	The blade has developed a crack and will break soon. Expect the blade to break; when it does, stop the saw and replace the blade.

20. Blade will not stay on saw or will not stay near the center of the wheels

REASON	SOLUTION
A. Misaligned wheels	(See Chapter 5.)
B. Poor tracking, too much forward tilt on the top wheel	Line the wheels up with a straightedge and let the blade find its own equilibrium on the wheels.

C. Tires are worn

If the tires are worn, there will be a concavity in the middle of the tire and the blade will refuse to track in the concavity. Resurface the tires so that the crown is created again. This is discussed on page 167.

D. Too much blade tension

Excessive blade tension can cause the blade to come off the wheels. Relax the tension.

E. Too little blade tension

Increase the blade tension to the recommended amount.

9
Safety Procedures

A friend of mine recently said, "People don't think about safety until after an accident." In many ways, this statement is true. When reading a book it is very easy to flip through the safety section or totally ignore it. But you should be aware of and always follow the safety procedures discussed in this chapter.

Obviously, you want to avoid cutting your hand. A bad cut can remove a finger or two. Safety, however, should be considered more than simply avoiding an accident. It is a system that should be reflected in the entire way that you work.

The band-saw has several safety advantages. The blade is small; only the front of the blade is dangerous. The band-saw blade applies a downward force to the workpiece, and cannot "Kick back" the way a circular blade can.

In a recent study, it was found that woodworking tools were involved in about half of all industrial accidents. Most of these accidents involved a circular saw blade in one form or another. Table-saw accidents are more common, but radial arm saws inflict the most severe injuries. The least serious accidents occur with the friendly band saw, and they are not nearly as common.

The best safeguard against accidents in the shop is a clear mind. Don't work when you are tired, sick, or on medication. Even a bad cold can be a hazard around equipment. The most dangerous time to work is after a meal, which is also the best time for a short nap.

Woodworking is time-intensive, requiring long hours. Noise is fatiguing, so wear some type of hearing protector. Be careful working late at night when you are tired. A deadline isn't worth a finger. And remember, a cold beer is good for washing down the sawdust *after* the work is done, not before.

Following are some safety aspects that you should be aware of when using a band saw.

Blade Guard

The blade guard is attached to the top guide assembly and is adjustable up and down. It should be about a ¼ inch above the workpiece. This doesn't allow the operator access to the blade, an important safety feature.

Push Sticks

The most dangerous time to use the band saw is at the end of the cut, when the cutting is completed and the blade is exposed. This is especially true of narrow blades when a rip fence is used.

The safest and often the most convenient approach is to use a push stick at that end of the cut. It is best to lay the push stick on the table and then pick it up and use it for the last inch or two of the cut. (See Illus. 360.) Although there are commercially available push sticks, it is easy to make one out of wood. (See Illus. 361 and 362.)

Illus. 360. Keep a push stick on the table. This way, you can use it when it is needed. At the end of the cut, use it to push the workpiece forward. The push stick is extremely useful when you are using a rip fence on a small workpiece.

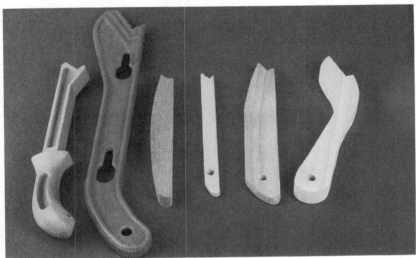

Illus. 361. The two push sticks on the left are commercially available plastic models. The four push sticks on the right are made of wood and were made by the author.

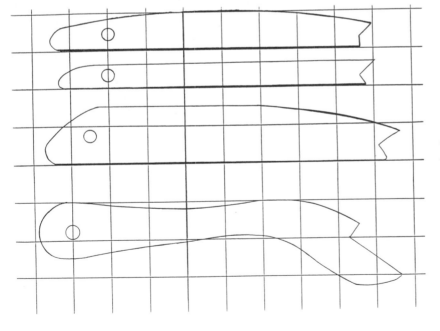

Illus. 362. A pattern for shop-made push sticks. Each square equals one inch. (Drawing by Chris Morris)

175

Pulling the Work

Pulling the work through a cut would be considered dangerous with a table or radial arm saw, but is comparatively safe with the band saw. (See Illus. 363 and 364.) Still, be careful when making this cut.

Safety Devices

Besides cutting yourself, you can injure yourself in other ways when using woodworking equipment. Always wear eye protection when using power tools. (See Illus. 365.) Also use hearing protection, especially with routers and planers. (See Illus. 366.)

Something that many woodworkers are negligent about is protection from the air in the workshop. Long-term exposure to wood sawdust is not healthy. The band-saw cut creates a fine dust. The best approach is to wear a dust mask and use a vacuum on the machine. This will also help to keep the shop clean. (See Illus. 367–370.)

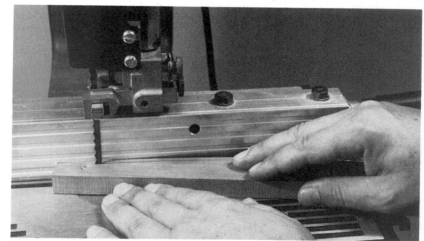

Illus. 363. One option is to pull the workpiece through the cut. This should only be done with a band saw, never with a table or radial arm saw. Use two hands to pull the work through. The hand nearest the blade acts as a pivot.

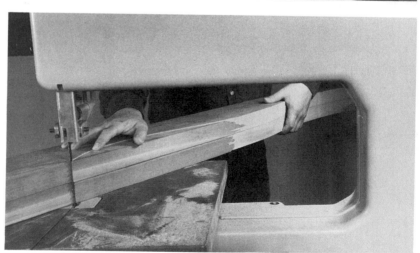

Illus. 364. On large workpieces, the operator controls the work with two hands that are spread apart from each other; this allows for more leverage. Hold heavy pieces up at the end of a cut. A roller stand will work well for straight cuts, but not as well when curves are being made.

Illus. 365. Protect your eyes with either safety glasses or goggles. Most woodworkers prefer safety glasses.

Illus. 366. Although the band saw is quieter than most other woodworking machines, wear hearing protection. Noise creates hearing loss and adds to fatigue. The ear inserts shown on the left are becoming increasingly popular. The hearing muffs shown on the right work well but are bulky, especially when used with glasses.

Illus. 367. Because the band saw creates fine dust, you should use a dust mask. The model shown on the left is disposable. The one shown on the right is plastic and features a replaceable filter.

Illus. 368. The vacuum filter can become coated with a thick layer of the fine dust that the band saw produces. This is hard on the vacuum motor and decreases its efficiency. The finer the blade used, the finer the dust. Check and clean the filter every couple of hours of use.

Illus. 369 (above). Plastic yogurt cups make good vacuum adaptors. Illus. 370 (right). The band saw is attached to a centralized vacuum system that is made of plastic plumbing pipe. A wood gate is used to control the vacuum. The gate shown here is between the floor and the band saw. It consists of two pieces of wood with a ¼-inch of plywood sandwiched between them. The moveable piece of plywood has a large hole in it. The vacuum draws when the plywood hole corresponds with the hole in the pipe.

10
Basic Cutting Techniques

It is not hard to use the band saw. Many people get satisfactory results the first time that they try to saw—especially if they don't try to make intricate or tight cuts. It does take some practice and a certain understanding of how the blade and workpiece work to become proficient. This can be accomplished over time with patience and concentration. Also remember that to get the best performance out of this tool you must tune it.

Following is an exploration of basic cutting techniques.

Following the Line

The key to using a band saw efficiently is to develop a slow, smooth rhythm. You must have good control of the workpiece. Hold the workpiece securely with both hands. Most people find that standing slightly to the side of the blade is the most comfortable way to work. Eye protection is important. (See Illus. 371.)

The usual practice is to draw the cut line on the workpiece. Pencil lead is often used because it can be erased and because it doesn't leave a permanent mark.

There are a number of ways to cut a line. Most woodworkers prefer to cut next to the line. (See Illus. 372.) This leaves the line intact, so you know where the line is if you are going to sand.

If you are going to sand the edge smooth, don't sand too much. Sanding about ⅟₃₂ inch is about average—depending on if you are sanding by hand or by power tool. If you are using power tools such as a disc sander, you may want a little more material between the edge of the cut and the finish line.

Make the cut on the outside of the workpiece. At times, you may be standing to the side of the saw; if you are in this position, the line will be between you and the saw blade.

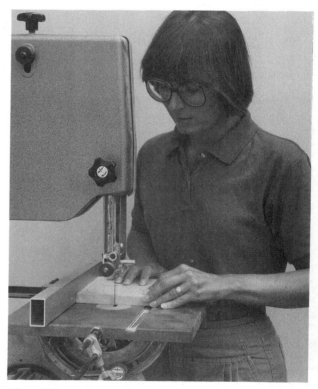

Illus. 371. Many woodworkers prefer to stand slightly to the side of the blade when cutting. Use both hands when feeding wood into the band saw. Eye protection should be used.

Illus. 372. The usual method of sawing is to cut to the outside of the pencil line. This keeps the line intact and allows you to sand away the material to create the final edge.

Hand Position

The hand position that you use is important for both comfort and safety reasons. There are three basic hand positions. Illus. 373 shows the most common one. One hand is used to shove the workpiece forward, and the other hand is used on the side to guide the work. Illus. 374 shows another approach: a hand on each corner shoves the workpiece. This allows for the easy sideways movement of the workpiece for turns. Use the position shown in Illus. 375 when you will rotate the piece often or make a tight turn. When you use this position, your hands will hold the workpiece on opposite ends, making rotation of the workpiece easy.

It must be remembered that the workpiece has to be advanced into the blade as it is rotated. If it is rotated without moving into the blade, it will twist the blade and possibly break it.

The way you use your fingers is important. Basically, they work as three separate groups. The thumb is by itself in one group, the index and large finger form the middle group, and the ring and little fingers form the third group. (See Illus. 376.) At times the ring and little finger will be used as a unit opposite the other groups. (See Illus. 377.) At other times, they will be tucked completely out of the way. (See Illus. 378.)

As you saw, you will change the positions of your hands. With practice, you will change the positions naturally without any conscious thought. You will often start a cut with your hands in one position (Illus. 379) and then change them during the cut. At the end of the cut, your hands may assume another position. (See Illus. 380.) The important thing is that they are not near the line at the end of the cut.

Using the Correct Blade

To use the band saw efficiently, you have to use the correct blade. If the blade is too large, it will prevent tight curves. To decide which size blade to use, you have to evaluate the work correctly. You can do this easily by using two coins and a pencil to size the curves. (See Illus. 381.) A ¼-

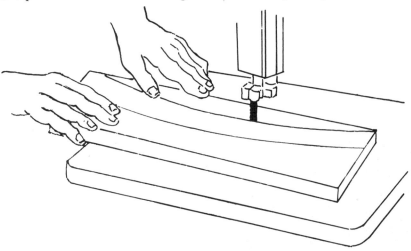

Illus. 373. When you are feeding the work, one hand should feed the work and the other hand should control the work from the side.

inch blade cannot make a cut tighter than a circle the size of a quarter. The smallest curve that a 3/16-inch blade can make is the size of a dime. (See Illus. 382.) A 1/8-inch blade can make a turn that's the width of a pencil. (See Illus. 383.) A scale of blade widths is shown in Illus. 181 on page 91.

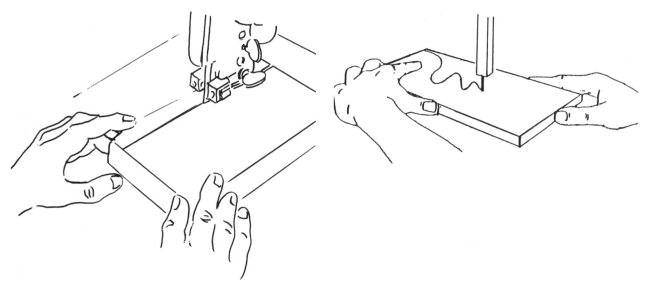

Illus. 374 (above left). When hand-feeding short pieces, place a hand on each corner. Illus. 375 (above right). If a design has many turns, place a hand on its opposite corners.

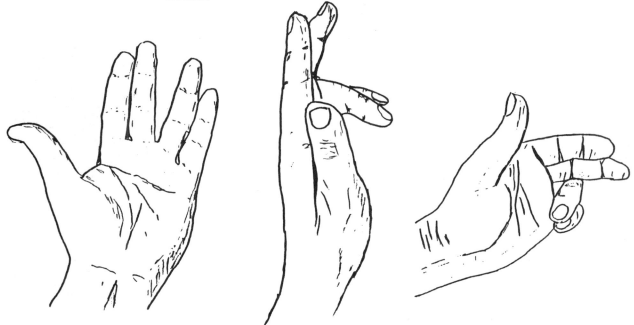

Illus. 376 (left). The fingers should work in three distinct groups. The thumb is one group. The index and large finger form the middle group. The ring and little finger form the third group. Illus. 377 (middle). The small fingers are often used opposite the other groups. When you position your hand as shown here, you form a 90-degree angle, which is good for holding the corners of boards. Illus. 378 (right). At times the thumb and large fingers should form a 90-degree angle. At these times, move your smaller fingers out of the way.

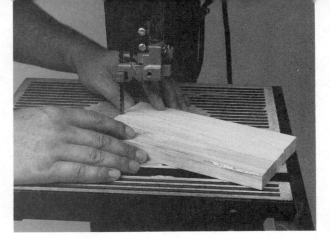

Illus. 379 (above left). Start the cut with your hands on each side of the board. This position will give you control over the forward and sideways motion of the piece. Safety note: The guide in this photograph has been raised so that you can get a clear view of the cut. Illus. 380 (above right). As the cut progresses, slowly move your hands to the back of the workpiece. Use your thumb to move the piece forward. By the end of the cut, your thumbs should be controlling the workpiece. Your index finger should be resting on top of the work. The other fingers will work as a group.

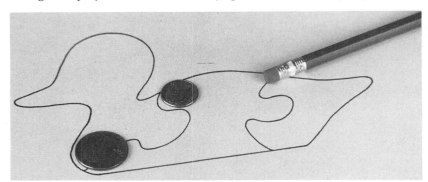

Illus. 381. Use coins and a pencil to size curves. The curves in this pattern correspond to the size of a pencil eraser, which means that a ⅛-inch blade is the appropriate blade for this project. This duck pattern is from Pat and Patricia Spielman's Scroll Saw Pattern Book, published by Sterling Publishing Company.

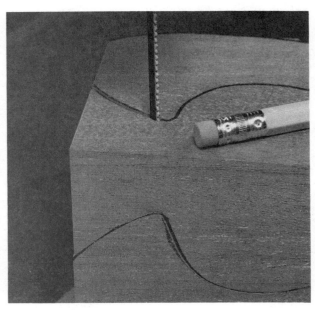

Illus. 382 (above left). The tightest curve that a ³⁄₁₆-inch blade can make is equal to the size of a dime. Smaller curves require smaller blades. Illus. 383 (above right). This ⅛-inch blade is making the tightest cut it can possibly make on a cabriole leg.

Workpiece Rotation

When you are making your cuts, it is important that you think ahead. Always try to rotate work away from the column rather than into the column. This may require that you plan ahead when deciding which side of the workpiece the pattern will be on. (See Illus. 384–388.)

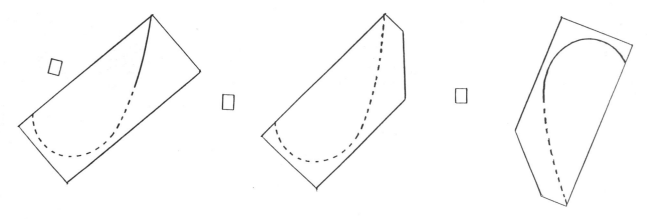

Illus. 384 (left). If you use the approach outlined here, the workpiece will hit the column before you complete the cut. Illus. 385 (center and right). This approach works better. Trim the waste first.

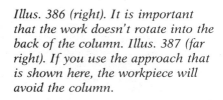

Illus. 386 (right). It is important that the work doesn't rotate into the back of the column. Illus. 387 (far right). If you use the approach that is shown here, the workpiece will avoid the column.

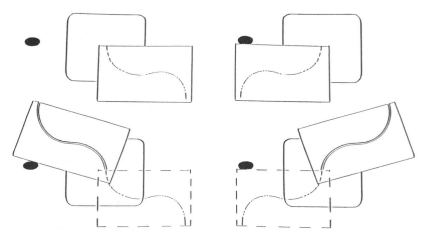

Illus. 388. You may have to trim off some of the waste before starting the cut.

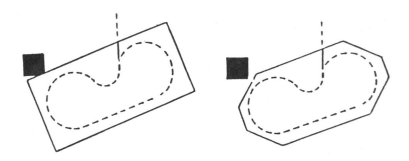

Release Cuts

A release cut is used so that the waste piece can be easily separated from the workpiece. Release cuts are designed to break up long cuts and make the removal of waste easier. A good example of a release cut is used when a heart pattern is being cut.

In some situations, multiple release cuts are used to expedite the removal of waste. (See Illus. 397.)

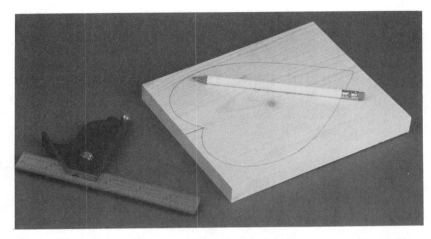

Illus. 389. The release cut ends in the middle of the heart. Because the workpiece was accurately squared, the release cut and the edge of the board are parallel.

Illus. 390. Release cuts should be as straight as possible. A straight cut makes it easier to retract the work-piece. Mark the cut path with a ruler or square.

Illus. 391. Start the cut at the end of the workpiece opposite the release cut.

 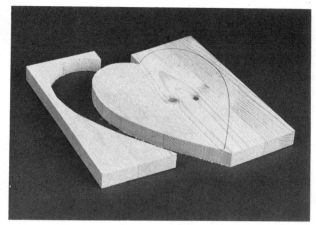

Illus. 392 (above left). Make the cut by following the line. Illus. 393 (above right). The cut intersects with the release cut, which frees the waste piece.

 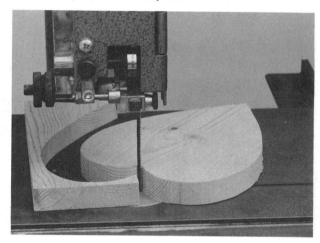

Illus. 394 (above left). Cut the opposite side in a similar fashion. Illus. 395 (above right). The completed cut.

 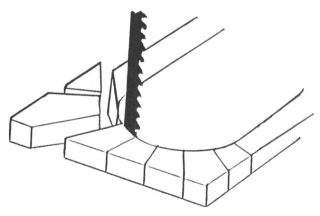

Illus. 396 (above left). The completed heart and the two waste pieces. Theoretically, the two waste pieces can be glued back together. Illus. 397 (above right). Multiple release cuts are used for small waste pieces. This technique is used when you want to make a tight turn with a wide blade.

Cutting Sequence

The sequence of the cuts is important. It is easiest to maneuver a small piece, so it is best to cut the largest pieces of waste off first. As the larger pieces are cut off, the more delicate cuts are left.

A few years ago, a friend of mine, Jim Langlois, gave me a square that he had made as a Christmas present. It is a copy of an antique tool that functions both as a square and as a French curve. (See Illus. 398.) This tool has a shape that is a good illustration of the cutting sequence described earlier. (See Illus. 399.)

Illus. 398. This antique square is both a French curve and a square.

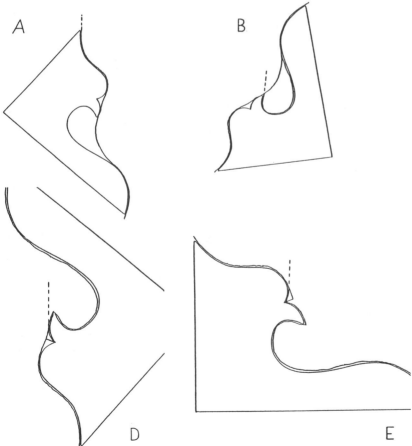

Illus. 399. A. The first cut separates the workpiece. B. The second cut removes the remaining large piece of waste. C. The third cut is a release cut that separates the waste into two separate pieces. D and E. The last two cuts remove the waste.

Backing and "Nibbling"

We are all familiar with the idea of painting oneself into a corner. It is also possible to saw oneself into a corner. In this situation, the best approach is to back up the workpiece and either turn a corner or "nibble" more material out of the way. Nibbling is when you use the band-saw blade to remove small pieces of material. Illus. 400–417 show backing and nibbling techniques used on a project.

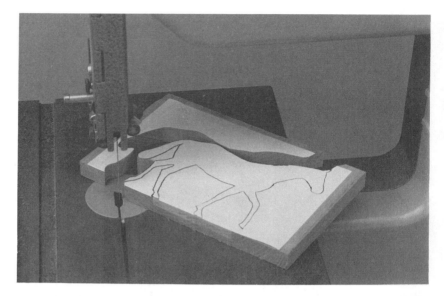

Illus. 400. The first cut separates the waste from the workpiece. This decreases the bulk of the workpiece and makes it easier to control.

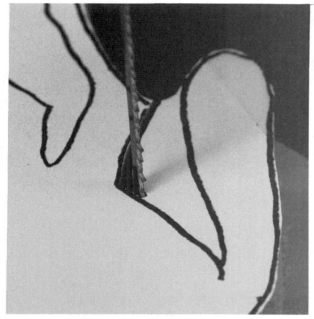

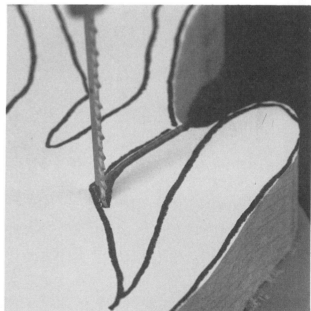

Illus. 401 (above left). First make a straight cut into the corner because it is too square to allow the blade to rotate. Then back the workpiece up and make multiple cuts the width of the blade, as shown here. This technique is called "nibbling." This creates enough room so that the workpiece can be rotated without twisting the blade. Illus. 402 (above right). Then rotate the workpiece so that the blade is in line with the pencil line.

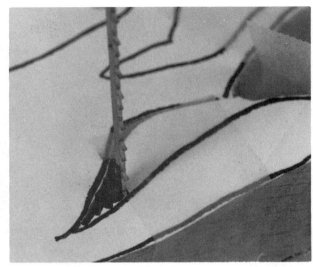

Illus. 403 (above left). Next, make a straight cut into the corner. Place tape over the previous cut to keep the pattern in place. Illus. 404 (above right). Nibble the corner out with the band-saw blade.

Illus. 405 (above left). Nibbling creates a rough surface. Cut along the pencil line with the blade to remove the rough nibbled surface. Illus. 406 (above right). Next, rotate the workpiece into the space that has been created.

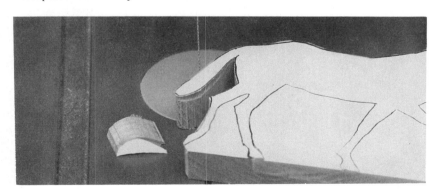

Illus. 407. Finish the cut and remove the waste piece.

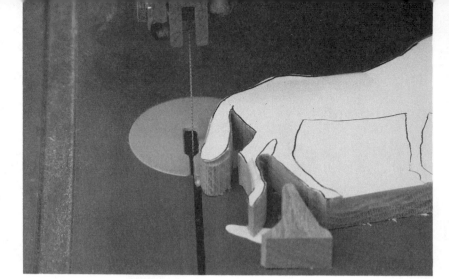

Illus. 408. Remove the piece of waste between the back legs with one cut. Make this cut about as tight as the ⅛-inch blade can turn.

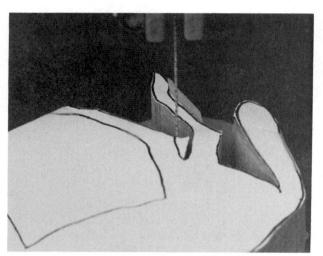

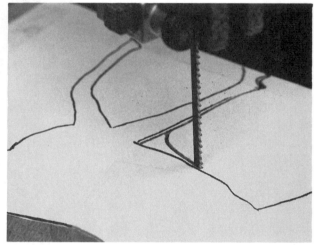

Illus. 409 (above left). Because one cut line is fairly straight, you can use it as a release cut. It is best to use a straight line as a release cut because it makes backing out easier. The cut shown here releases the waste piece. Illus. 410 (above right). It is impossible to turn a square corner with a ⅛-inch blade, so cut into the corner and then back up. Then make a curve to the next line. You can finish the corner later.

Illus. 411. Also use the back-up-and-turn-technique in the opposite corner. This will free the last waste piece between the front and back legs.

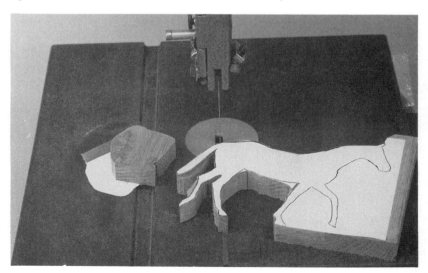

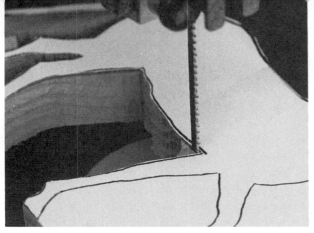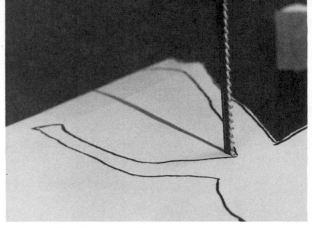

Illus. 412 (above left). Finish the corners with a cut from the opposite direction. Illus. 413 (above right). Because both of the cuts for the front legs are long and curved, make a straight release cut first.

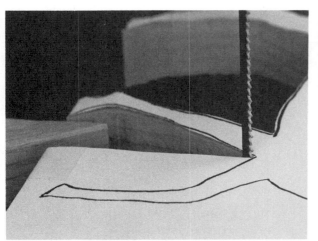

Illus. 414 (above left). This cut ends at the release cut and frees the waste piece. Illus. 415 (above right). This cut separates the last waste piece.

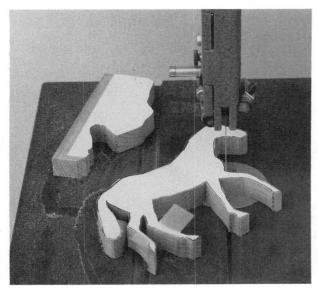

Illus. 416 (above left). The last cut trims the corner. Illus. 417 (above right). The completed horse. As you remove the waste, retape the paper pattern to the workpiece.

Circular Cuts

One technique for making sharp corners is the use of circular or semicircular cuts. With these techniques, small circular or half-circle cuts are made that create sharp corners with minimum waste (See Illus. 418–420.)

Turning Holes

Drilling a hole is often a very useful technique when the band saw is being used. The hole facilitates the removal of the waste wood. (See Illus. 421.) It makes turning the workpiece at the end of the cut much simpler because it often prevents the need to back out of the cut. It is especially useful for patterns that have long, curved cuts. (See Illus. 422.) Some designs have circular elements and drilling a hole the correct size saves time and energy. (See Illus. 423 and 424.) This technique is useful for some types of carving. (See Illus. 425.)

One advantage to using holes is the consistency and quality of the curves that are created. Because the holes are smooth, it also saves the time spent sanding the inside corners. A good example is the cutting of the letter F using two different sizes of turning holes. (See Illus. 426–433.)

Illus. 418 (above left). When you are making a very sharp curve, it would be useful if you make a circular cut. Illus. 419 (above right). Here the cut is continued into the corner.

Illus. 420. When you complete the cut, a half-circle of waste will be released and fall through the throat plate into the band saw. It is important that the waste piece falls opposite the bottom wheel. If the waste piece falls between the blade and wheel, it can kink or break the blade.

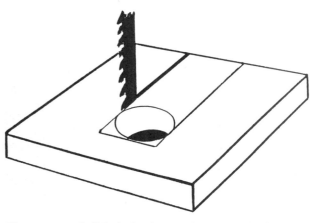

Illus. 421. A drill hole facilitates the removal of waste.

Illus. 422. This is an architectural bracket. Two drill holes were made at the end of the spirals.

Illus. 423 and 424 (above). You can make this miniature anvil more easily by drilling holes that correspond to the concave curves in the design.

Illus. 425. This dulcimer piece was made more easily when three holes corresponding to the curve in the design were drilled. (Photo courtesy of Orion Designs of Milwaukee, Wisconsin)

Illus. 426. The letter F presents some of the typical band-saw problems in that it has multiple curves and corners.

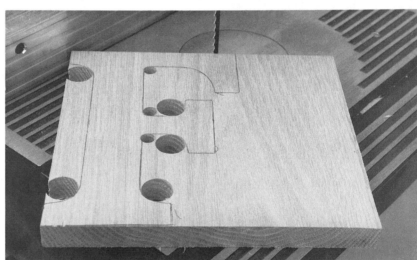

Illus. 427. Two sizes of holes were used for this design.

Illus. 428. Make the straight cuts with a rip fence.

Illus. 429 (above left). The hole is big enough so that the workpiece can be rotated freely around the blade. Illus. 430 (above right). Remove the large waste pieces first.

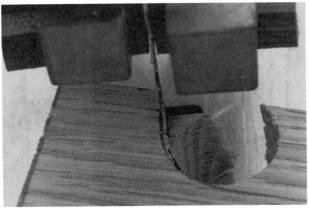

Illus. 431 (above left). You can trim the small pieces later. Illus. 432 (above right). Use the rip fence for the straight cuts.

Illus. 433. This completed letter is ready for sanding. The turning holes improve the efficiency of the cuts and the quality of this job.

11
Patterns and Templates

Patterns

It is easier to trace an outline with a pencil than to cut one with a band-saw blade. For this reason, a drawing of the desired object is placed on top of the workpiece. The design or the drawing of the design is called the pattern. The pattern is a two-dimensional representation. It can either be drawn directly onto the workpiece. (Illus. 434 and 435) or on a piece of paper (Illus. 436). If you are reproducing a piece, which is often the case in furniture repair, you can use the original to trace a pattern. (See Illus. 437.) A broken chair leg is often glued together to provide the pattern for its replacement.

Some shapes can be copied with a profile gauge. (See Illus. 438.) If multiples of a pattern are needed, such as with a set of cabriole legs, it is best to use a template. (See Illus. 439.) Some patterns are very simple pieces of wood, but once painted they can transform an ordinary piece of pine into something much more appealing. (See Illus. 440.)

Sources of Patterns

Patterns are often found in books and magazines. Prepared plans are also available by mail or in stores.

For some objects, it is handy to use a full-size pattern. Some companies specialize in full-size plans. (See Illus. 441 and 442.)

 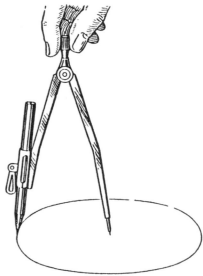

Illus. 434 (above left). This pattern is an image of an object drawn on the workpiece. Illus. 435 (above right). The pattern can also be drawn onto the work by mechanical means.

Illus. 436. The best way to attach a paper pattern to the workpiece is with tape.

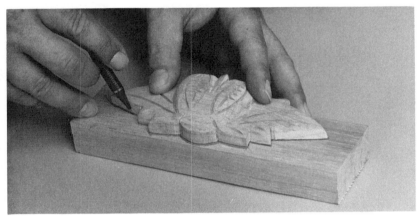

Illus. 437. Here a wood drawer pull is being used to draw the pattern on the workpiece. Broken pieces can be glued together and used as a pattern.

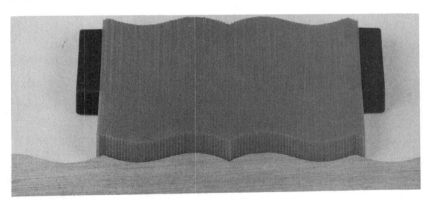

Illus. 438. You can copy and transfer the shape of a curve onto a workpiece with a profile gauge. (Photo courtesy of John Cosperdot)

Illus. 439. Use a clear plastic template to trace a pattern of a cabriole leg.

Illus. 440. Paint adds character to cutouts. (Photo courtesy of Yvonne Barnes of Canton, Pa)

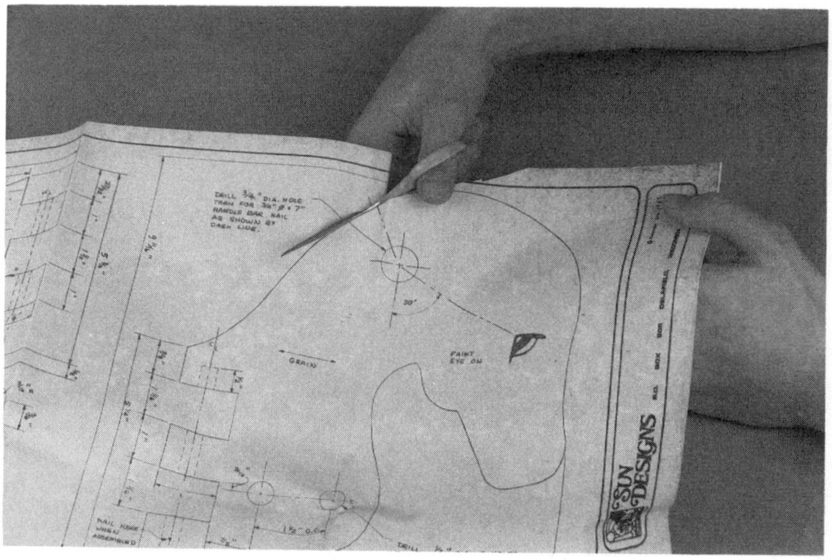

Illus. 441. A full-sized plan being cut out with scissors.

Illus. 442. The completed horse. (Photo courtesy of Sun Designs)

Enlarging Patterns

Because of limitations in space, patterns in books and magazines are often printed at a reduced size. (See Illus. 443.) You will have to draw the pattern at its full size. This is not a difficult task. The magazine drawing of the object is reduced in size and is covered with a grid. To enlarge the drawing, you have to make a grid that has inch-square blocks. Almost all patterns use a one-inch grid. You can either use graph paper or make your own grid. At each point where the pattern in the magazine intersects a grid line, make a dot. (See Illus. 444.)

After all of the dots are completed, connect them. It is often useful to use French curves for this purpose because it is much easier to get a smooth line. (See Illus. 445.)

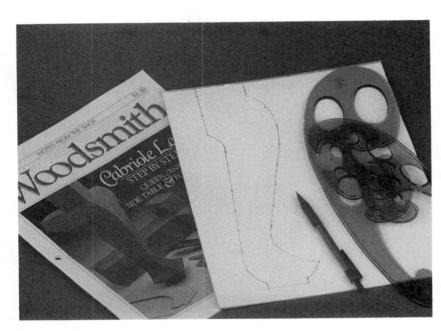

Illus. 443. Books and magazines are a good source for patterns.

Illus. 444. Transpose the intersection of the pattern and the grid lines onto a full-sized 1-inch grid.

Illus. 445. Connect the dots to complete the pattern. French curves help to create a smooth line.

Using Patterns

The pattern is extremely useful for layout work. Layout refers to the positioning of the pattern on the workpiece. If multiple pieces are planned, place the patterns as close together as possible to avoid wasting material. (See Illus. 446.)

When you are cutting, it is possible to get confused as to which is the waste and which is the workpiece. This is especially true if you have been cutting for hours. It is a good idea to mark the waste area of a pattern. A red crayon makes a good marker. Lumberyards often sell a "lumber crayon," that is, a huge, hard crayon specifically made for marking lumber.

When laying out the pattern on the workpiece, it is very important to consider the direction of the wood grain. (See Illus. 447.) The pattern should be used in such a way that maximum strength is achieved. This is especially important when thin sections are used.

With some patterns, it is hard to decide which orientation of the grain is better because there is a weakness either way. At times like this, the best approach is to use plywood, especially if the design has a sharp curve and will be subject to stress. (See Illus. 448 and 449.)

Drawings are often used as patterns. When using a drawing, photocopy or copy with carbon or tissue paper the original drawing. This keeps the original copy intact.

Drawings often have three views. (See Illus. 450.) This is the traditional drafting approach. Complicated drawings such as those used in patternmaking often have more views. (See Illus. 451.) Some objects will only require a front and a side view. (See Illus. 452 and 453.) When you buy a drawing or use a book or magazine drawing, you will note that the creator often saves space by placing all of the parts on one piece of paper.

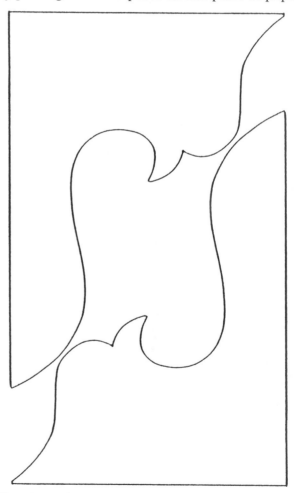

Illus. 446. When you put patterns close together, you save material by decreasing the amount of wood you will waste.

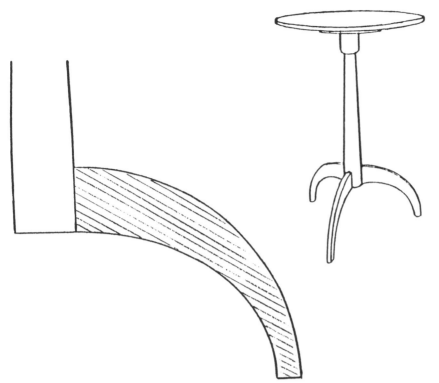

Illus. 447. When you are laying out the pattern, grain direction should be an important consideration.

Illus. 448 (above left). The rockers on this horse will be weak no matter which way the grain is oriented. The body of this horse is solid wood. The rockers and leg piece are plywood. Because the piece is painted, the plywood is inconspicuous. Illus. 449 (above right). Because the wood in this piece is under considerable stress from the tensioned strings, the inside lamination is made of plywood. Solid wood is glued to the outside. (Photo courtesy of Jim Kirchner of Orion's Creations in Milwaukee)

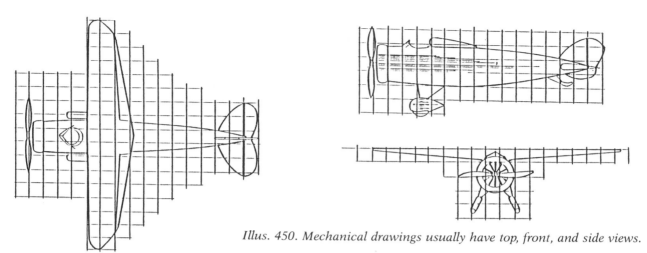

Illus. 450. Mechanical drawings usually have top, front, and side views.

Illus. 451. Complex pattern drawings are given in multiple views. This is the mahogany pattern used to make the manifold for the 390 cubic inch Ford V-8 engine. The individual pieces were cut out on a band saw and glued together.

Illus. 452 (right). This pattern shows the front and side views of the deer. Cut the side-view pattern first and then reattach the waste that contains the front view to the workpiece with tape, glue, and/or brads. Then cut the front pattern. Illus. 453 (far right). The completed deer makes a popular Christmas ornament.

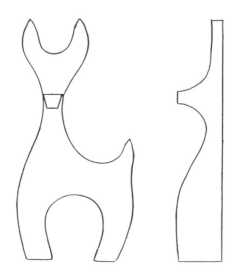

Types of Patterns

When both sides of an object are exactly the same, use a half pattern. You draw both sides with the same pattern by flipping it over. To do this technique well, you will need a pattern in the form of a template. A good example is the heart design shown in Illus. 454 and 455. The top and front views on a drawing used for carving are given using the half pattern technique. (See Illus. 456 and 457.)

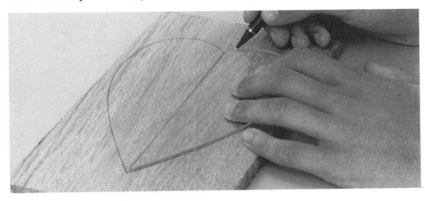

Illus. 454. Here a half pattern is being used to draw two identical sides of an object.

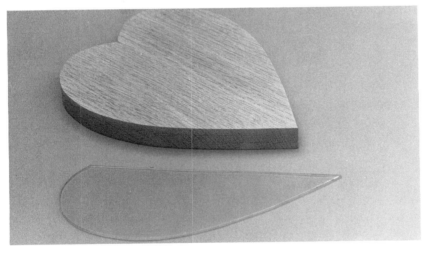

Illus. 455. This view shows the clear plastic half pattern and the completed heart.

Illus. 456. Half patterns are often used in carving projects such as a duck decoy.

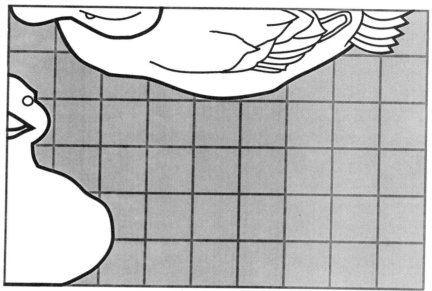

Illus. 457. The top and front views of this decoy are given in the half pattern form.

A quarter pattern is a pattern that shows one quarter of an object. It is used when all four corners have exactly the same design. A quarter pattern is often used to save space.

A double pattern is used in a situation where the object will have the same profile from two different sides. This is the case with the cabriole legs and Chinese-style legs shown in Illus. 458 and 459.

Some objects can be created by using the same design twice. This technique was used on the mirror shown in Illus. 460. The sides are the same. The reflection of one side in the mirror creates the pattern for the other half of the body. This unique mirror was made by Sharon Grossman, a student of mine in a summer program at the University of Akron.

Create Your Own Patterns

With a little practice, it is not hard to create your own patterns. Certainly drawing ability helps, but good patterns can be created even if you are not that talented. With a handful of mechanical drawing tools, you can do an amazing job of creating useful patterns. (See Illus. 461.) Like anything else, it takes practice.

Circular work can be drawn either with a compass or a circle template. (See Illus. 462.) When you combine circles of different sizes, interesting curves can be created. (See Illus. 463.)

French curves are useful for drawing smooth, curved lines. (See Illus. 464.) They are especially useful for drawing an ellipse. (See Illus. 465.) An ellipse can also be drawn by mechanical means. (See Illus. 466.)

When you are drawing curves, an adjustable "ruler" is very useful. One type of ruler is flexible and holds its shape, If need be, its shape can be changed slightly. This type of ruler is commonly called a "snake" ruler. A flat flange on the bottom makes it easier to hold a pencil next to the ruler. (See Illus. 467.)

The ACU-ARC is a drafting tool that is adjustable. The patented mechanism is very clever. The curve is adjustable from a radius of 7 inches to 200 inches. (See Illus. 468.)

The company that makes the ACU-ARC also makes an adjustable ruler. The snake ruler can make a tighter curve, but this adjustable ruler is probably better at making long, gentle curves. (See Illus. 469.)

Changing Pattern Size

At times it is important to either reduce or enlarge a pattern. Perhaps the easiest way is to use a photocopy machine. Most large copiers can reduce or enlarge. A clear acetate sheet can also be reduced or enlarged on the machine. A clear pattern is useful because it allows one to see the pattern and the workpiece simultaneously. (See Illus. 472.)

A more tedious approach is to proportionally

202

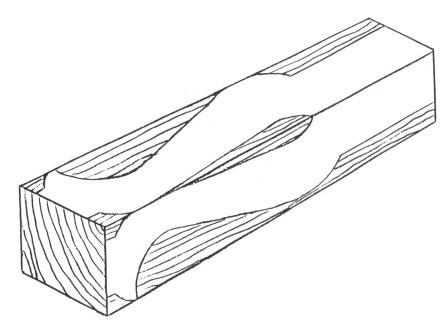

Illus. 458. When you are making a cabriole leg, use the same pattern on two adjacent sides.

 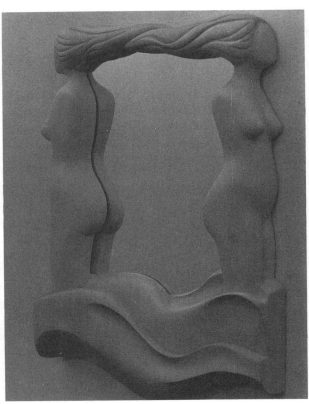

Illus. 459 (above left). Chinese-style legs such as the ones shown on this uncompleted table are similar to cabriole legs. Use the same pattern on two adjacent sides. Illus. 460 (above right). The two sides of this mirror are the same. You can see the shape of the side reflected in the mirror. (Photo courtesy of Sharon Grossman of Cleveland Heights, Ohio)

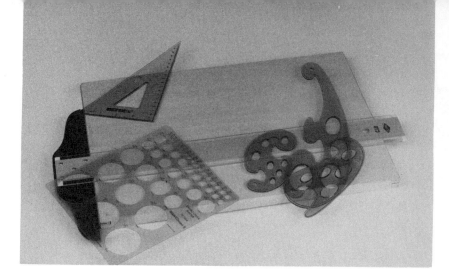

Illus. 461. The basic drafting tools used to create patterns are a T square, a clear drafting triangle, a circle template, and a set of French curves.

Illus. 462. The circle template is useful for making circles or sections of circles.

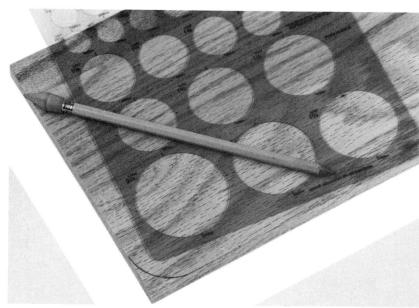

Illus. 463 (far left). Different-sized arcs are often combined to make interesting curves. Illus. 464 (center and right). French curves come in a set of three different sizes. These designs offer the user a variety of options. A couple of French curves are often used to make a smooth, gradually curving line.

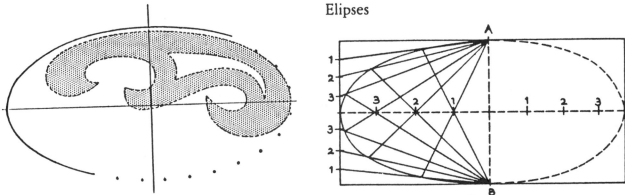

Elipses

Illus. 465 (above left). This ellipse was drawn with a French curve in a manner similar to a quarter pattern. Illus. 466 (above right). The ellipse can also be drawn using a technique that divides each quarter into four different spaces. The dots are then joined together, preferably with a French curve.

Illus. 467. A "snake" ruler. This adjustable ruler has a flat flange that makes it easy to draw a curve with a pencil.

Illus. 468 ((above left). The ACU-ARC ruler is adjustable for a radius of 7 to 200 inches. Illus. 469 (above right). It is good for long, gentle curves, particularly if the curves reverse in the opposite direction.

Illus. 470. You can also use a metal yardstick and a string to make curves. Twisting the string bows the yardstick and increases the curve. Here it is being used to mark the curve on a chair back.

Illus. 471. The adjustable yardstick was used to make the curve on the middle stretcher on these Shaker tables. The curve is similar to a catenary curve, which is the kind of curve a hanging chain makes. The ends are not as curved as the middle. This is often preferable visually to a true radius, which often looks very mechanical.

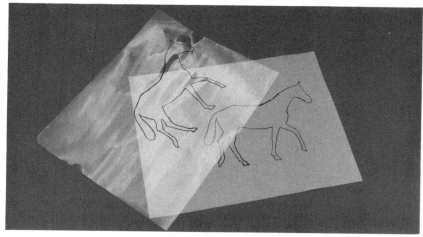

Illus. 472. Some copy machines can Xerox clear acetate sheets. A clear pattern allows you to visualize the workpiece and the pattern at the same time.

reduce and enlarge the pattern. This is not as complicated as it may appear. A mechanical approach is the use of the panograph. (See Illus. 473.) The arms are adjustable and allow a variety of ratios to be used. You can make something three times its original size when you use this machine. (See Illus. 474.)

You can shorten or elongate a design by splicing a pattern—that is, by removing or adding squares. Illus. 475 shows the half pattern for the chair leg shown in Illus. 476. When the pattern was spliced, the legs were made longer or shorter. (See Illus. 477.)

Positive mechanical transfer (PMT) is a technique used in the printing trade. The pattern is printed on plastic rather than paper. It can be enlarged or made smaller. The detail is kept in proportion and is very sharp. (See Illus. 478.)

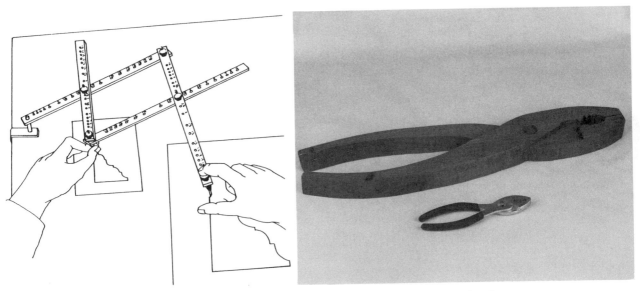

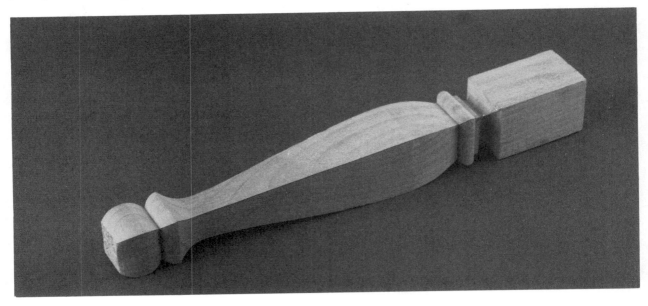

Illus. 473 (above left). A pantograph is a mechanical device used to change the scale of a drawing. It is used to either enlarge or reduce the size of a drawing. (Drawing courtesy of Lee Valley Tools, L.T.D., Ottawa, Canada) Illus. 474 (above right). The larger wooden pliers were made from a pattern enlarged with a pantograph.

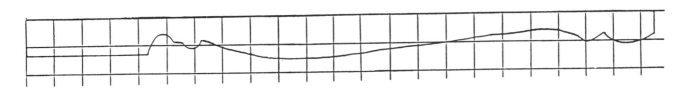

Illus. 475 (above). This is a half pattern for a leg design. Each square is equal to one inch. You can shorten or elongate the design by adding or removing squares. Illus. 476 (below). The chair leg based on the pattern shown in Illus. 475.

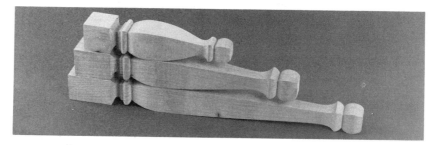

Illus. 477. You can make the top leg by splicing the pattern, and the bottom leg by elongating it.

Illus. 478. P.M.T. is a technique used in the printing trade. The clear, photo-like characteristics that can be achieved with this process are important when you are enlarging a pattern or object.

Templates

Paper patterns are not very durable. For this reason, it is advisable to make a pattern of a more durable material such as plastic, plywood, or masonite. This is especially important if the pattern will be used often.

Illus. 479 shows a clear plastic template used for a cabriole leg. Illus. 480 shows a plywood lathe template that was cut and sanded on a band saw. A template is especially important when the pieces have to be uniform.

Some templates are rather simple and can be used to make only one type of curve. An example is the clock shelf made by my friend, Ed Hinza. (See Illus. 481 and 482.) Because he makes a variety of shelf designs, he has a plywood template for each variation.

When using more complex templates, it is important that you lay out the pattern first. Next, cut the joinery such as grooves, dadoes, mortises, etc. It is easier to cut joints before cutting the curves. Dry-assemble the piece (without glue) to check the fit. Finally, cut the curves. (See Illus. 483–485.)

Designs that are complex often require multiple patterns. (See Illus. 486 and 487.) It is important to remember that each template has two sides. You may have to rest a template on one side, and then flip it over for the opposite side, a technique that is similar to a half-pattern technique.

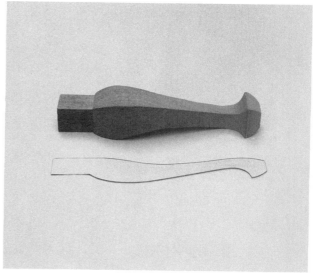

Illus. 479. A clear-plastic template being used to make cabriole legs.

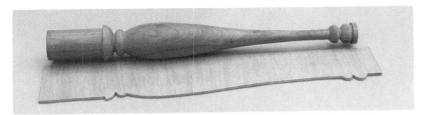

Illus. 480. This plywood template is being used with a lathe duplicator to make multiple turnings of the same size and shape.

Illus. 481 (above left). A variety of plywood shelf bracket templates used by Ed Hinza to make shelves. The template on the left was used to make the shelf shown in Illus. 482.
Illus. 482 (above right). This clock and shelf were made by Ed Hinza with plywood templates. (Photo courtesy of Ed Hinza, Green Bay, Wisconsin)

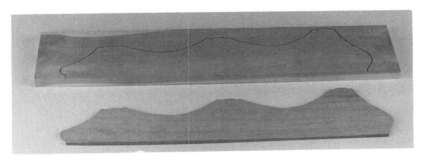

Illus. 483. A plywood template used to make cherry shelf sides.

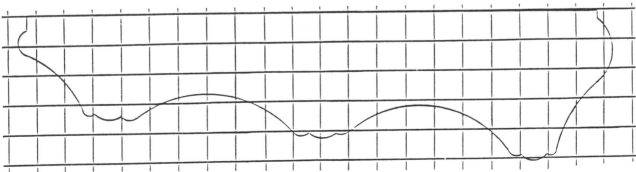

Illus. 484. The pattern for the shelf side. Each square equals one inch.

209

Illus. 485. The completed shelf that was made with the plywood template. (Photo courtesy of David Morris, Austin, Texas)

Illus. 486 (above left). This butternut mirror was made with the templates shown in Illus. 487. (Photo courtesy of Ed Hinza) Illus. 487 (above right). The templates for a mirror are used in a manner similar to the way a half pattern is used.

Making Clear-Plastic Templates

If you are going to use a pattern often, it is well worth it to make a template. The best material for templates is clear plastic. Because it is clear, you can visualize the grain of the wood underneath the pattern.

Clear plastic is not easy to draw on, so it is best to tape the pattern onto the clear-plastic material. You can either trace the pattern onto paper or you can use a photocopy machine to capture the image of the pattern. (See Illus. 488.)

Tape the pattern onto the piece of plastic (Illus. 489), and cut it out in the usual manner. (Illus. 490). The plastic pattern is very useful for laying out the pattern. (See Illus. 491). Illus. 492 shows a table made out of oak. The plastic templates on top of the table are either half or quarter patterns.

Illus. 488. A photocopy machine was used to make copies of this completed workpiece. The copy on the right was made with the machine set on a light setting.

Illus. 489. Tape the photocopy to a clear plastic sheet to make a template.

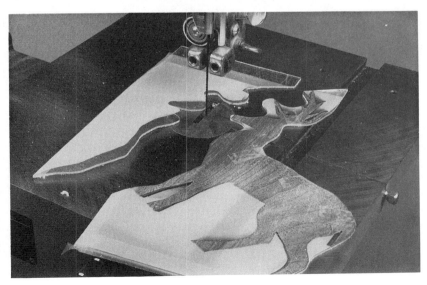

Illus. 490. Cut out the pattern in the usual manner. As you cut, retape the pattern to the workpiece.

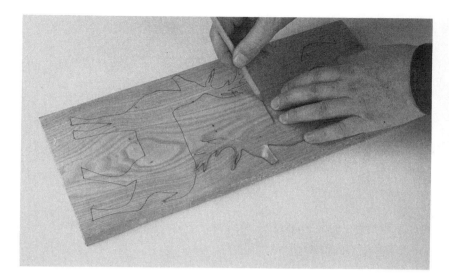

Illus. 491. Using the plastic pattern for layout work.

Illus. 492. Half and quarter patterns made of clear plastic were used to accurately lay out this table. This table was made by a music teacher during a week-long summer class at the University of Akron.

Pattern-Sawing

The term pattern-sawing refers to a technique in which the pattern is attached to the workpiece. The cut is made around the pattern with a guide or "rub block." This is particularly useful when one is making a number of workpieces with the same irregular shape—as, for example, when making a gentle curve such as that which would be used for a cabinet door top.

When pattern sawing, clamp a rub block with a curved end to the saw table. (See Illus. 493.) The curved end should have a notch in it. The notch fits over the blade, extending past it about 1/16 inch. (See Illus. 494.) Cut out the rub block so that the workpiece can slide underneath it.

The pattern should be made of plywood. Tape it to the workpiece with double-faced tape. (See Illus. 495 and 496.) The pattern will rub against the rub block during the cut. Because the blade is about 1/16 inch short of the pattern, the workpiece is cut about 1/16 inch away from the pattern. (See Illus. 497–499.)

You can easily trim the 1/16-inch waste with a router table and a "flush cutter," which is a straight bit with a bearing on the top of it. The bearing rubs against the pattern as the cutter trims the waste. (See Illus. 500.) The finish is smooth and requires little sanding.

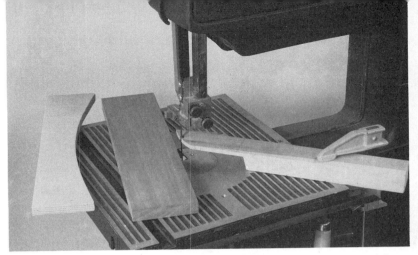 

Illus. 493 (above left). Clamp the rub block to the table. Illus. 494 (above right). The notch in the rub block fits over the blade and protrudes past it by about 1/16 inch.

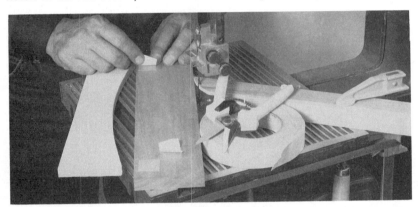

Illus. 495. Use double-faced tape to attach the template to the workpiece.

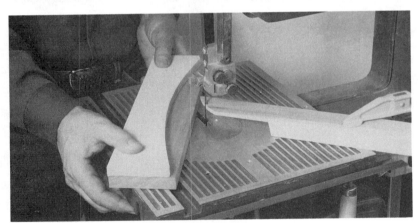

Illus. 496. Press the template firmly onto the tape. Be careful not to use too much tape or it will be difficult to get the template off.

Illus. 497. Begin the cut with the template touching the rub block.

Illus. 498. As you continue cutting, use slight pressure to keep the template against the rub block.

Illus. 499. The completed cut. The workpiece should extend about $\frac{1}{16}$ inch past the pattern.

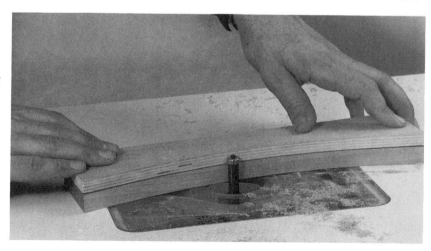

Illus. 500. While the template is still attached to the pattern, trim off the waste with a router. The router bit being used for this operation is called a flush-cutting bit. The bearing on top of the bit rides against the pattern.

12
Making Curves

One of the unique qualities of the band saw is its ability to cut curves, particularly in thick stock. Curves are often used as a design element. This can be seen in the modern chair and bookcase. (See Illus. 501.) The curve softens the lines.

Curves are often used as decorative mouldings to enhance a plain design. (See Illus. 502.) They also serve a complex structural purpose, particularly when used in musical instruments. Curves are usually cut, but you can also create them by using forms, in which the wood is either steamed or laminated to form the curve. (See Illus. 503.)

 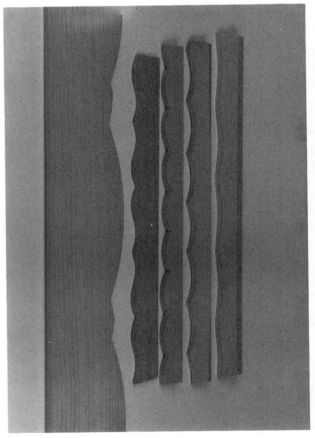

Illus. 501 (above left). A rocking chair made of black walnut. This inviting piece has no straight lines. A chair of this calibre requires substantial skill. (Photo courtesy of Wayne Francis, of Marquette, Michigan) Illus. 502 (above right). These mouldings all have a simple curve or a combination of curves. A curved design often adds zest to a simple workpiece.

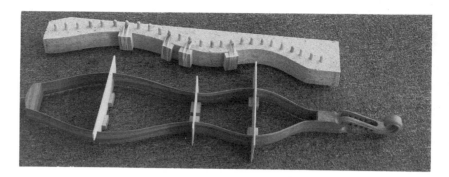

Technique for Making Curves

Cutting a curved piece out of wood is often very wasteful. A technique that wastes no wood is the "cut and glue" technique. Cut the pieces so that they have one curve. (See Illus. 504.) Then glue

Illus. 505. If you plan to use dowels or biscuits, mark the piece with lines before cutting it. If you pay attention to the grain, the joint will be almost impossible to see.

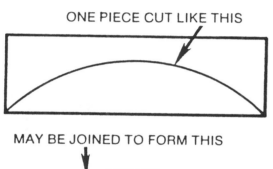

ONE PIECE CUT LIKE THIS

MAY BE JOINED TO FORM THIS

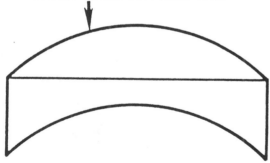

Illus. 504. In this technique, the cut pieces are glued, and form a curved piece with parallel sides.

the pieces together with the straight sides against each other. If you choose the piece of wood carefully, its grain will hide the glue line. (See Illus. 505.)

At times you may want to accentuate the glue line. This is a technique used often by Neil O'Reilly of Milwaukee. A piece of dark veneer is glued between the two curves. (See Illus. 506.)

Two different types of woods are often used

Illus. 506. Here a dark veneer strip has been placed in the glue line to accentuate the joint. It becomes a design detail. (Photo courtesy of Neil O'Reilly, of Milwaukee, Wisconsin)

next to each other as a decorative design. When veneer is used, the technique is referred to as marquetry. (See Illus. 507.) When solid wood is used, it is called intarsia. (See Illus. 508.)

To use the techniques of marquetry or intarsia, you usually have to cut the two mating pieces simultaneously. Place one piece on top of the other and then cut both at the same time. (See Illus. 509.) Then glue the pieces together, with the top piece mating with the bottom piece. (See Illus. 510.) If more than two pieces are used, you can use a variety of different species of wood. (See Illus. 511.)

When the cuts are long or gentle curves, the two pieces will fit exceptionally well if the blade and table are at 90 degrees to each other. If the curves are tight or the design is small, the fit between the two pieces will be better if the table is slightly angled. The angle accurately helps to compensate for the wood lost to the saw kerf. You will have to experiment with scrap wood to get the right angle. The angle will depend on the saw width and the wood thickness.

Recently, the Wisconsin Woodworkers Guild published a drawing and a chart (Illus. 512) after one of its members, Stan Austin, did a demonstration of intarsia. The drawing shows how the top piece of wood mates with the bottom piece after the angled saw cut is made.

Table 2 is a chart that was created by Beau Lowerr, an engineer for the Alan Bradley Company. Using this chart, it is easy to determine the right degree of table tilt that is needed to create a tight fit.

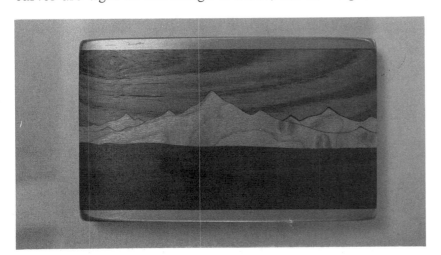

Illus. 507. This belt buckle is made out of veneer and is an example of marquetry.

Illus. 508. This wildlife piece was made by Glenn Elvig of Minneapolis. This is an example of intarsia. Solid wood, rather than veneer, is used.

Illus. 509. Tape the two pieces together with double-faced tape. Then make the saw cut.

Illus. 510. If the saw cut is a gentle curve, you can glue and fit the opposite pieces tightly together.

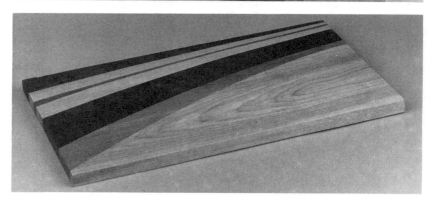

Illus. 511. Three different species of wood can be glued together, as shown by this cutting board.

Illus. 512. Two pieces will fit tightly together if you cut tight curves and tilt the table. This drawing was first published in the December 1988 Wisconsin Woodworkers Guild newsletter. (Drawing by Beau Lowerr)

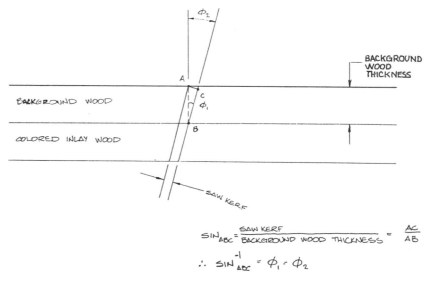

$$SIN_{ABC} = \frac{SAW\ KERF}{BACKGROUND\ WOOD\ THICKNESS} = \frac{AC}{AB}$$

$$\therefore\ SIN^{-1}_{ABC} = \phi_1 = \phi_2$$

218

"BACKGROUND" WOOD THICKNESS

DEGREES TABLE TILT FROM HORIZONTAL

SAW KERF	0.125	0.250	0.375	0.500	0.750
0.015	6.9	3.4			
0.016	7.4	3.7			
0.017	7.8	3.9			
0.018	8.3	4.1			
0.019	8.7	4.4	2.9		
0.020		4.6	3.1		
0.021		4.8	3.2		
0.022		5.0	3.4		
0.023		5.3	3.5		
0.024		5.5	3.7		
0.025		5.7	3.8	2.9	1.9
0.026			4.0	3.0	2.0
0.027			4.1	3.1	2.1
0.028			4.3	3.2	2.1
0.029			4.4	3.3	2.2
0.030			4.6	3.4	2.3

Table 2. This chart gives the table tilt angle for different thicknesses of wood. It was created by Beau Lowerr and first published in the Wisconsin Woodworkers Guild newsletter.

Parallel Cuts

Many times you will have to make parallel cuts. For example, parallel curves are made on chair parts. (See Illus. 513.) Cut the tenons before cutting the curves. Make the concave cut first. (See Illus. 514.) When making the convex cut, use the rip fence to establish uniform workpiece thickness. (See Illus. 515.)

Making Multiple Cuts

It is easy to make multiple pieces exactly the same when you use the rip fence to guarantee uniform workpiece thickness.(See Illus. 516.) The piece contacts the rip fence about ⅛ inch in front of the blade. (See Illus. 517 and 518.) This is a rotation point, and it allows the operator a little leeway when making the cut.

Single-Point Cutting

Using the rip fence to make multiple cuts is very useful. A similar technique called "single-point cutting" uses the same principle. This technique has all of the advantages you will get from using the rip fence, and it also helps to make cuts that cannot be made with the rip fence.

The procedure is very simple. Clamp a board with a round point to the saw table. (See Illus. 519.) The round point should be located ⅛ inch in front of the blade. (See Illus. 520.) This allows the workpiece to touch the point before it touches the saw blade. (See Illus. 521.)

Cutting Multiple Curves

The single-point technique is used to cut multiple curves. Thus far, we have focused on single curves with a uniform radius. Some workpieces have more than one curve that change in direction. A chair leg is a good example.

Start the multiple curve cut by making the initial cut. (See Illus. 522 and 523.) Then place the resulting curve against the point and make the cut. (See Illus. 524–526.) The single-point technique allows the piece to "fishtail" back and forth. Multiple cuts use the same technique.

Concave Cuts

When making concave cuts, use the waste piece as a jig. Clamped to the table, it makes a good surface against which to move the workpiece. (See Illus. 527–529.) The blade has to cut straight for this technique. If it pulls to one side or the other (blade lead), it is difficult to get a uniform cut. This is especially important when making narrow strips because there is not much room for error. You may have to experiment to find the best clamping angle for the jig in relationship to the blade.

Illus. 513. Chair backs have parallel curves.

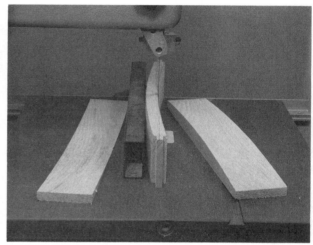

Illus. 514 (above left). When creating parallel curves, first cut the convex curve. Safety note: in this photograph, the top guard is elevated to show the cutting operation. Illus. 515 (above right). Here a rip fence is being used to make a parallel cut that will form the concave side. Safety note: In this photograph, the top guard is elevated to show the cutting operation.

Illus. 516. Using this technique, it is easy to make multiple parallel cuts.

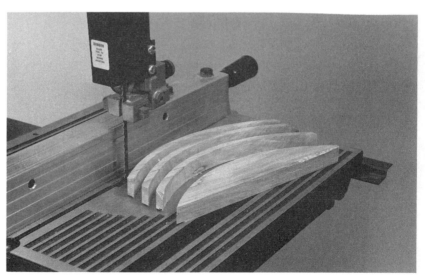

Illus. 517 (above left). It is best to contact the fence with the workpiece slightly in front of the blade. This is the pivot point. Illus. 518 (above right). Always rotate the piece by touching the same pivot point.

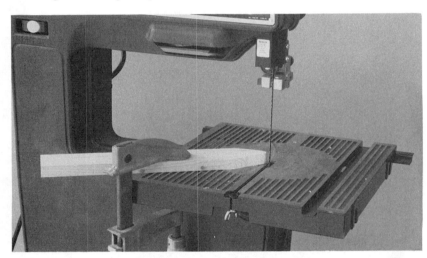

Illus. 519. The single point is used to do a variety of work. It is simply a board with a round point clamped to the table.

Illus. 520 (above left). Place the tip of the point, as indicated by the pencil, about ⅛ inch in front of the blade. Illus. 521 (above right). The workpiece contacts the point before the blade.

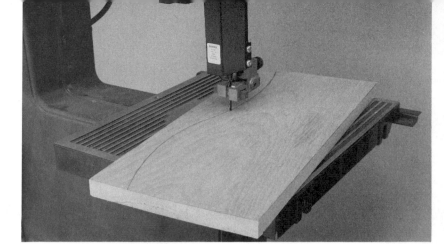

Illus. 522. Make the first cut in the usual manner.

Illus. 523. Complete the first cut. Make it as smooth as possible.

Illus. 524. Start the cut with the corner against the single point. Proceed with the cut by exerting light pressure against the point. It is not enough to just hold the piece against the point and shove. Moving the workpiece back and forth (fishtailing) is very important in this situation.

Illus. 525. The completed first piece.

222

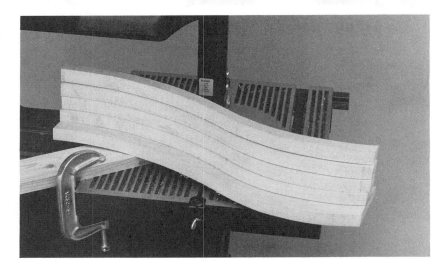

Illus. 526. Multiple pieces that are exactly the same can be made with the technique.

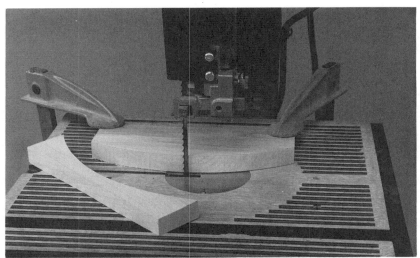

Illus. 527. When you are making concave cuts, you can use the waste piece as a jig. Clamp it to the table.

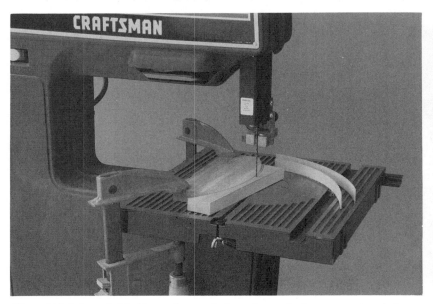

Illus. 528 (above left). Move the workpiece through the cut, maintaining contact with the jig. Illus. 529 (above right). A close up of Illus. 528.

Making Curved Mouldings

Curved mouldings are often used as decorative elements. Illus. 530 shows one of the many clocks my father has made since he retired from his patternmaking career. Illus. 531 shows the detail of a curved moulding.

It is standard procedure to do the router or shaper work first. This is the safest way to proceed because you are working with a large piece of wood. Then cut the moulding off the larger piece. If the moulding is curved, cut off the finished edge using the single-point technique. (See Illus. 532.)

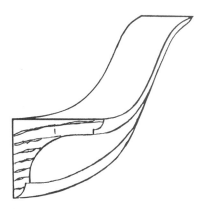

Illus. 530 (above left). Note the standard curve moulding that has been used on this grandfather clock. Illus. 531 (above right). The side detail of the moulding.

Illus. 532. First make the moulding and then cut it off with a band saw using the single-point technique.

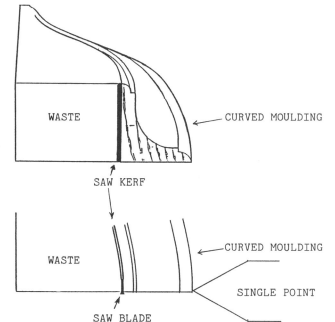

224

Using Jigs

Some curved cuts are best done using a jig to support the work. It will often take longer to make a jig than to actually use it. Illus. 533–537 show the procedures used to make a bevel cut on a curved piece. Make the initial cut with a jig to support the work as it is being cut. Make the second cut without the jig. Illus. 538 and 539 show a jig being used to support the work as a curved bevel is cut.

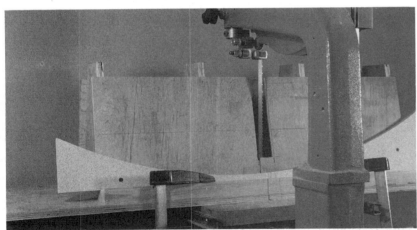

Illus. 533. A bevel cut on a curved piece.

Illus. 534. The bevel cut shown in Illus. 533 was made with this jig. The jig holds the piece at the correct angle.

Illus. 535. During the cut, the curved bottom of the workpiece slides along the curved bottom of the jig.

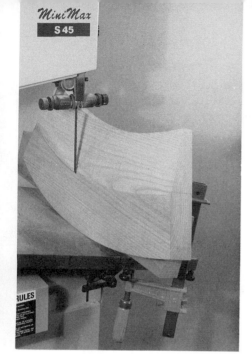

Illus. 536 (left). Make the opposite bevel cut with the workpiece resting on the table. Illus. 537 (above). The completed double-bevel cut. This piece is a curved stair rail.

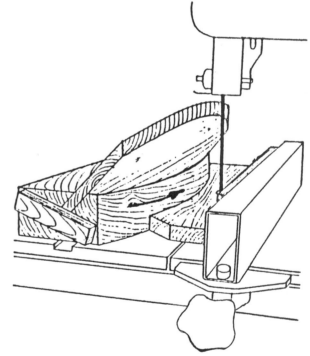

Illus. 538 and 539. Bevelled curves are cut with these jigs. (Drawings courtesy of INJECTA INCA of Switzerland)

Making Tight Turns

The size of the blade determines the maximum potential for a tight turn. For years, the smallest blades available were ⅛ inch wide. With the recent development of Cool Blocks, it is now possible to use ¹⁄₁₆-inch blades on an ordinary band saw. (See Illus. 540–542.) The non-metal Cool Blocks decrease friction between the blade and the guide blocks. A dry lubricant in the Cool Blocks actually lubricates the blade. The blade runs cooler and thus lasts longer. A side effect is

that the saw is quieter than when used with metal guides.

With Cool Blocks and a ¹⁄₁₆-inch blade, you can do "scroll" work with the band saw. It is possible to do almost everything that can be done with a scroll saw except make inside cuts. The band saw has the advantage of cutting much faster than the scroll saw.

The small blades on the band saw will do an amazing variety of work. For example, you can use a 1/16-inch blade to "cope" a mitre. (See Illus. 543–545.) The small blade is actually quite durable and capable of cutting very thick stock. (See Illus. 546.)

There is one important safety factor that the woodworker who uses 1/16- and 1/8-inch blades should be aware of. The blades will last longer if the top guides and thrust bearing are kept about an inch or two above the work. This allows the blade to flex rearward through a gentle arc rather than a sharp curve below the top thrust bearing. Because this technique exposes about an inch of blade, it is a potential safety problem. So be careful.

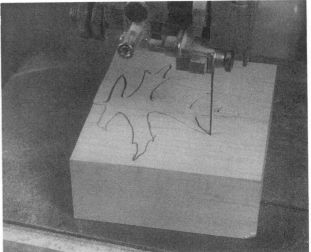

Illus. 540 (left). This band saw is fitted with a 1/16-inch blade and Cool Blocks. Cool Blocks are replacement guide blocks that allow the use of small blades and prolong normal blade life. Illus. 541 (above). The 1/16-inch blade will cut tight curves like a scroll saw. Small blades such as 1/8- and 1/16-inch blades last longer if the top guide is kept an inch or two above the work. This is a potential safety problem that the saw user has to be aware of.

Illus. 542. This 1/16-inch blade cuts much faster than a scroll saw blade, particularly in thick hard wood such as the two-inch hard maple shown here.

Illus. 543. For the first part of the cope cut, make one square and one mitre cut.

Illus. 544. Cut off the mitre cut with a ¹⁄₁₆-inch blade.

Illus. 545. When the piece is fitted together, there is no gap. If the piece were to shrink or move, there would not be a gap like one that would occur if the corner were made with two mitres.

Illus. 546. The ¹⁄₁₆-inch blade is very durable if treated corrected. It is also capable of very deep cuts. This 10-inch-deep cut was made with a ¹⁄₁₆-inch blade by Brad Pachard from Atlanta, Georgia.

228

13
Circular Work

Many projects require either complete circles or a portion of a circle, commonly called an arc. Circles and arcs can either be cut freehand or with the use of jigs. This chapter will explore both approaches.

A circle is often cut to prepare work for turn-ing on the lathe. If a circle is to be cut freehand, make the outline of the circle on the top of the work forming the cut line. The usual approach is to use a compass for this type of work. (See Illus. 547.) A novel approach is the use of a clear plas-tic disc with spaced lines. This helps you locate

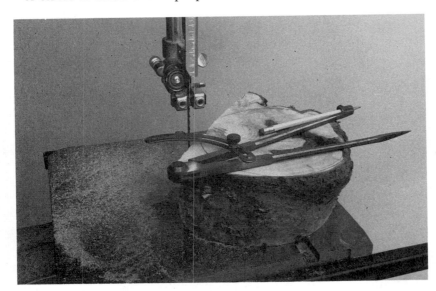

Illus. 547. When cutting a circle freehand, mark the top of the work-piece with a compass.

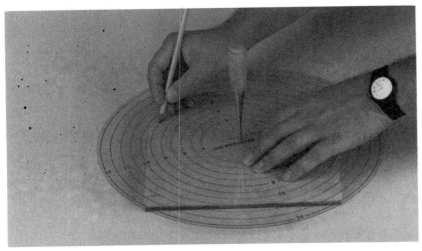

Illus. 548. This clear-plastic center finder is used to first find the center of the circle and then to mark it.

Illus. 549. The completed circle in the middle of the workpiece.

the exact center of the work. Each line, spaced at ½-inch intervals, has a hole that accepts a pencil for drawing a circle. (See Illus. 548 and 549.)

Circle-Cutting Jigs

Circle-cutting jigs are commercially available or can be shopmade. Although the design of each jig varies slightly, the basic principle is the same. The work is rotated around a point similar to the way a compass rotates around a center point. The point can be either on the bottom or top of the workpiece. (See Illus. 550.) To get a perfect circle, make sure that the pivot point is at 90 degrees to the front of the saw tooth. (See Illus. 551.) If the rotation point is either greater or less than this angle, it will cause the blade to lead either into the circle or out of the circle. Illus. 552 shows the design of a shopmade top-mounted pivot point.

Often, it is important to make a number of circles that are the same size. In this case, it is best to use the pivot point on the bottom of the workpiece. Locate the pivot point with a jig. (See Illus. 553.) The circle-cutting jig slides in the mitre slot. (See Illus. 554.) Mount the workpiece on the center point. Slide the whole assembly, both the workpiece and the jig, into the saw blade. (See Illus. 555.) As the workpiece slides into position, the initial cut is straight. A stop on the jig is preset so that the pivot point stops moving forward when it is even with the front of the blade. At this time, rotate the work. This creates a circle. (See Illus. 556.)

A simple circle-cutting jig is not hard to make. It is just a matter of nailing two boards together.

One board should be a piece of plywood (a good use for scrap wood) and the other piece a strip of wood the size of the mitre slot. Cut the end of this wood off. Clamp the cutoff piece onto the mitre slot strip to create a stop. (See Illus. 557.) To make the jig, nail the two pieces together and advance the jig almost halfway into the blade. Stop the saw and make a pencil line 90 degrees to the saw cut. The rotating point should be on this line. The point can either be a nail or a screw that starts from the bottom of the jig. (See Illus. 558–560.)

In a fashion similar to the commercial jig, mount the workpiece onto the rotation point and advance it into the work until the stop prevents any further movement. (See Illus. 561.) A note of caution: It is important that the stop always be in contact with the table. Be particularly aware of this because as you rotate the workpiece forward you are creating a slight rearward pressure on the rotation point. If the jig slides rearward, you will not get a round circle. (See Illus. 562 and 563.)

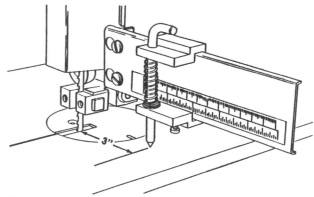

Illus. 550. The radius of the circle is the distance between the blade and the rotation point.

230

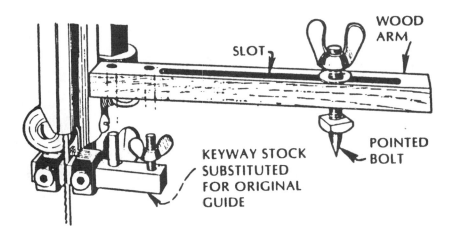

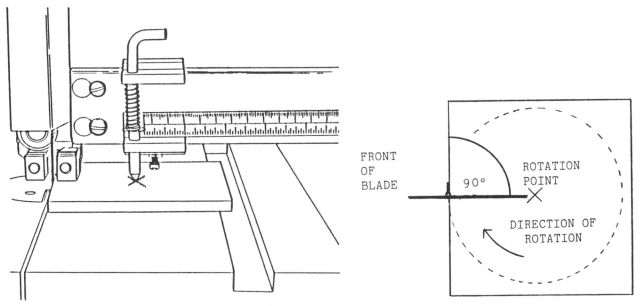

Illus. 551. A shop-made, top-mounted pivot point.

FRONT
OF
BLADE

90°

ROTATION
POINT

DIRECTION OF
ROTATION

WOOD
ARM

SLOT

POINTED
BOLT

KEYWAY STOCK
SUBSTITUTED
FOR ORIGINAL
GUIDE

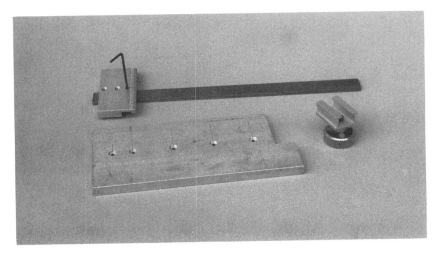

Illus. 552. Locate the pivot point
with the jig.

Illus. 553. A commercially available
circle-cutting jig made by INCA for
its band saws. The jig is adjustable
for any radius.

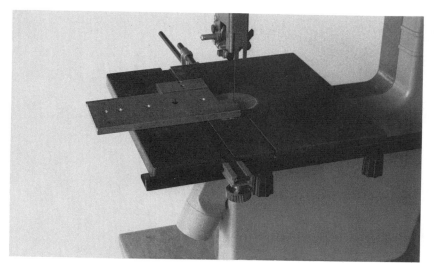

Illus. 554. The jig slides in the mitre slot. A stop at the end of the mitre is adjustable.

Illus. 555 (above left). When using the bottom pivot point, move the jig and workpiece forward to create a straight line. When the rotation point is even with the front of the saw blade, rotate the work to create the circle. Illus. 556 (above right) The completed circle. Remove the waste by sliding it through the initial straight cut.

Illus. 557. A shop-made plywood jig. To create a stop, clamp a piece of scrap wood to the mitre guide piece. The stop should stop the jig when the rotation point is 90 degrees to the front of the saw blade.

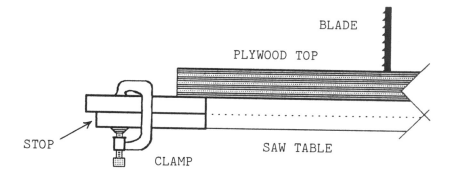

Illus. 558 (above left). Measure the desired radius with a ruler and place a nail at that point. Illus. 559 (above right). Cut off the head of the nail with a pair of pliers.

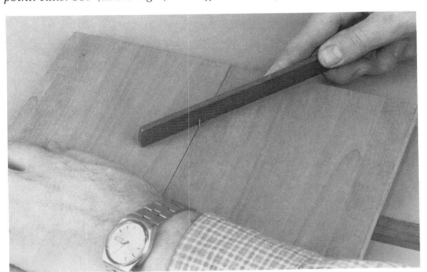

Illus. 560. File the nail to a point.

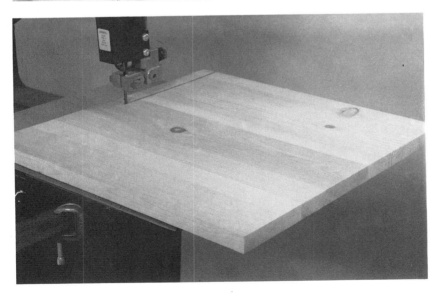

Illus. 561. Advance the workpiece into the blade.

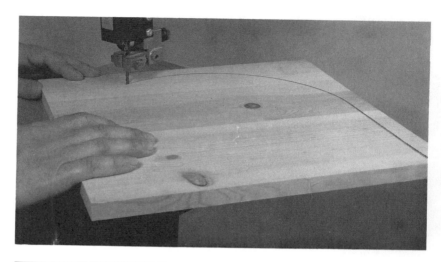

Illus. 562. Rotate the workpiece. Make sure that the stop is in place during the cut. Rotating the piece can cause the pivot point to come rearward towards.

Illus. 563. A perfect circle that was cut with the shop-made jig.

Cutting Circles in Thick Stock

Solid bowls are usually cut into circular shapes before being mounted onto the lathe. (See Illus. 564.) Circle-cutting jigs can be used for this chore. They are particularly useful when you want two pieces with the same diameter. (See Illus. 565.)

It is important that the band-saw blade used is coarse enough. If the bowl is 6 inches or larger in diameter, a 3 TPI hook or hook-skip blade is a good choice. Refer to the chart on page 89 if you have any questions. Pieces smaller than 6 inches should be cut with the largest blade possible. Since the finish is not important, the coarser the blade the better. This is especially true if the wood is green or is laminated, because in both cases the wood will quickly dull a blade that is too fine. (See Illus. 567.)

Tilted-Table Circles

You can add a new dimension to circle-cutting by tilting the table. (See Illus. 568.) Large, rough pieces used for turning bowls can be cut to shapes closer to the finished product. (See Illus. 569 and 570.)

Cutting multiple rings and then gluing them back together is another useful technique for making bowls. (See Illus. 571 and 572.) When using this technique, you have to move the pivot point for each cut. Then glue the cut back together before gluing the rings.

Partial Circles

Some projects require the use of a partial circle. (See Illus. 573–575.) Use the circle-cutting jig for this. Instead of advancing the work into the blade, simply rotate it. Clamp the jig into posi-

Illus. 564. A walnut bowl made from a commercially available bowl blank.

Illus. 565. A circle-cutting jig is particularly useful when you are using two circles of the same size, such as the top and bottom of this walnut and maple turned container used to hold change.

Illus. 566. Interesting small turnings are often made from waste wood or fire wood. The birch piece shown second from the right came from burl.

Illus. 567. Laminated bowls are a good project on which to use scrap pieces of different species. (Photo courtesy of David Morris, Austin, Texas)

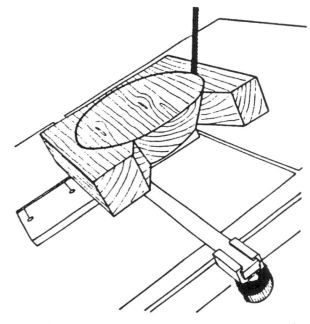

Illus. 568. Angling the table causes the piece to be wider on the top than the bottom. (Photo courtesy of INCA, Switzerland)

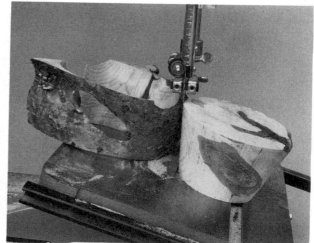

Illus. 569 (above left). This piece is being cut freehand with the table tilted. Illus. 570 (above right). The completed workpiece. Making the straight top and bottom cuts is discussed in the next chapter.

Illus. 571. Each one of these mahogany boards was made from a piece of 1-inch stock that was cut at an angle and glued into these shapes. A lathe was used to true the shapes and for sanding. (Photo courtesy of Rick Hartom of Marquette, Michigan)

Illus. 572. The glue lines in this piece are accentuated with a dark veneer. (Photo courtesy of Rick Hartom of Marquette, Michigan)

Illus. 573. This Shaker table features half circles as a design element.

Illus. 574. It is often easier to cut a quarter circle before gluing the piece together. Shown here is half of a side from a Shaker step stool.

Illus. 575. You can easily sand the large end grain curve if you use the sponge sander shown here.

tion with the front of the blade even with the pivot-point line. If the piece is long and will hit the column, place the point between the blade and the column. (See Illus. 576.)

The mirror in Illus. 577 is almost a complete circle. The tape dispenser is a half circle. (See Illus. 578.)

The circle-cutting jig should be used to guarantee accuracy. Start the cut in the usual manner, as a straight entry cut. After you have com-

pleted the desired portion of the circle, stop the band saw. Lift the workpiece off the jig and remove the jig from the saw. Then finish the cut. If it is a straight cut, it may be advisable to use a rip fence or mitre guide.

Some design elements require a circular cut. If you carefully lay out the pivot point, you can make numerous designs. Here again it is a good idea to clamp the jig to the table and rotate the work into the blade. (See Illus. 579.)

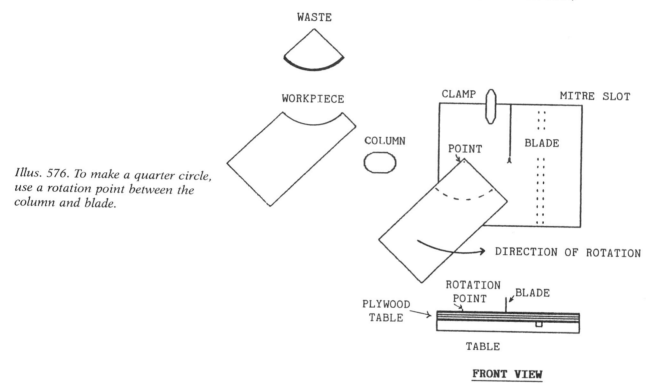

Illus. 576. To make a quarter circle, use a rotation point between the column and blade.

FRONT VIEW

Illus. 577. This mirror is an incomplete circle. You can cut the circular part with a circular jig.

238

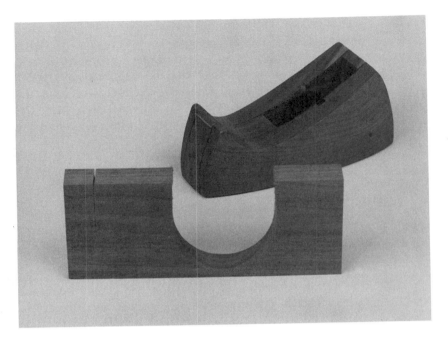

Illus. 578. This tape dispenser is laminated. The middle piece has a half circle cut designed to accent the tape. (Photo courtesy of Lyle Kronberg)

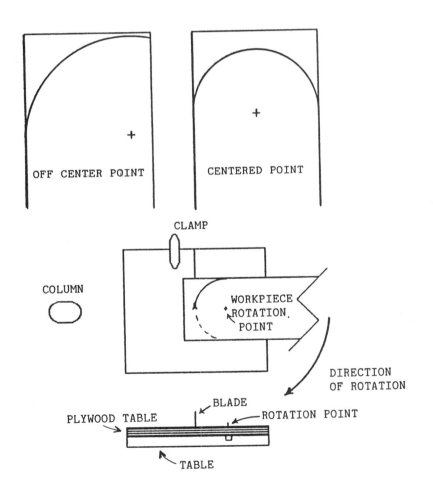

OFF CENTER POINT

CENTERED POINT

CLAMP

COLUMN

WORKPIECE
ROTATION
POINT

DIRECTION
OF ROTATION

BLADE

ROTATION POINT

PLYWOOD TABLE

TABLE

Illus. 579. These curved objects show the result of various rotation point locations.

Radius Cuts

When a corner cut is made, thus forming a quarter circle, it is referred to as a "radius" cut. To make a "radius" cut, mark off the piece so that the center of the circle is the same distance (radius) from the edge of the board. (See Illus. 580.)

To make radius cuts, mark the center point by making two equal measurements, one from each edge. Illus. 581 shows the center point being marked. Use an awl to mark the point and to make a hole. Move the jig nail or point to the proper location from the blade, which is the same measurement as the radius. Place the workpiece hole over the jig point and make the cut. (See Illus. 582.)

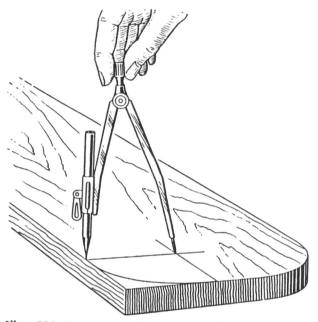

Illus. 580. A quarter circle cut is usually referred to as a "radius" cut.

Radius Jigs

You can easily make a radius jig by attaching two strips of wood to each side of a complete piece. (See Illus. 583.) This will save the effort of having to mark, punch, and locate each corner. Simply hold the workpiece against the jig sides and rotate the jig. (See Illus. 584.) It is important that the jig does not move during this operation, and for this reason you may want to clamp it to the table. You can also use this jig in conjunction with a sanding belt to sand the corners.

Making Round Tenons

At some time you may have to make a round tenon or a dowel of a nonstandard size. You can do this quickly and accurately if you use a V jig and a stop block. (See Illus. 587–589.)

Illus. 581. Mark the rotation point by measuring an equal distance from each edge. In this case, the rotation point is an inch from the edge.

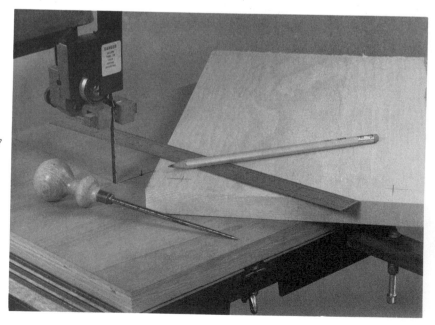

Illus. 582 (above left). Rotate the piece into the saw blade, thus making a quarter circle cut with a half-inch radius. Illus. 583 (above right). You can make a radius jig by adding a wood strip to each side.

Illus. 584 (above left). Hold the workpiece in the corner of the jig and make the cut. Illus. 585 (above right). You can make the cut without having to measure, mark, or make a hole.

Illus. 586. The four corners can be accurately cut in a matter of seconds.

Illus. 587. Use a V block to support the work when cutting round tenons. Use a stop block to determine the length of the cut.

Illus. 588. Make multiple cuts by rotating the piece slightly for each cut. Continue this process until the piece is done.

Illus. 589. The completed round tenon. The radius is determined by the distance the blade is from the center of the dowel.

Making Cones

Cones are made by tilting the table. Advance the piece of wood into the blade, preferably with a rip fence. (See Illus. 590.) After cutting the piece halfway through, remove the rip fence and slowly rotate the workpiece. (See Illus. 591–593.)

You can make a double cone by rotating the workpiece around two points. (See Illus. 594.)

You can make a cone puzzle by making curved cuts around the cone. (See Illus. 595 and 596.) A cone puzzle is a fun toy that doesn't need electricity or batteries.

Illus. 590. Start the cone with the table tilted. Using a rip fence ensures a straight entry cut.

Illus. 591 (above left). Make the cut to the middle of the piece. Illus. 592 (above right). Slowly rotate the piece without moving it.

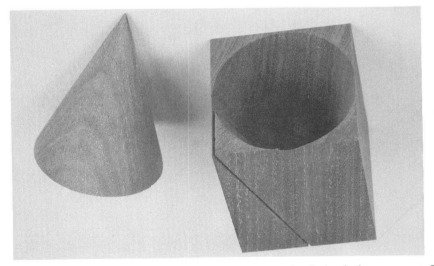

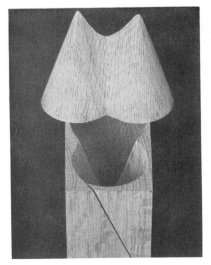

Illus. 593 (above left). At the end of the rotation, slowly back the cone out. Shown here is the completed cone. Illus. 594 (above right). Make a double cone by using two rotation points.

Illus. 595 (above left). You make a cone puzzle by cutting curves along the side of the piece. Illus. 596 (above right). The completed cone puzzle.

14

Making Straight Cuts

Though the band saw is usually thought of as a tool for making curves, a well-adjusted band saw with the correct blade for the job will very accurately make straight cuts. One advantage in using the band saw for straight cuts is the fact that it is safer than either the table or radial saw, particularly when small pieces are being cut. Following is a description of some of the straight cuts you will be making with a band saw.

Ripping

Ripping is defined as cutting along the grain. When you are making a rip cut, the band saw usually doesn't cut perfectly straight, but instead tends to cut at a slight angle. This is referred to as "lead." Rather than fighting this tendency, it is best to learn how to compensate for it. Feed the wood into the blade, matching the angle at which the blade wants to cut. A single point is often used to guide the wood. This gives the operator a chance to change the angle slightly. (See Illus. 597.)

The single-point approach is acceptable if you are cutting a minimal amount of work. If you are doing a lot of ripping, it is best to change the rip fence to match the cutting angle of the blade. Although it may sound complicated, this is quite simple to do and well worth the minute or two that it takes. First, make a knife line along the edge of the test board. (See Illus. 598.) Darken the line with a pencil. (See Illus. 599.) Feed the work into the blade as you cut down the edge of

the line. (See Illus. 600.) You may have to angle the board to make a straight cut. Stop cutting halfway through the cut and mark the angle. This is the angle at which the saw blade cuts best. (See Illus. 601.)

Change the angle of the fence to correspond to the angle of the workpiece. (See Illus. 602.) At this angle, the saw should cut straight without the workpiece pulling to one side or the other. Start the saw and finish the cut. (See Illus. 603.) Observe to see if the cut followed the pencil mark. (See Illus. 604.)

Next, make a test cut. Joint the side straight. Stop the cut halfway through and observe the workpiece and the fence. There should be no gap between the two. (See Illus. 605.) If the cut has veered off towards the fence, the blade will

Illus. 597. The single point method allows the wood to be fed into the blade at a slight angle. The angle compensates for blade lead.

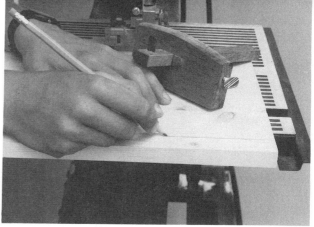

Illus. 598 (above left). The first step in correcting the fence angle is to prepare a test board. Make a straight knife line near the edge of the board. Illus. 599 (above right). Darken the line with a pencil.

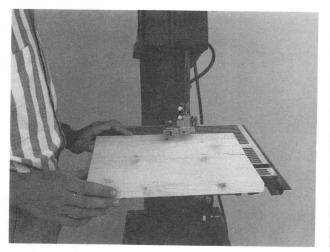

Illus. 600 (above left). Feed the work freehand into the blade by following the pencil line. Illus. 601 (above right). Shown here is the difference between a rip fence that is parallel to the table slot and the best cutting angle for this particular blade.

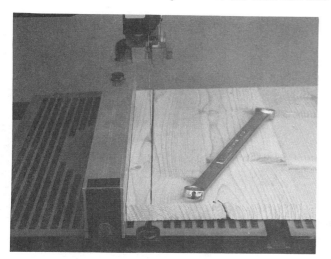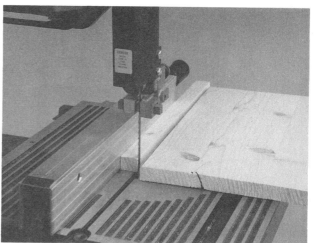

Illus. 602 (above left). Loosen the fence bolts with a wrench and change the angle of the fence so that it corresponds to the angle of the test cut. Illus. 603 (above right). Start the saw and finish the cut.

Illus. 604 (above left). Observe the last half of the cut. This cut has followed the line perfectly. Illus. 605 (above right). Make a test cut and stop the saw in the middle of the cut. The fit between the workpiece and the fence should be tight.

spring the wood back to its normal position and pull the workpiece away from the fence. This means that the fence is angled too far. This problem is discussed on page 247.

Continue the saw cut until you reach the end of the workpiece. (See Illus. 606.) At the end of the

Illus. 606. At the end of the cut, the workpiece should just touch both the rip fence and the blade, as shown here. This means that the fence is parallel with the cut.

cut, the workpiece should just touch both the blade and rip fence. This means that the rip fence is parallel with the cut. If the workpiece is thicker than the distance between the blade and the rip fence, the cut has veered away from the fence. This means that there wasn't enough fence angle.

It is important that you understand what happens in each of the situations described. These situations are shown in Illus. 607–609. Illus. 607 shows the desired situation, in which the cut angle (the angle at which the blade cuts best) and the rip fence are parallel to each other. At the end of the cut, the workpiece is the same width as the distance between the rip fence and the blade (X). Illus. 608 shows a situation in which there is too much fence angle. The workpiece is less than X at the end of the cut. During the cut, the workpiece will have a tendency to pull away from the fence. This is corrected by moving the fence away from the blade.

Illus. 609 shows a situation in which there is not enough rip fence angle. In this situation, you will cut a taper that's wider at the back of the cut. This will deflect the blade and force the workpiece against the rip fence. You can correct this by moving the fence towards the blade.

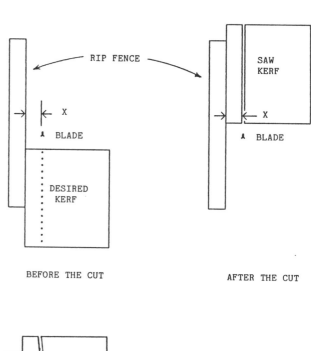

Illus. 607. In an ideal situation, the rip fence and the angle of the cut are parallel to each other. At the end of the cut the workpiece is the same as the distance between the rip fence and the blade (X).

RIP FENCE

SAW KERF

X

BLADE

DESIRED KERF

X

BLADE

BEFORE THE CUT   AFTER THE CUT

INCORRECT FENCE ANGLE   CORRECTED ANGLE   INCORRECT FENCE ANGLE   CORRECTED ANGLE

Illus. 608 (above left). In this situation, the rip fence is not at the correct angle. At the end of the cut the workpiece is less than desired. You can correct this by changing the angle of the fence as shown on the right. Illus. 609 (above right). In this case, the fence is incorrectly angled and the workpiece is wider than the distance between the blade and the fence at the end of the cut. You can correct this by angling the fence as shown on the right.

Making a Rip Fence

The rip fence is usually an accessory on an American saw. Illus. 610 shows a very simple, easy-to-make rip fence. It has a bolt that allows for angular adjustment. The bevel gauge can be used to set an angle. To make this rip fence, drill a hole in both pieces of scrap wood. Attach a piece of sandpaper to the top of the bottom piece. The sandpaper prevents any rotation of the two pieces. A carriage bolt holds the pieces together. (See Illus. 611.) The rip fence is held in position by a clamp. (See Illus. 612.) Another piece of wood could be attached to create a higher fence if one were needed.

Illus. 610. This adjustable shop-made fence is made from scrap wood. You can set the angle with a bevel gauge.

Illus. 611. A piece of sandpaper on the top of the bottom piece prevents the rotation of the two pieces. A carriage bolt is used to hold the two together.

Illus. 612. Hold the fence in place with a clamp.

MICROADJUSTERS

At times, it is useful to be able to move the rip fence a "hair" or two, especially when fitting a tenon or dovetails. The word hair is used to indicate a fine adjustment. In reality, a strand of hair is about .004 inch, about the same thickness as a dollar bill or a piece of paper. Rulers usually are spaced in 64ths of an inch, which is about .015 inch or 4 strands of hair.

A microadjuster is an accessory that fits onto the rip fence. It moves the fence by rotating a thread. (See Illus. 613 and 614.) It is an extremely useful device and is available for most European machines. Why American machines don't have microadjusters is a mystery to anyone who has used one.

Shopmade Microadjusters After using an INCA band saw with a microadjuster for about ten years, I would find it difficult to get along with-out one. At times I've wished that my drill press and router table had the same microadjusting ability.

After years of experimentation, I've made a jig that will provide the solution to this problem. (See Illus. 615–620.) The jig is made from scrap plywood. It has two angled surfaces that slide against each other, much like the surfaces on a jointer table. (See Illus. 616.) The angle is about 80 degrees (a one:to:six ratio, which means that for every inch laterally that the fence moves, it moves vertically ⅙ inch). The fence stays parallel as it moves, which is a big advantage.

If you want to, you can change the angle to a one:to:eight ratio. In this case, moving the fence forward (or rearward) an inch would change its position by ⅛ inch. This would be a better ratio to use if you were going to calibrate the adjustment with a ruler.

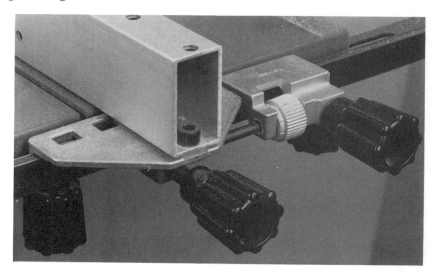

Illus. 613. The INCA rip-fence microadjuster.

Illus. 614. The microadjuster is an accessory that rotates threads into the rip fence.

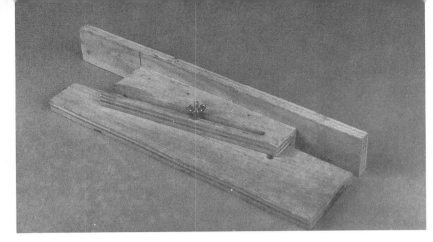

Illus. 615. This shop-made microadjuster is made from scrap plywood.

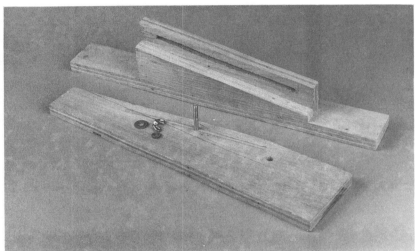

Illus. 616. Each piece has an angled side. To change the fence position, move it forward or rearwards.

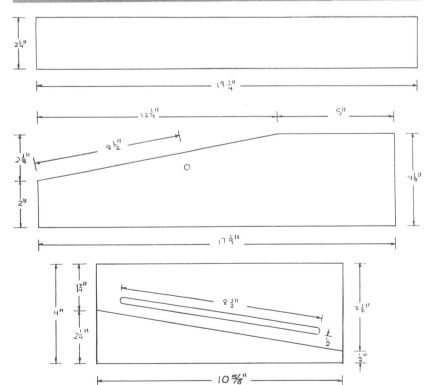

Illus. 617. The dimensions for the jig.

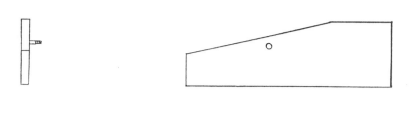

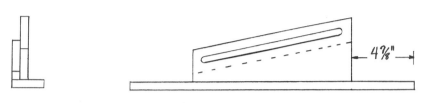

Illus. 618. Side view of the jig.

Illus. 619. The fence can also be adjusted for the correct cutting angles. To do this, add a bottom piece with sandpaper on top of it. Use a carriage bolt.

Illus. 620. Attach the jig to the table with a clamp.

Ripping with the Fence

A well-adjusted band saw with a correctly adjusted fence is an accurate tool. When ripping, put the "good" piece between the fence and the blade. (See Illus. 621.) This is especially true when you are making multiple pieces of the same size. (See Illus. 622.) In this situation, the piece on the side of the blade opposite the fence is the waste piece. This is called cutting on the "inside." At other times, especially when you are cutting thin pieces, the workpiece will be the piece on the side of the blade opposite the fence. (See Illus. 623.) This is called "outside" cutting.

Table Tilt

Rip cuts on bevelled and angled pieces can best be made with the table tilted. This is the position for making the "X" cut often used for preparing turning stock. (See Illus. 624.) It is also the best approach for cutting round stock. (See Illus. 625.)

Illus. 621 (above left). Most often, the distance between the rip fence and the blade determines the size of the workpiece. This is called the "inside." In this case, the waste is the piece on the side of the blade opposite the fence. Illus. 622 (above right). Shown here is the usual procedure for making multiple pieces. All of the pieces are cut on the "inside."

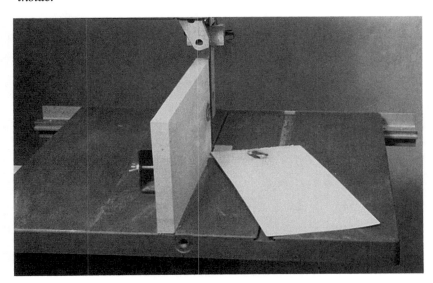

Illus. 623. Some workpieces, especially narrow ones, are best cut on the "outside." The outside is the piece cut on the side of the blade opposite the rip fence.

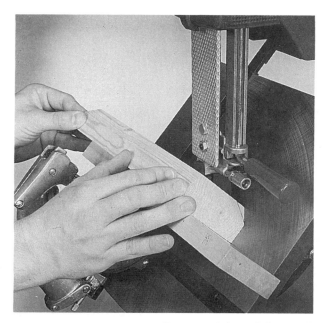

Illus. 624 (above left). Cut bevels with the table tilted. Illus. 625 (above right). The high fence and the tilted table cradle a round workpiece. (Photos courtesy of Shopsmith)

RIPPING JIG

At times, it is inconvenient to tilt the table. At these times, you should make a jig to support the work. Illus. 626 shows a long jig being used to support a 3 × 12 oak piece during a long bevel cut. Another jig used for ripping is the V block. This is used to support unusually shaped pieces. (See Illus. 627 and 628.) At times it is useful to tape an unusually shaped item to a V block and cut both the workpiece and the V block in half.

Crosscutting

Crosscutting is defined as cutting across the grain. This can be done freehand, with a fence (Illus. 629), or with a mitre guide (Illus. 630). If you use a mitre gauge, make sure that it is square in the usual manner. (See Illus. 631.) The mitre gauge will help you to crosscut accurately.

A simple square jig can also be used in conjunction with the fence. This jig is simply a square board with a handle. One end of the square rests against the fence, and the other square face supports the work. (See Illus. 632 and 633.)

The biggest problem with accurate crosscut-

ting is blade lead. The mitre guide may be perfectly square, but if the blade leads to one side or the other the resulting cut will not be square. (See Illus. 634.)

This potential problem can be dealt with in several different ways. You can use a blade that

Illus. 626. This bevel jig is being used to rip a long piece of 3 × 12 oak. This jig is 4 feet long and extends past the saw table on each end to support the work.

Illus. 627. This turning is being cut in half. The V block is used to support the work.

Illus. 628. The completed cut. The V block is positioned so that the work is supported on each side of the blade.

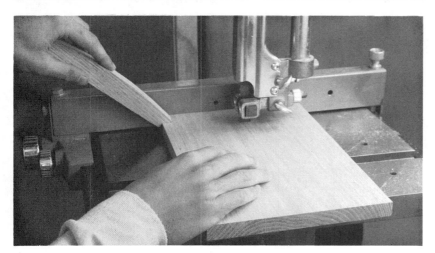

Illus. 629. Crosscutting with the rip fence. Use a push stick if the fence is close to the blade.

Illus. 630. Crosscutting with a mitre guide.

Illus. 631. Square the band-saw mitre with the usual method of using a square.

Illus. 632. Crosscutting using a square jig against the fence.

Illus. 633. A round knob functions as the handle. The jig is kept in contact with the fence. The other side is kept in contact with the workpiece.

Illus. 634. If the blade leads to one side or the other, the mitre cut will not be straight.

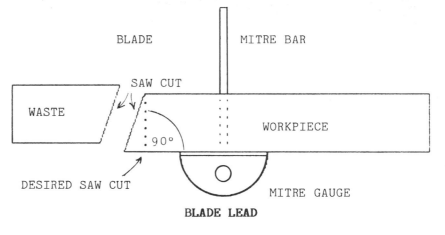

doesn't lead, or you can very easily check the accuracy of the cut. You can also use the square jig that was discussed earlier. Because it follows the fence rather than the mitre slot, it can be correctly set for blade lead. If the fence is correctly adjusted for the blade lead, the square jig will provide an accurate crosscut. Of course, the longest square cut is limited by the post. (See Illus. 635 and 636.)

Narrow-Blade Crosscutting

Perhaps the best approach for dealing with the potential problem of blade lead is to use a narrow blade such as a ⅛-or ¹⁄₁₆-inch blade. (See Illus. 637 and 638.) These blades are less susceptible to blade lead. You can enhance this accuracy by keeping the top thrust bearing an inch above the work. This allows the blade to flex rearwards slightly during the cut.

Illus. 635. A square jig with a plane-type handle.

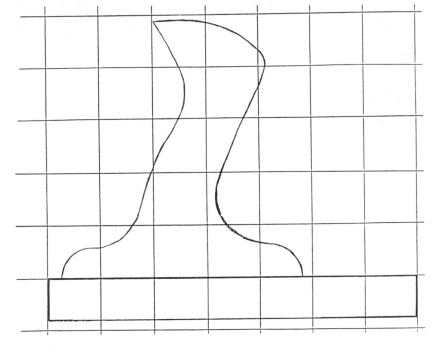

Illus. 636. The design for the jig shown in Illus. 635. Each square is equal to 1 inch.

Illus. 637. Smaller blades such as the 1/8- and 1/16-inch blades are less likely to lead. Keep the top thrust bearing about an inch above the work; this increases the saw's accuracy because the blade flexes rearwards in a straight line. This technique exposes more blade, so be careful.

Illus. 638. These straight cuts were made with a mitre guide and a 1/16-inch blade.

Checking for Squareness

It is important that the cut be square both from top to bottom and from front to back. You can check for squareness either with a square or by checking the accuracy of the cut by comparing the sawn pieces to each other. The latter is done by making a pencil mark on the cut. (See Illus. 639.) Next, turn one piece upside down and mate the pieces back together to check the fit. This is a means of checking the squareness of the blade and table. If it is square, the fit will be good. Any error will be doubled. (See Illus. 640.) Rotate both pieces on the adjacent side to check for squareness in the opposite direction. This checks the squareness of the mitre or square jig. (See Illus. 641.)

Cutting Mitres

Mitres are angled crosscuts made by either using the mitre guide or by using the table-tilt mechanism. (See Illus. 642 and 643.) A stop block can be used to accurately cut mitres to length. (See Illus. 644.) When cutting compound mitres, tilt the table and angle the mitre. (See Illus. 645.) A plywood jig can also be used to cut compound angles. Cut and fit the mitres first before making the curve cuts. (See Illus. 646 and 647.)

258

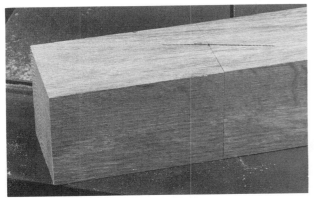 

Illus. 639 (above left). To check the accuracy of the saw cut, first mark the top of the cut with a pencil mark. Illus. 640 (above right). After you have made the cut, flip one piece upside down. This is a means of checking for table-blade squareness. Any error will be doubled.

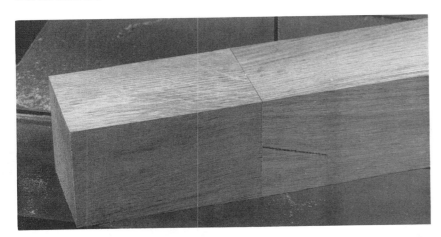

Illus. 641. Next, rotate both pieces onto an adjacent side. This is a means of checking the squareness of the mitre or square jig.

Illus. 642 (above left). The mitre here is being made by using the mitre gauge in an angled position. Clamp the work to prevent the wood from slipping during the cut. Illus. 643 (above right). This mitre is being cut with a table-tilt mechanism. Keep the mitre guide at 90 degrees. Clamp the work to prevent it from slipping.

Illus. 644 (above left). Use a stop block to accurately cut mitres to length. Illus. 645 (above right). To cut a compound angle, use the mitre gauge in an angled position and tilt the table.

Illus. 646 (above left). When you have to mitre a piece that is curved, cut and fit the mitre first. Illus. 647 (above right). A close-up of the clock mitre.

Cutting Tapers

There are basically three types of jigs used to cut tapers. The simplest is a tapered piece of wood. (See Illus. 650.) This jig has a brass screw as a stop. (See Illus. 651.) The stop can be used in front or in back of the workpiece.

The step jig, as its name implies, is a jig with notches or steps. (See Illus. 652.) To use it, first mark the start of the taper. Place the workpiece on the first step. Then start the cut. Stop the piece after an inch of cutting and start over again. You can do this more than once. When you use this method, you prevent the blade from deflecting rather than cutting. (See Illus. 653–655.)

If you want two tapers, rotate the workpiece to an adjacent side and make another cut. (See Illus. 656 and 657.) If you want to make a taper on the opposite side or a leg with all four sides tapered, use the next step. (See Illus. 658.)

The step jig is very easy to make. Just machine a piece of wood and make three cuts about 3 inches long off the end. Glue the pieces together with about a quarter of an inch per step. (See Illus. 659.) Tapers are usually given in ratios per foot such as "one inch per foot." This means that the waste piece will be a foot long and an inch wide. To make this jig, use a one-inch-wide board. The first step should be 12 inches from the opposite end of the long piece.

The third type of taper jig is an adjustable one that is sold commercially. (See Illus. 660.) This design has a hinge on one end. It also has a gauge for setting the angle in degrees. (See Illus. 661.) To adjust the jig to an "inch per foot" ratio, measure 12 inches from the hinge end. Mark this point and make a square mark across both legs

Illus. 648. The taper on the bottom of this boat adds to the character of the piece.

Illus. 649. A taper jig was used to cut off the top two corners of these plywood pieces that function as truss gussets. (Photo courtesy of Tom Klosinski)

Illus. 650 (above left). The simplest taper jig is an angled piece of wood. Illus. 651 (above right). A brass screw at the wide end of the jig functions as a stop. Use brass because it is soft. It is less likely to damage the blade if it accidentally hits it.

Illus. 652. The step jig is a piece of wood that has three staggered pieces glued to it.

Illus. 653 (below left). Rest the workpiece on the second step. This location angles the workpiece in relationship to the blade. Illus. 654 (below right). Start the initial cut at the marked line. Restart the first cut several times to make sure that the blade has not deflected sideways.

Illus. 655. The completed first cut. The waste is as wide as the first step.

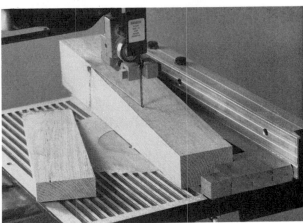

Illus. 656 (above left). Using the second step again, cut the adjacent side. Illus. 657 (above right). A leg with two tapers is a popular design, especially on Shaker furniture.

Illus. 658. Make tapers on the four sides by using the third step for the last two cuts.

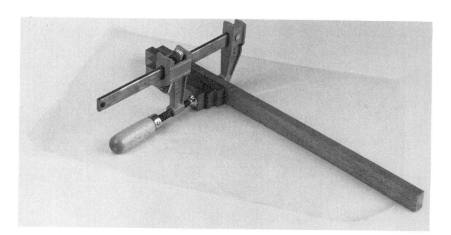

Illus. 659. Glue the pieces together, leaving about a quarter of an inch per step.

Illus. 660 (above left). The commercially available jig is adjustable. It has one-inch-per-foot taper. Illus. 661 (above right). There is an indicator for the degree of the taper.

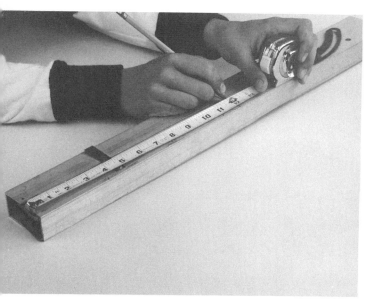

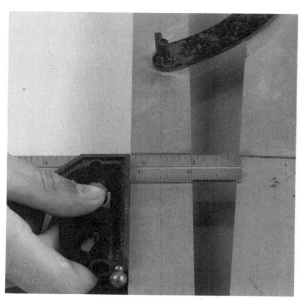

Illus. 662 (above left). To use a foot-per-inch ratio, measure the foot from the hinged end. Illus. 663 (above right). Measure the inch part of the ratio at the one-foot mark.

Illus. 664. To cut the opposite side of the taper, double the inch-per-foot ratio. Rotate the piece before making the cut.

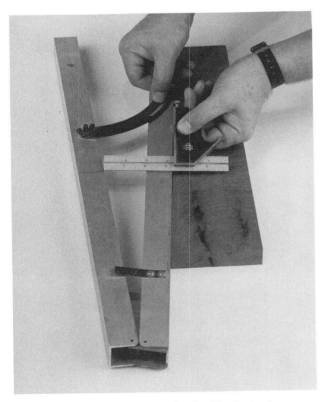

Illus. 665. To double the angle, double the inch measurement.

of the jig. (See Illus. 662.) To adjust the jig for a ratio of inches per foot, measure the inches between the two legs at the one foot mark. (See Illus. 663.) To make a cut on the opposite side of a piece, rotate the workpiece and double the ratio. (See Illus. 664 and 665.)

Resawing

The term resawing means cutting a board in half through its width. (See Illus. 666.) This exposes the inside of the board. Both halves will be a mirror image of each other. (See Illus. 667.) These two halves are often glued together. This is called bookmatching. (See Illus. 668.)

Resawing is used to cut off waste or to cut veneer. (See Illus. 669 and 670.) It is very useful when a design requires woods of nonstandard thicknesses. (See Illus. 671–673.)

Resawing uses the same techniques as ripping. It is just that the work being sawn is thicker. You still have to deal with the potential problem of blade lead. Test the setup with a piece of scrap first. Many people use a single-point jig for resawing. (See Illus. 674–676.)

Because the board is on its edge, it is important that the piece be well supported so that it doesn't tip. The best way to support the piece is to use a fence. If your saw is well-aligned and cuts straight, you can use a high fence. (See Illus. 677.)

Resawing Technique

Feed rate is very important when you are resawing. The blade should be kept busy, but not too busy. There can be a problem if the work is overfed (too fast) or underfed (too slow). A sharp blade is also important.

Square the fence and the blade to the table.

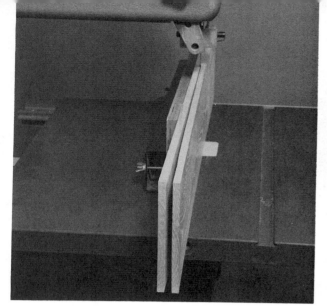 

Illus. 666 (above left). Resawing is cutting a board in half throughout its width. Illus. 667 (above right). Resawing exposes the inside of the board. Each side is a mirror image of the other side. When the pieces are glued together, it is called a bookmatch.

Illus. 668. This piece is book-matched, with the heartwood sides glued together. (Photo courtesy of Fal Wing, Sturgeon Bay, Wisconsin)

Illus. 669. Cutting the waste off saves time thickness-planing.

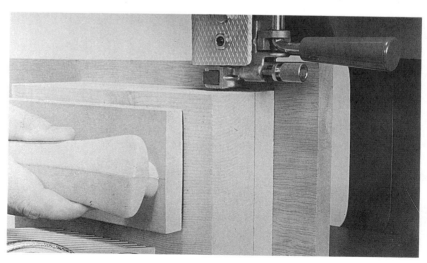

Illus. 670. To make veneer, cut the wood through its width.

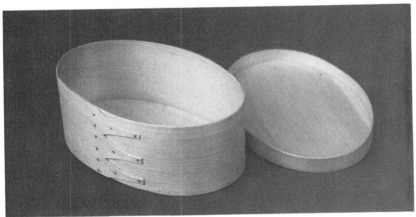

Illus. 671. Maple veneer is used to make oval Shaker boxes.

Illus. 672 (above left). Scrap wood can be resawed and glued into blanks. The variety of wood widths makes this design more interesting. Illus. 673 (above right). You can resaw scrap wood to make a variety of small projects. My nephew and shop assistant, Chris Morris, made coasters for Christmas presents out of scrap oak and walnut. He resawed the stock to dimension.

Illus. 674. This square piece of wood clamped to the table functions as a single-point resaw fence.

Illus. 675. This single-point fence is used for high work.

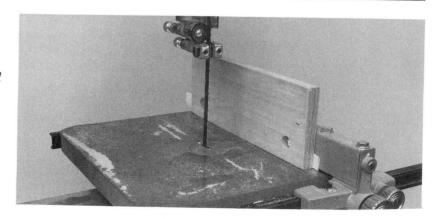

Illus. 676. A T-shaped piece is designed to clamp to the standard rip fence.

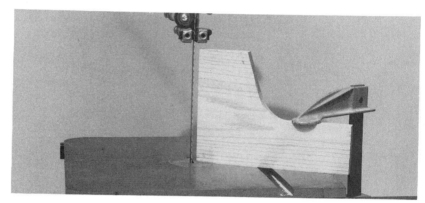

Illus. 677. A piece of plywood bolted to the rip fence extends to the height of the fence. A paper shim between the plywood and the fence keeps the fence square.

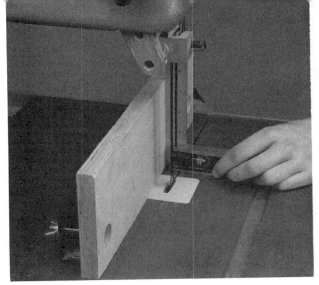

Illus. 678 (above left). It is imperative that the blade be square to the table. Illus. 679 (above right). When the fence is square to the table, the blade and fence are parallel to each other.

Illus. 680 (left). Assume a position on the side of the work. Press the work against the fence with one hand and advance it with the other. Illus. 681 (above). If the work is centered accurately both pieces will be the same thickness.

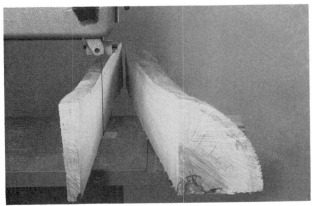

Illus. 682. Resawing thick stock is particularly useful way to harvest wood. This piece was quartered with a chain saw that has a lumbering attachment.

269

(See Illus. 678 and 679.) Support the work just behind the blade and slowly feed the work with the other hand. (See Illus. 680). If the blade is centered, the pieces should be the same thickness. Resawing is extremely useful when harvesting green wood—wood cut directly from the tree. (See Illus. 682.)

Cutting Irregularly Shaped Pieces

It is not easy to make perfectly straight cuts on irregularly shaped pieces. One technique that works well is to use the waste cutoff as a jig for holding the work. Use a rip fence, mitre guide, or taper jig to support the waste piece at the appropriate angle. (See Illus. 683 and 684.)

Cutting by Eye

Some pieces are not easily supported with a jig. (See Illus. 685.) A good technique that works extremely well in this situation is to use your eye as a guide. As the cut progresses, look past the blade at the saw kerf. (See Illus. 686 and 687.) Focus on the back of the workpiece. If this is in line, so is the rest of the workpiece.

Round stock should be jointed flat on one side. (See Illus. 690.) Always cut round stock down the middle or else the piece will rotate. Focus on the back corners of the cut. The workpiece often separates, allowing you to see the sides of the cut. As long as you can see the sides of the cut, you are cutting straight. (See Illus. 691 and 692.)

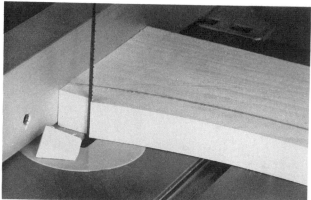

Illus. 683 (above left). This piece is being ripped straight, and the waste is being used as a guide. Note: The guard in this operation has been raised so that you can see the operation clearly. Illus. 684 (above right). This piece is being crosscut; the waste is being used to position the piece during the cut.

Illus. 685. This odd-shaped burl was cut perfectly straight by eye.

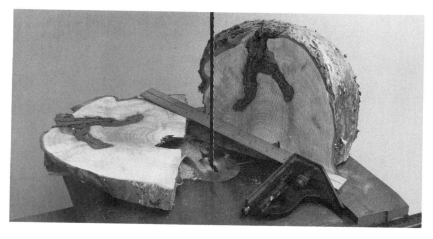

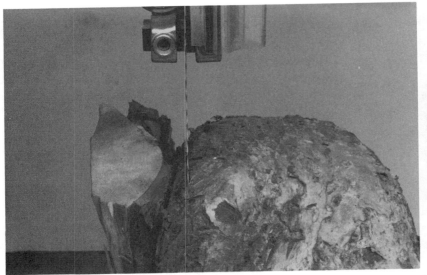

Illus. 686 (above left). Many people focus on the blade during the saw cut. This is wrong. Illus. 687 (above right). When you cut "by eye," you should focus one eye on the back of the workpiece. As long as you can cut the kerf, as shown here, you are cutting straight. The blade here is out of focus because you are looking past it. Occasionally focus on the blade to see how much of the cut is left.

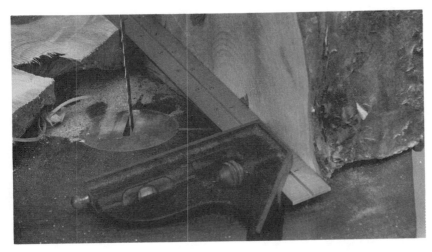

Illus. 688. This cut, which was made "by eye," is perfectly straight.

Illus. 689. You can test the accuracy of the cut by placing the cut surface on the table.

Illus. 690. When cutting round stock, joint one surface first.

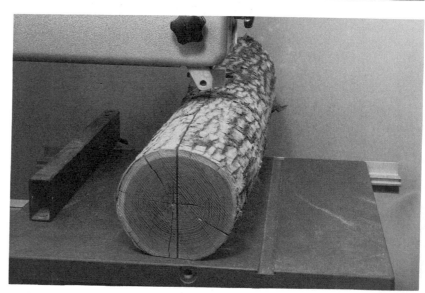

Illus. 691. Place the flat surface on the table. Always cut down the center of round stock to prevent the piece from rotating. This piece is being cut by eye. You can nail a 2 × 6 onto the side of the log and use the rip fence.

Illus. 692. The cut should be down the pith, the center of the log.

15

More Advanced Techniques

There are a number of techniques and procedures that are particularly well suited to the band saw. They will be explored in detail here. Some, particularly those used for making the dovetail, may appear complicated. Don't expect to get perfect results the first time you try these techniques. However, with practice you will soon master them and will be able to, for example, make a well-fitted dovetail box in about ten minutes.

Making Boxes

Making boxes with a band saw is a technique that has become quite popular. Illus. 693 shows a band-saw box made from a piece of walnut firewood. To make the box, mark the pattern on the top of the workpiece. (See Illus. 694.) Cut out the outline and then saw the top off. (See Illus. 695.) Cut out the inside plug by entering from the stem area of the leaf. (See Illus. 696.) You will cut two pieces off the plug. Cut one off each side of the plug and label it with a letter. The piece cut off the bottom of the plug will be the bottom of the box, so mark it B. The piece cut off the top of the plug will be attached to the top later, and should be labelled T. (See Illus. 697.)

To mark the correct position of the lid base, place the body over the top and mark the inside. (See Illus. 698 and 699.) Tap in two brads that will later be used to locate the top.

Next, glue the bottom in place and glue the body together in the area of the stem. Gap-filling

Illus. 693 (above left). This band-sawed box was made from a piece of walnut fire wood. The inside of the box was finished with spray-on suede. Illus. 694 (above right). A maple leaf was used as a pattern for this box.

Illus. 695. Cut out the outline of the box and then saw the top off. This is an example of with-grain cutting. This technique gives the smoothest finish, which is important in this situation.

Illus. 696 (above left). Cut out the plug by entering through the stem area of the leaf. Glue this seam back together later. Illus. 697 (above right). Cut a piece off each side of the plug. Glue one piece to the bottom and the other piece to the top.

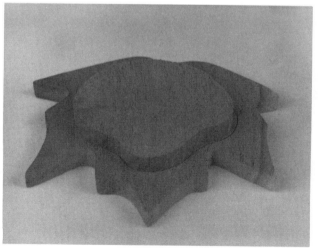

Illus. 698 (above left). To mark the position of the top base, place the body on the top and mark the inside. Illus. 699 (above right). The pencil line marks the correct position for the base of the top.

glue is best for this. At the same time, finish the underside of the top and then finish the inside of the box, the top base, and the edge of the top with a spray-on suede lining. (See Illus. 700.)

After the top oil finish dries, glue the base to the top. The brads should extend about 1/16 inch from the base. The brads help to locate the top exactly. (See Illus. 701.) Next, finish the bottom of the cover base and the inside and the bottom of the box with the spray-on suede lining. (See Illus. 703 and 704.)

Illus. 700. The three different processes involved. The body seam is glued together. The bottom is also glued together at this time. The bottom of the top is finished with oil. The edge of the top is finished with spray-on suede finish.

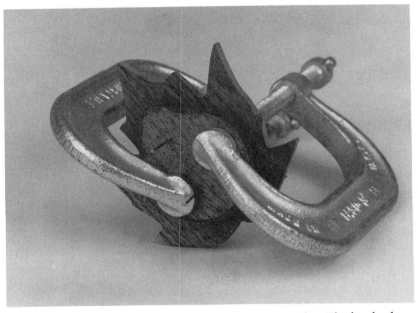

Illus. 701 (above left). Glue the base and the top together. The brads shown are used to locate the exact position of the base. They extend through the base into the top by about a sixteenth of an inch. This prevents the base from slipping out of position. Illus. 702 (above right). Here the bottom is glued in place. It will later be covered with spray-on suede. The glue used was 202 GF gap-filling glue from Garrett Wade.

Illus. 703. Apply the adhesive for the spray-on suede with a brush.

Illus. 704 (above left). Here is the completed box with the spray-on suede finish on the cover base and the inside of the box. Illus. 705 (above right). The band-saw box with its top in place.

Making Dovetails

Cutting dovetails with a band saw has numerous advantages. It is a lot like cutting dovetails by hand. It is quieter, safer, and more enjoyable than using a table saw. In fact, the band saw is the ideal tool for the woodworker who is making his first dovetails.

Dovetail Design

The exposed dovetail is both a structural and a design element in modern furniture. The idea is to expose the construction detail and to incorporate it as part of the design. This is in direct contrast with the goals of past woodworkers, who hid structural elements. Mouldings were used to cover the crude structural dovetail, and then ornamentation in the form of carving was added. A joint that is meant to be *seen* is different than a covered joint, which is there only to add strength. An exposed dovetail requires more technical expertise and a feel for aesthetics.

The relationship between design and technique is complex. Good work requires a compatible blending of the two. Design without technical skill or consideration is superficial; it places the cart in front of the horse. When we begin to design things, we usually avoid creating pieces beyond our technical abilities. As we gain skill and confidence, we can expand our repertoire. As our understanding increases, we develop a better grasp of design considerations.

Part of the design process is the visualization of the options available. Good design involves making the best choice of options.

Following is an exploration of the various factors that affect dovetail design. The quality of your work will reflect how you've dealt with these factors when making the dovetail. Alternatives in design are offered, each slightly different from one another. The drawings presented should help you visualize the options available when designing a dovetail joint.

ANATOMY

First, let's start with a review of dovetail anatomy. The dovetail is a locking joint consisting of two elements: the pin and the tail, for which the joint is named. The pin and tail only fit together from one direction.

The single dovetail joint can either be a complete pin or a complete tail. (See Illus. 706.) The

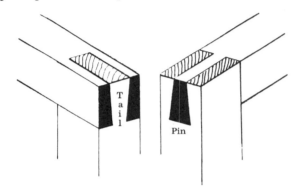

Illus. 706. The simple dovetail can either be a complete tail or a complete pin.

multiple dovetail usually ends with a half pin on the corner; the half tail is usually avoided. (See Illus. 707.) The tail board is a mirror image of itself. Each side is identical, and can function as either the inside or the outside of a box. The pinboard sides are not identical, and thus not rever-

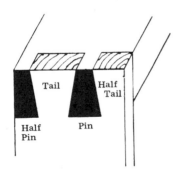

Illus. 707. The multiple dovetail ends with either a half pin or a half tail on the corner. The half tail should be avoided if possible because it has a tendency to split.

sible. The outside of the pin board is the side towards which the pins are tapered. (See Illus. 708.)

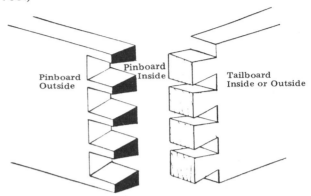

Illus. 708. The tail board is a mirror image of itself. It is reversible. Each side can function as either the inside or the outside of the box.

ANGLE

The dovetail angle provides the mechanical lock. The angle of the pin (shown in black in Illus. 706–719) mates with the angle of the tail, and that contact point is the foundation of the joint. If the angle is too slight, the pin can slide between the tails, and the locking mechanism is insufficient. (See Illus. 709.) If the angle is too great, the wood at the corner becomes too fragile and will easily break under the stress. (See Illus. 710.)

Illus. 709. The dovetail angle provides the mechanical lock. If the angle is too slight, the pin can slide between the tails.

Illus 710. If the angle is too great, the corners become brittle and break off too easily.

The angle at which the dovetail will best function is approximately 80 degrees. (See Illus. 711 and 712.) It does not matter if this angle is off a couple of degrees either way. What is important is that the pin and tail have the same angle and fit closely without gaps. On some of the softer woods such as pine, an angle of 82 to 83 degrees is suggested. (See Illus. 712b.) The dovetail

Illus. 711. The best compromise between the two extremes is the 80-degree angle. It will not slide and the corners will not break off.

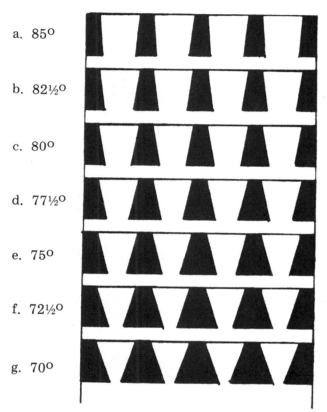

a. 85°

b. 82½°

c. 80°

d. 77½°

e. 75°

f. 72½°

g. 70°

Illus. 712. An illustration of the various pin angles.

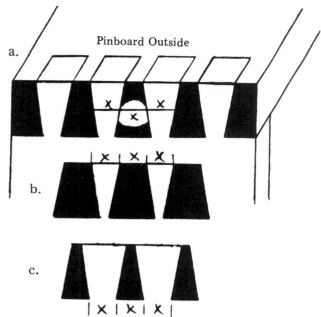

Illus. 713. One important design consideration is how the pins are spaced in relationship with each other.

router bit is at an angle of 14 degrees. (See Illus. 712e.) This angle is not the strongest, nor the most desirable, but the large surface area of the many pins and tails creates a strong joint. When using the 14-degree router bit be careful, particularly on hard wood, so that you do not break the corners off. The tendency for the corners to chip is particularly disturbing when the tails will show, as with through dovetails.

PIN SPACING

The spacing of the pins in relationship to each other is an important design consideration. The spacing is best measured from the center of the pin. (See Illus. 713a.) If the measuring is done, from the outside corner of the pin, the pins will be bigger than the tails. (See Illus. 713b.) If the

measurement is taken from the inside corner of the pin board, where the pin is the widest, the tail will be bigger than the pin. (See Illus. 713c.)

Variable Pin Spacing To avoid a mechanical look, you can space pins so that the tails are not equal in size. Illus. 714 shows various possible arrangements. The design created should be consistent with the need for structural strength. If the pins are not evenly spaced, as shown in d, the pins should be closer to the edge of the piece as in e, f, g, and h. The close proximity of the pin to the half pin on the corner provides extra strength. A dovetail will usually fail on the corner rather than the middle, so it makes good sense to reinforce the corner. If the pins are too close to the middle of the board, as shown in a, they provide little more strength than a large single pin. Example e is the one that I find most visually interesting.

Illus. 715 shows various pin-spacing ratios. The 1:to:1 ratio of the pins and tails is very mechanical looking. This is the type of joint created by a router and jig or an industrial dovetail machine. This mass-produced look is not consistent with high-quality work. It is often used and is acceptable for kitchen cabinets.

The other pin-spacing designs shown in Illus.

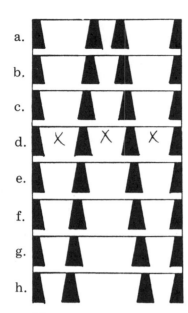

Illus. 714. Variable pin spacing.

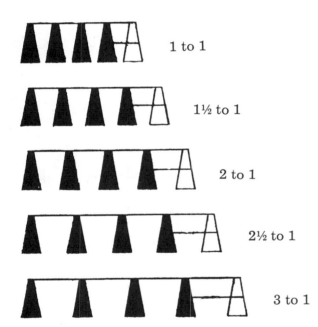

Illus. 715. Pin-spacing ratios.

a.

b.

c.

d.

e.

f.

g.

h.

1 to 1

1½ to 1

2 to 1

2½ to 1

3 to 1

pieces. They were considered elegant-looking. Examples b and c combine the strength of d and the looks of a. Examples f and g wouldn't be used because the tail is traditionally larger than the pin.

Illus. 716. An example of a one-to-one ratio of pin size.

Illus. 717. An example of a one-to-one ratio of pin stock thickness.

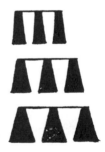

Illus. 718. An example of a one-to-one ratio of dovetail angle.

PIN-TO-TAIL RATIOS

Illus. 719 shows various spacing ratios of the pins (black) and the tails (white). The strongest joints would be the two middle examples (d and e), because the pins and tails are similar in size and are therefore strong. The weakest joints would be examples a and h, the two extremes. The small pins of a and the small tails of h would both break easily under stress. It is interesting to note that small pins such as the one shown in example a were in vogue for a period of time in

715 are much more attractive. A ratio of more than 3 to 1 should be avoided, as the strength of the joint becomes questionable as the pin size decreases in relationship to the tail sizes.

Three factors have an effect on the spacing of one pin to another: pin size (Illus. 716), stock thickness (Illus. 717), and dovetail angle (Illus. 718.) Illus. 716–718 are examples of 1:to:1 ratios.

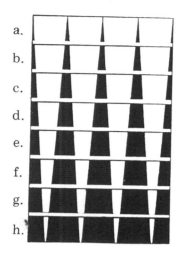

a.
b.
c.
d.
e.
f.
g.
h.

Illus. 719. Various pin-to-tail ratios.

expensive European pieces. They were considered elegant-looking. Examples b and c combine the strength of d and the looks of a. Examples f and g wouldn't be used because the tail is traditionally larger than the pin.

Making Dovetails with Spacing Blocks

With the present emphasis on exposed joinery, the hand-cut dovetail has become a symbol of craftsmanship and taste. The hand-cut method offers unlimited design flexibility. Unfortunately, it is too time-consuming for most professional use.

The accepted alternative for efficient small shop work is the dovetail router jig. The router jig was developed for thin stock-and-drawer construction, and most models have stock width and thickness limitations. Router jigs take time to set up. Their tendencies to tear out wood can be very disturbing. The tail angle is 14 or 15 degrees, depending on the bit; the standard (1 to 6) ratio of 10 degrees is more functional and is better aesthetically. The pins have to be at least the width of the bit; this oftentimes makes the design look chunky. I like small, thin pins like those that are hand-cut. The jigs, collars, and routers can be expensive. In spite of these drawbacks, however, the router jigs are efficient when properly set up.

For a long time, I searched for a technique that was an ideal compromise between the hand and the router jig methods. It would combine the design flexibility of cutting by hand with power

tool accuracy and efficiency, allow any tail angle to be used, would not be limited to stock width or thickness, and would be inexpensive and easy to use. With this in mind, and after about five years of experimentation, I've developed the following technique for use in my shop. It provides hand-tool flexibility with power-tool speed and accuracy. (See Illus. 720.)

Illus. 720. The band-saw dovetail has a flexible design that can be efficiently made.

To properly cut dovetails, you have to solve two distinct problems. First, you have to accurately space the cuts for the interlocking pins and tails. This is accomplished with the router jig. There are also a number of ways to accurately measure and mark the spaces when using the hand method.

To facilitate the correct spacing of the cuts, I started using wood spacing blocks. When used with a simple guide, the blocks function as the jig for precisely spacing the angled band-saw cuts.

Secondly, you have to cut at the correct angle. When you use a router, the angle of the dovetail bit ensures this. When you use the block method I've adopted, you use a simple angle jig to cut the

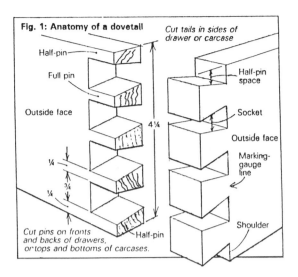

Fig. 1: Anatomy of a dovetail

Cut tails in sides of drawer or carcase

Half-pin

Full pin

Outside face

4¼

¼

¾

¼

Cut pins on fronts and backs of drawers, or tops and bottoms of carcases.

Half-pin

Half-pin space

Socket

Outside face

Marking-gauge line

Shoulder

Illus. 721. To cut an accurate dovetail, make sure that the angles of both pieces are identical. The spacing between the angles must be the same on each piece.

tails, and angle the table to cut the pins. (See Illus. 721.)

With the technique I've adapted, you can vary both the width and the spacing of the pins and tails for practically any aesthetic effect. The blocks that set the spacing are self-centered and will produce perfect-fitting, interchangeable joints. This eliminates the need to mark boards so that individual joints will fit, as is done when hand-dovetailing.

To make dovetails with this technique, begin by preparing your stock accurately. The piece of wood upon which this technique is being per-

formed in the illustrations is green elm that was cut off a quarter log and then resawn through using a bookmatching technique attributed to Sam Bush of Portland, Oregon. (See Illus. 722.) Mark each corner on both pieces. (See Illus. 723.)

After preparing the stock, score the material with a gauge line. (See Illus. 724 and 725.) The gauge line prevents tear out and makes the cut area easier to see.

SPACING THE CUTS

You can easily make accurate dovetails when you use wood blocks to space the saw cuts. After each cut, remove a spacing block and make a different series of cuts. (See Illus. 726.) Illus. 727 shows the relationship between the blocks and the saw cuts. Each block spaces the distance from the corner of one tail to the corner of the next tail. The difference between the total width of the blocks (4 inches) and the width of the workpiece (4¼ inches) determines the size of the pin and half pin (¼ inch).

You can alter tail size by changing the block size. When you use tails of different sizes you affect the design of the joint. (See Illus. 728.) By changing the block sizes and the width of the workpiece, you can create completely different designs. (See Illus. 729.)

Following are some different formulas to use when considering different dovetail designs: WIDTH = total width of blocks and the pin size. PIN SIZE = width of workpiece minus the total block width. TOTAL BLOCK WIDTH = width of workpiece minus the pin size.

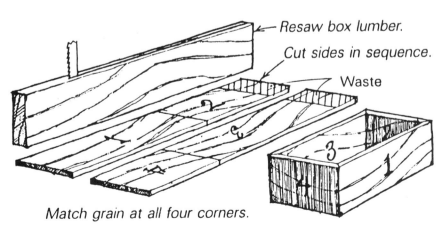

Resaw box lumber.

Cut sides in sequence.

Waste

Match grain at all four corners.

Illus. 722. (Drawing courtesy of Fine Woodworking *magazine)*

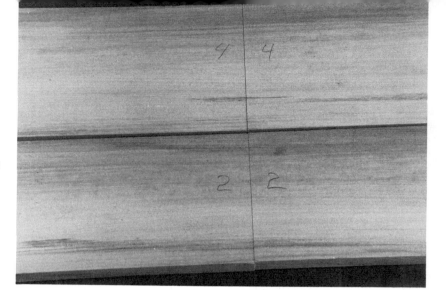

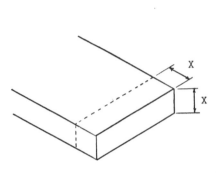

Illus. 723. Mark the corner on each piece.

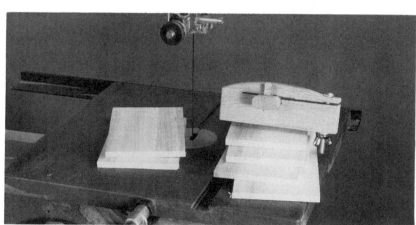

Illus. 724 (above left). Use a gauge line to mark the depth of the cut and to prevent tearout. This mark should be the same distance from the end of the board that the wood is thick (X). Illus. 725 (above right). Use a marking gauge to score the angle line. This Japanese-style gauge is a project in Chapter 16.

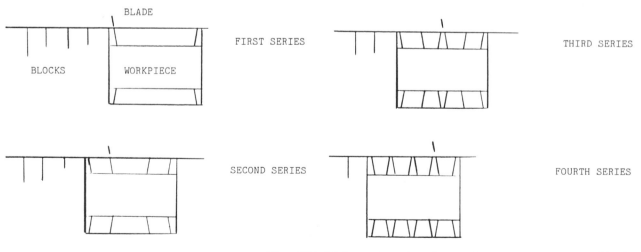

Illus. 726. Make each series of cuts after removing a spacer block.

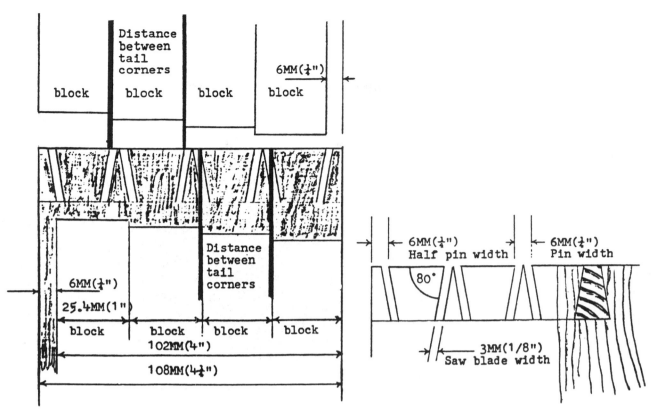

Illus. 727. *If you use wood blocks to space the saw cuts, you can cut accurate dovetails with the band saw. Here the relationship between the blocks and the saw cuts is shown. Each block spaces the distance from the corner of one tail to the corner of the next tail. The workpiece shown is 4¼ inches wide. Each block is 1 inch wide. The difference between the width of the workpiece (4¼ inches) and the width of the blocks (4 inches) is ¼ inch. One-quarter inch is the size of the pin and the half pin.*

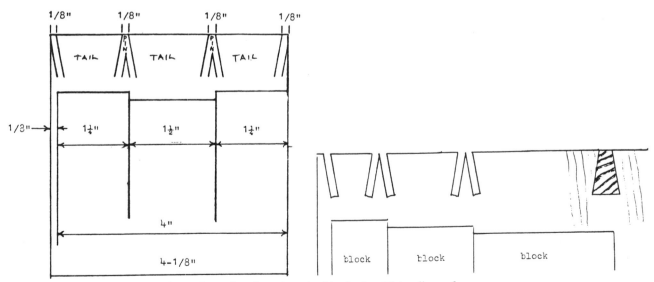

Illus. 728. *You can change the tail size by changing the block size. This allows for variable pin spacing. Here the pins are ⅛ inch, which is the difference between the blocks (which total 4 inches) and the 4⅛-inch board.*

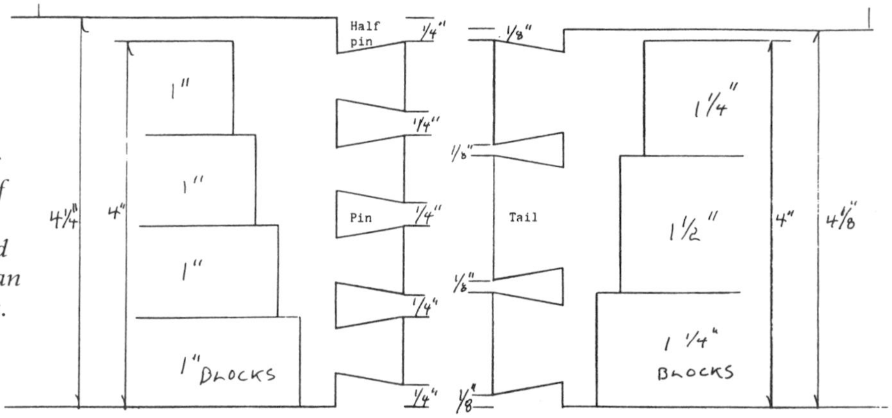

Illus. 729. Both of the examples shown here employ a total of four inches of blocks for the spacing of the cuts. When you change the width of the individual blocks and the width of the workpiece, you can create completely different designs.

(Diagram labels: Half pin, ¼", ⅛", 1", 1", 1", 4¼", 4", 1" BLOCKS, ¼", ⅛", Pin, ¼", Tail, ½", ¼", ½", ⅛", ¼", 1¼", 1½", 1¼", 4", 4⅛", BLOCKS)

CUTTING THE TAILS

Cut the tails first. Make individual cuts on the outside edge first. (See Illus. 730.) First, mark the pin size (the pin mark), which is the difference between the width of the blocks and the width of the workpiece. (See Illus. 731 and 732.) Next, position the blocks and the workpiece on the jig. Place the blocks on the side of the workpiece. (See Illus. 733 and 734.) The blade and the lead pin mark should be lined up with each other. (See Illus. 735.)

Make the first cut. Cut to the gauge line and then place a stop on the table so that the jig cannot go back any farther. (See Illus. 736.) Tilt the top saw wheel rearward far enough so that the blade rides against the thrust bearing. This will prevent the blade from wandering forward over the gauge line. Using a ⅛-inch blade seems to work best.

Next, rotate the board so that all four corners are cut. (See Illus. 737.) Remove a spacing block and repeat the process. (See Illus. 738.)

The next step is to widen the saw kerf between the two inside cuts. (See Illus. 739 and 740.) This will expedite removing the waste. Some people may prefer to remove the waste the traditional way, with a chisel. If this is the case, this step can be disregarded.

You can remove the waste by using the rip fence. (See Illus. 741 and 742.) This is where a microadjustable fence is very handy. (See Illus. 743.)

Illus. 730. Cut the tails first. Make the cuts on the outside first and proceed towards the middle.

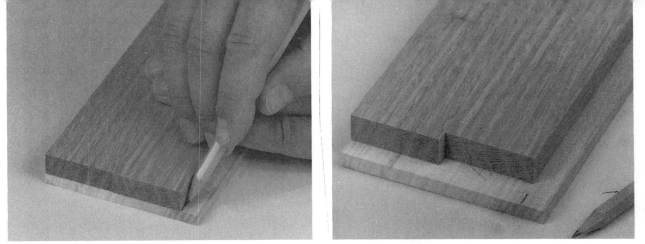

Illus. 731 (above left). Mark the difference between the total width of the blocks and the workpiece. The difference here is about ⅜ inch. Illus. 732 (above right). This pencil mark is where the first cut will be made. The half pin will be ⅜ inch wide and the pins will be ⅜ inch wide.

Illus. 733. Hold the blocks and the board at a 10-degree angle to the blade. The fence is adjustable and can be tightened with wing nuts.

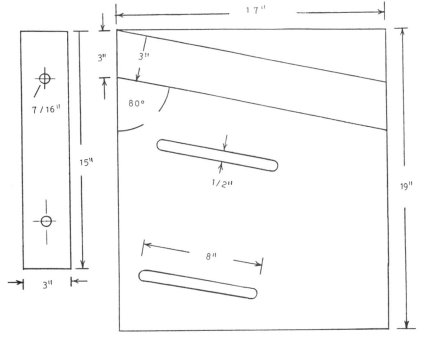

Illus. 734. A drawing of the tail jig. It was designed for the INCA bandsaw, which has the column on the right. If the column on your saw is on the left, reverse the design.

Illus. 735 (above left). Start the first cut on the pencil mark. The actual position of the blade is not critical. Illus. 736 (above right). Cut to the gauge line and place a stop behind the jig.

Illus. 737 (above left). Cut all four corners of both tail boards. Illus. 738 (above right). Remove a block and repeat the cuts.

Illus. 739 (above left). Move the workpiece away from the block and widen the saw kerf. Illus. 740 (above right). Here the tail pieces are being cut on the jig. The waste area between the tails is wide enough to accept a ⅛-inch saw blade.

Illus. 741 (above left). Cut the waste off using the fence. This is where a fence that has a microadjuster is very worthwhile. Plans for a fence with a fine adjustment are included in Chapter 11. Illus. 742 (above right). Place the blade in the wide kerf and crosscut the kerf. Flip the piece over and trim the opposite corner.

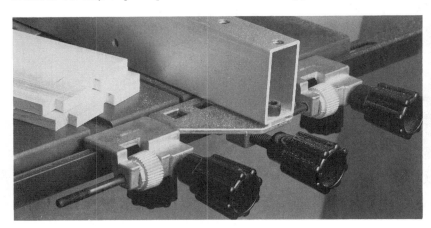

Illus. 743. When you use the extra microadjuster as a stop, you locate the exact position that you will use later when you complete the pins.

CUTTING THE PINS

Cut the pins after completing the tails. There are two processes to cutting the pins. The first cutting series is done with the board tilted at 10 degrees. The next series is cut with the table tilted the opposite way. (See Illus. 744.) The tilting can be done with either the table or the jig. (See Illus. 745–747.)

The cutting sequence for the pins is different than that for the tails. Start the pin cut on one side and progress to the opposite side. (See Illus. 748.) Position the piece on the jig or place it against a fence.

Line up the corner of the blade with the outside corner of the tail. (See Illus. 749.) Another option is to clamp the fresh pin board to the tail board and mark the area to be wasted. (See Illus. 750.) Cut in the waste area.

Start the first cutting sequence without a spacing block. (See Illus. 751.) In this sequence, blocks are added instead of subtracted. A stop

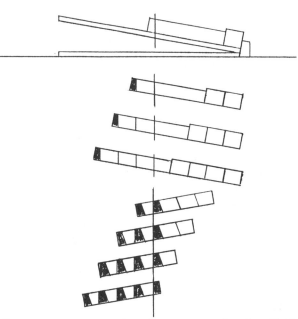

Illus. 744. Use two series of cuts to cut the pins. Each series should be angled in the opposite direction.

287

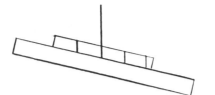
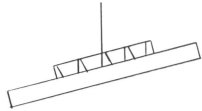

Illus. 745. The two series of cuts can be made on the band-saw table if your saw tilts in two directions.

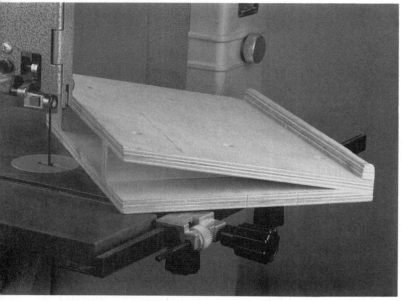

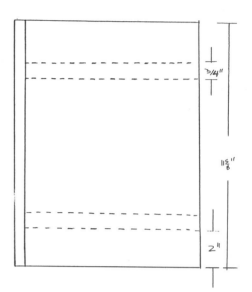

Illus. 746 (above). An angle platform can be used to tilt the pin piece. To match the tail angle, tilt the angle to 10 degrees. Illus. 747 (right). The plan for the tilted jig.

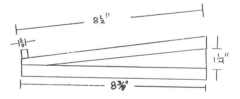

Illus. 748. Make the pin cuts from one side and progress to the opposite side. Make the cut and then expand it. The wide cut allows for easy entry of a ⅛-inch blade, so you can crosscut the waste.

Illus. 749. Line up the corner of the tail with the corner of the blade. You are going to cut out the space into which the tail will fit.

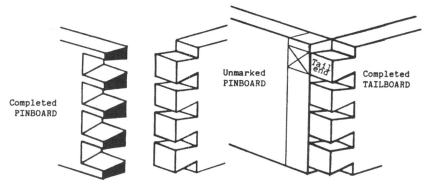

Illus. 750. It may help if you mark out the space. In this drawing, it is marked with an X.

Completed PINBOARD

Unmarked PINBOARD

Tail end

Completed TAILBOARD

Illus. 751. Make the first cut with a spacer block.

should be used to stop the forward progress of the pin board. (See Illus. 752.) A square block of wood works well. You can also clamp the jig to the saw table if you are using one.

Make the first series of cuts. Cut the opposite corner instead of all four corners, which is what you did when you cut the tails. Widen the cut because you will remove the waste later with the band-saw blade. (See Illus. 753.) Next, add a block. This will space the next cut. Then repeat the cutting process. (See Illus. 754 and 755.)

Make the second series of pin cuts with the table or the jig tilted in the opposite direction. (See Illus. 756.) Align the blade so that it's just short of the tail corner. You can always take more off later. (See Illus. 757.) Use the spacing block for this cut. (See Illus. 758.) With this cut, you are making the final fitting for the entire batch of dovetails. Make one cut to see if the dovetail fits. If it does, you can finish the rest of the cuts. If it doesn't fit and you haven't made a microadjuster, do the final fitting by using paper shims on the opposite side of the block. If the fit is too tight, remove a paper shim. (See Illus. 759.)

Illus. 752. Use a stop to set the depth of the cut. A large square block of wood works well. It is a good idea to clamp the platform to the saw table. Note: If your saw column is on the left, reverse this procedure.

Illus. 753. Widen the saw kerf so that the waste can be easily removed later.

Illus. 754. Add a block for the next series of cut.

Illus. 755. Expand the kerf for all of these cuts.

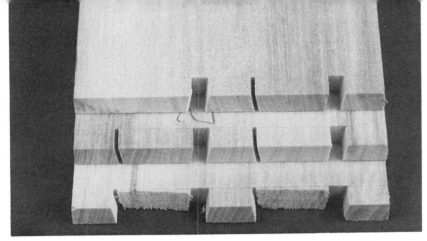

Illus. 756. Make the second series of cuts with the table or jig angled in the opposite direction. The single cuts shown here are those made in the second series. The bottom piece shows the last step. Remove the waste with a coping saw to see if the joints fit.

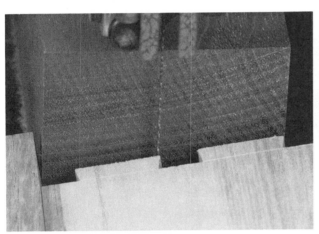

Illus. 757 (above left). Using a spacing block for this series, line up the blade so that it is just shy of the tail corner. You can always take off more later. Illus. 758 (above right). Make the cut on one edge of the board.

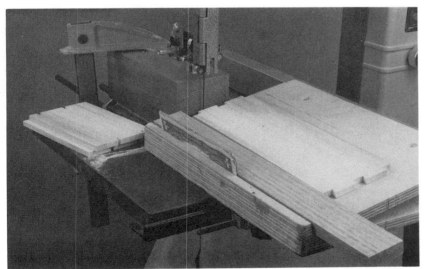

Illus. 759. Fit the dovetails with a set-up piece. To fit the joint, remove the paper shims or use a microadjuster. When you remove the paper shims, the area that accepts the tail is enlarged.

Make the second series of pin cuts in the same manner as the first pin series. (See Illus. 760.) With a coping saw, cut off the waste. Fit the tails to the pin board. (See Illus. 761.) If it is too tight (which is what you want), make another cut. Take a "hair" off. Make the adjustment with a microadjuster or a paper shim. When it fits, cut off the waste using the rip fence. (See Illus. 762.) You may have to tilt the piece slightly to start and end the waste cut. (See Illus. 763.)

Illus. 760. The completed second series of cuts.

Illus. 761. Remove the area between the pins with a coping saw. Check the fit. If it is too tight, take more off the side of one pin by using shims or a microadjuster.

Illus. 762 (above left). When the joint fits, remove the waste with the fence. Illus. 763 (above right). You may have to tilt the workpiece slightly to start and finish the cut.

292

Illus. 764. The completed tails and pins. All of the work was done with the band saw.

Illus. 765. The completed box.

Making Letters

The band saw can cut letters more quickly than the jigsaw, though the jigsaw can make interior cuts. When making letters it is much easier if you use a template to lay out the design. Two scroll saw companies sell letter templates. (See Illus. 766 and 767.) Lance Nybye, the person who makes letter templates for AMI, has developed a technique for cutting letters and separating them with a saw cut. (See Illus. 768.)

Sanding

Band saws are designed to use sanding belts. It takes a special attachment to support the sanding belt. (See Illus. 769.) The new small belt sanders can also be used. (See Illus. 770.) This would save the time of changing from the belt to the blade.

Illus. 766. These transparent, orange, plastic letter templates are distributed by Seyco Sales, 2107 So. Garland, Box 47 27 49, Garland, Texas 75047.

293

Illus. 767. These templates are a clear plastic with a brown-paper backing. Peel off the brown paper before using the template. These templates are sold by A.M.T., P.O. Box 312, New Castle, Delaware 19720.

Illus. 768. The letters on this brass key chain were separated with a shallow cut that was made with the piece standing on end. This shallow cut provides the line for the other cuts that are made with the piece laying flat. The brass key chain was made by Lance Nybye.

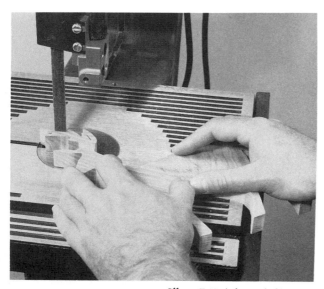

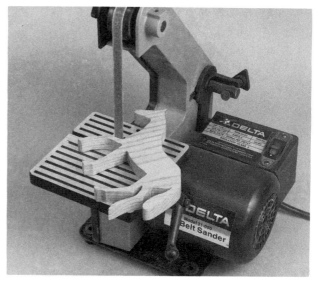

Illus. 769 (above left). One of the accessories available for the band saw is a sanding belt. Illus. 770 (above right). The small sanders can also be fitted with smaller belts. Shown here is a fine ½-inch belt. The sanding platen has been removed.

Interior Cuts

Wood-cutting band saws are not designed to do interior cutting. Metal-cutting band saws have welders, so the blade can be threaded through a hole and rewelded.

With some planning, you can make and sand many interior cuts with the band saw. A good example is the letter P. (See Illus. 771.) Make the entry cut and remove the waste. (See Illus. 772 and 773.) Make the rest of the cuts, but leave a square corner to support the clamp. (See Illus. 774 and 775.) Glue the entering cut, and after it dries cut off the square corner. It takes only a minute or two of extra work to make the interior cut and to reglue it. (See Illus 776 and 777.)

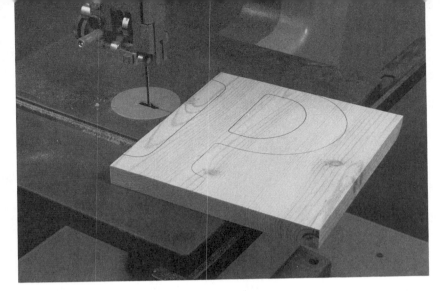

Illus. 771. The letter P is marked on the wood in pencil.

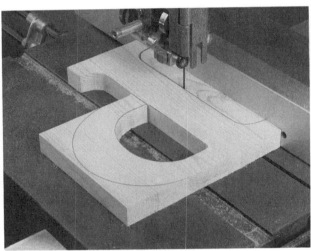

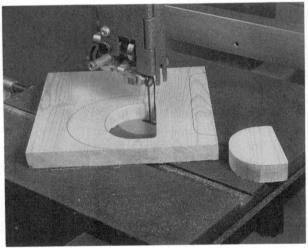

Illus. 772 (above left). Make the straight entry cut by using the fence. Illus. 773 (above right). Remove the waste.

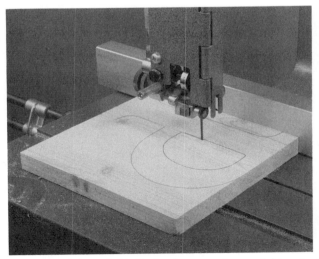

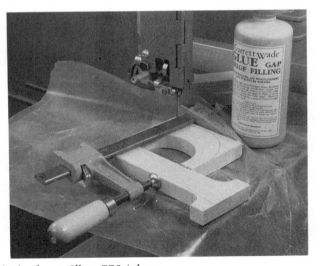

Illus. 774 (above left). Make the opposite straight cut with the fence. Illus. 775 (above right). Fill the saw kerf with glue and then clamp it. Leave a corner uncut. This makes the kerf easier to clamp.

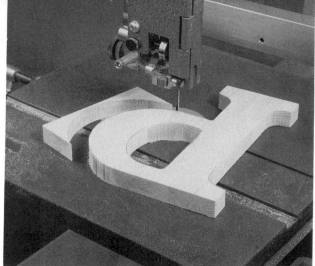

Illus. 776 (above left). After the glue dries, remove the square corner with a sharp chisel. Illus. 777 (above right). After removing the clamp, cut off the last piece of waste.

Making Multiple Pieces

The band saw is often used to make multiple pieces. This can be accomplished with a number of different techniques. When making straight crosscuts of the same size, use a stop. (See Illus. 778.) Multiple pieces are often cut sandwiched together; this technique is called "stack sawing." (See Illus. 779 and 780.) Other techniques include slicing thin pieces off thick stock (Illus. 781) and pattern sawing (Illus. 782), which is explored in detail in Chapter 8.

Making the Cabriole Leg

One job that is often intimidating for beginners is the making of a cabriole leg. This job is actually quite simple if the correct sequence is followed. Laying out the pattern correctly is critical. Since one often makes sets of four, it may get confusing. The knees and feet should be pointing towards each other. (See Illus. 783.)

Cut the straight lines first. (See Illus. 784.) Next, cut the backs of the legs (Illus. 785), and then the back corners. (See Illus. 786.) Make the long cuts last. (See Illus. 787–789.) It is best to have enough stock so that you don't cut through the pattern. (See Illus. 790.) When finishing the cut, stop it about 1/16 from the very end. (See Illus. 791.) This technique is called the "hinge" cut. If it is done correctly, the wood will open,

making it easy for you to back the blade out of the cut. (See Illus. 792.) If you accidentally go too far, you can tape the piece back on. It is important to have that long piece positioned well because it has the pattern for the next cut on the adjacent side.

Rotate the workpiece so that you can expose the pattern and finish the cut. (See Illus. 793.) Break the hinge cut; this will expose the completed leg. (See Illus. 794.) Sanding the leg takes a minimal amount of time if you use an inflatable drum sander. You can adjust the drum sander with air pressure so that it fits the shape of the leg. (See Illus. 795.)

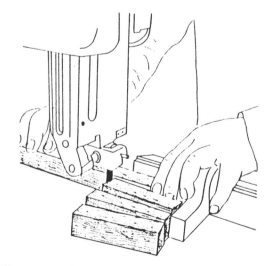

Illus. 778. When making multiple crosscuts, it is helpful to use a stop. (Drawing courtesy of INCA of Switzerland)

Illus. 779. These pieces of plywood are held together with rubber padding compound, a material used to make tablets. Rubber padding compound is usually available from office supply stores. It is a rubber, liquid-like paint that you paint on. It dries quickly. Tape, glue, screws, and nails can also be used to hold a stack securely.

Illus. 780. A completed stack of hearts.

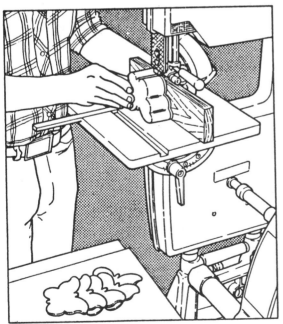

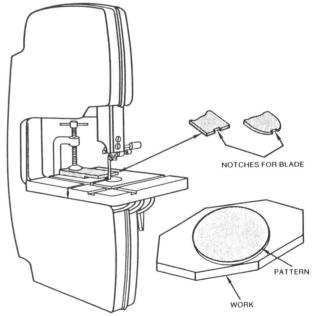

NOTCHES FOR BLADE

PATTERN

WORK

Illus. 781 (above left). Thin pieces can be sliced off of thick stock. (Drawing courtesy of Shopsmith) Illus. 782 (above right). Pattern sawing produces identical pieces. This technique is discussed in Chapter 8.

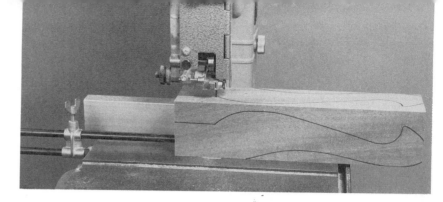

Illus. 783. Lay out the patterns so that the knees and feet point towards each other.

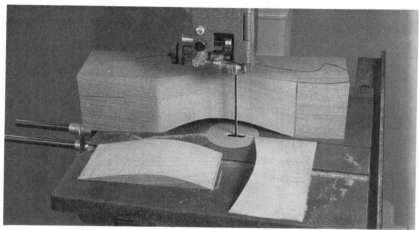

Illus. 784 (above left). Make the straight cuts first. Illus. 785 (above right). Then cut the backs of the legs.

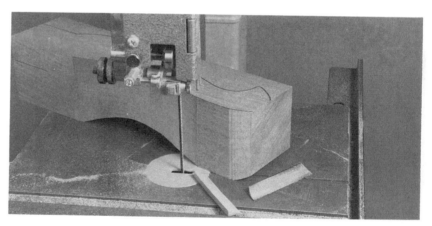

Illus. 786. Cut the heels off. Try to leave a flat area between the heels and the back of the leg. This can be rounded later.

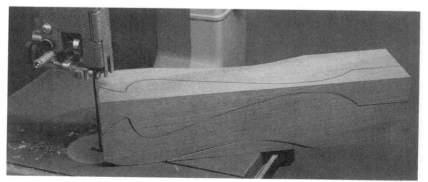

Illus. 787. Make the long cuts last.

Illus. 788 (above left). This is the tightest turn in this pattern. If you use a ⅛-inch blade, you can make the cut without backtracking. If you are using a wide blade, cut to the corner, back up, and then make a wide cut that will meet with the other curve. Illus. 789 (above right). If you keep the waste piece from the back of the leg under the workpiece, the piece won't have the tendency to tip off the edge of the table.

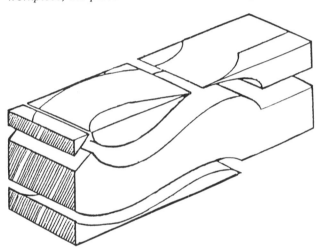

Illus. 790 (above left). When you make the first long cut, you remove the pattern for the adjacent side. If the pattern is too close to the edge of the work, remove it in three separate pieces. Illus. 791 (above right). When making the hinge cut, don't complete the cut. Leave about ¹⁄₁₆ inch of material between the cut and the straight release cut.

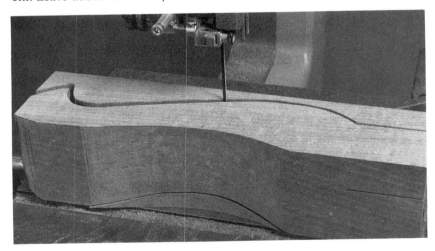

Illus. 792. The hinge cut allows you to open the kerf, which makes it easier for you to back the blade out. This allows the adjacent pattern to remain intact.

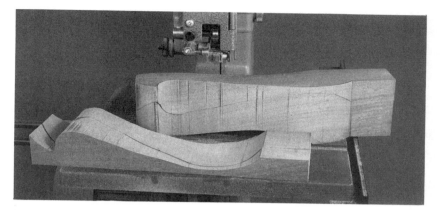

Illus. 793. Make the adjacent long cut.

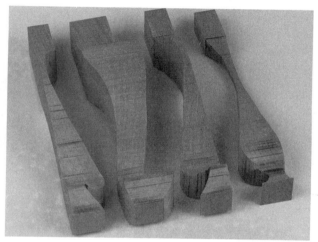

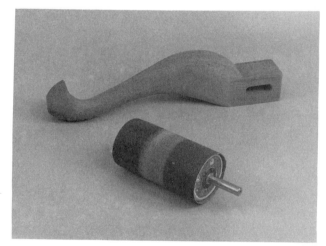

Illus. 794 (above left). The leg and the three waste pieces. Illus. 795 (above right). The leg can be easily sanded with an inflatable drum.

Cutting Tenons

The mortise-and-tenon joint and the dovetail joint are the two strongest joints. The dovetail is usually used for carcass work such as drawers and cabinets. The mortise-and-tenon is used for frame work such as chairs and tables (See Illus. 796–798.)

With the advent of powerful plunger routers, it is now easier to make the mortise. The mortise made with a router requires a tenon that will fit the round corner left by the router bit. The solution is to design a tenon that will fit the round mortise. One solution is to make the tenon corners angled. (See Illus. 799.) This solves the problem of fitting a square tenon to a round corner. It also solves the problem of releasing glue pressure. The 45-degree corner will snugly fit the round corner, but it will also allow for the escape of captured glue. This is the idea behind the fluted dowel.

The tenon requires two types of cuts. A crosscut is used to define the shoulder of the tenon. This can be done on the band saw, but is often done on the table saw.

After the crosscut is made, a rip cut is used to define the tenon. The band saw excels at this type of cutting because of its ability to cut into a corner. Another advantage is that the workpiece lays flat on the table for this process rather than having an end straight up in the air, as is the case when the table saw is used. It is often better to crosscut with the table saw so that the crosscut is slightly (1/32 inch) deeper than the rip cut. This ensures that the corner cut will be complete, and provides a place for the excess glue.

Cut the mortise first and then fit the tenon to it. The setup for doing the rip cut is the usual

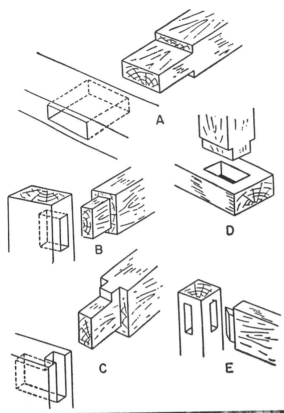

Illus. 796 (left). Mortise-and-tenon joints. A. Through mortise and tenon. B. Blind mortise and tenon. C. Haunched mortise and tenon. D. Stub mortise and tenon. E. Mitred mortise and tenon. Illus. 797 (above). The mortises on these chair pieces were made with a router. The tenons were cut with a band saw.

Illus. 798. This oak bench was made by my neighbor, Bob Umnus. It has a mortise-and-tenon construction.

Illus. 799. The corners on this tenon are bevelled. The bevelled corners fit the round mortise made by a router bit. The flat surfaces allow for a glue release that is similar to the flutes on a dowel.

setup for ripping, except a stop block is used to stop the cut. (See Illus. 801.) Using a microadjusting jig facilitates the final fitting of the joint.

Cut the short shoulder first. This is the less critical of the cuts, especially if the mortise is round. If the mortise is round, do the final fitting with the 45-degree bevel cut. (See Illus. 802.) Next, make the other shoulder cut. (See Illus. 803 and 804.) Make the cuts slightly oversized, and use the microadjuster for the final fit.

If you have a round mortise, you will want to bevel the corners. Tilt the table to 45 degrees (See Illus. 805 and 806.) Make the bevel cuts by cutting the opposite corners with the same fence setting. (See Illus. 807 and 808.)

Cutting Through Tenons

Through tenons are best cut with a ⅛-inch blade. If you use a ⅛-inch blade, you will find it easier to use when making the inside cut. (See Illus. 809.) Use only straight cuts when making the tenon. (See Illus. 810.)

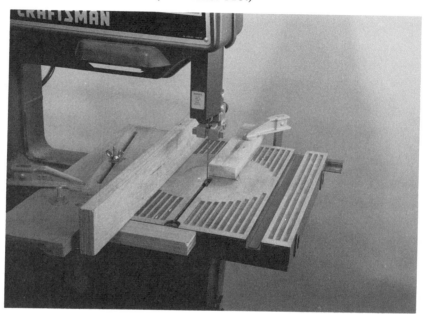

Illus. 800 (above left). The tenon requires two series of cuts. Cut the shoulder first with a crosscut, as shown on the bottom piece. Make the neck with a rip cut. Here the progression of these cuts is shown. Illus. 801 (above right). The setup for cutting the tenons is like that for making a rip cut. Use a stop block to stop the cut. If you use a fence with a microadjuster, you will be able to easily make a tight fit.

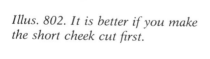

Illus. 802. It is better if you make the short cheek cut first.

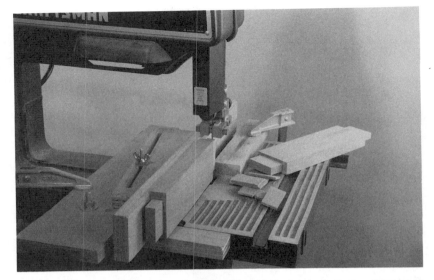

Illus. 803. Make the fit slightly over-sized and then slowly take off material until it fits.

Illus. 804. Shown here is the position of the stop block. The blade should be on the outside of the tenon so that the waste falls away from the fence rather than between the fence and the blade.

Illus. 805. Bevel the corners by tilting the table to 45 degrees.

Illus. 806. A close-up of the bevel cut.

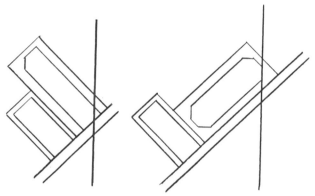

Illus. 807 (above). To make the four corners, use two fence setups. Each setup cuts opposite corners. Illus. 808 (right). Close-up of a bevelled corner tenon designed to fit the round mortise created by a router bit.

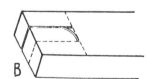 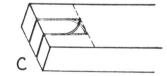 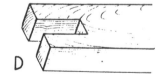 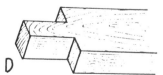

Illus. 809. When making a through tenon, make the inside cut first. (Drawing courtesy of INCA of Switzerland)

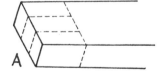 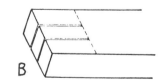 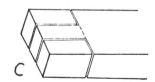 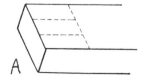

Illus. 810. Make the tenon last. (Drawing courtesy of INCA of Switzerland)

—16—
Projects

In this final chapter you will find projects that you can make with the band saw. These items were chosen because the making of each one incorporates a particular band-saw technique. Remember to think beforehand and follow the correct order of procedures when you are making a project from a plan such as those found in a book or magazine.

Wood Mallet

The wood mallet shown in Illus. 811 and 812 is a useful item around the shop. It is a good project on which to test your skill at making mortise-and-tenon joints. The head should be made from a piece of straight-grain hard wood such as maple or oak.

Make the mortise first, and then fit the tenon to the mortise. The technique for making the tenon is covered in Chapter 15.

Folding Basket

This is a very simple project that is made from one straight-grain board. The example in Illus. 813 and 814 is made from cherry. The handle can be cut, but it will be stronger if you make it by laminating pieces of veneer around a curve. The best blade for this project is a ¼-inch blade.

Illus. 811. A wood mallet with an oak head and a walnut handle. This is a good project on which to use mortises and tenons.

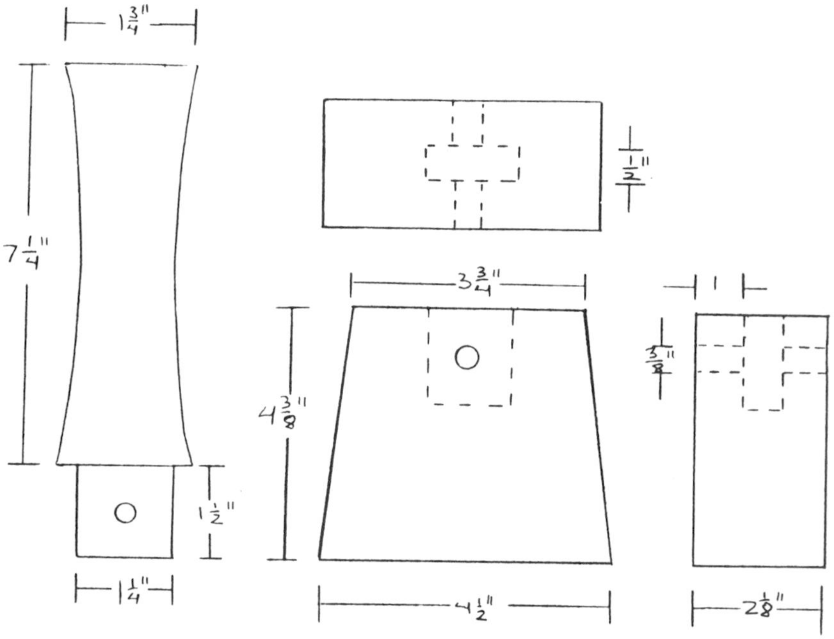

Illus. 812. The plan for the car-penter's mallet.

Illus. 813. A folding basket made from cherry.

Illus. 814. The basket in its folded position.

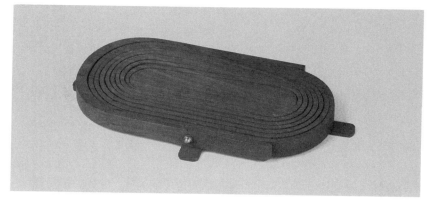

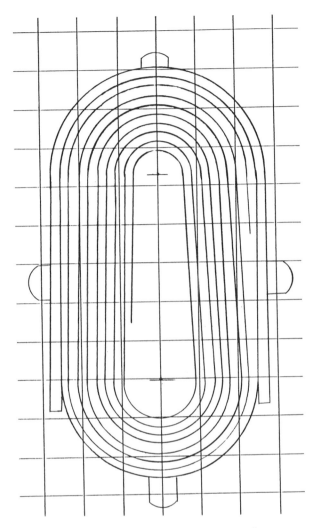

Illus. 815. The plan for the folding basket. Each square is equal to one inch.

Dovetail Tissue box

This project is a box that fits over the top of a standard-size tissue box. (See Illus. 816.) This box has an elm bottom with a black walnut top. The top is one piece of wood that is resawed and then glued back together in a bookmatched fashion. The bottom is made with dovetail corners using the technique shown in Chapter 15.

Decorative Deer

The decorative deer shown in Illus. 818 is an example of band-saw scroll work. You could use either a ¹⁄₁₆- or ⅛-inch blade. The cutting process is described in Chapter 8. The deer can be used for a number of decorative things, including a Christmas decoration. If you cut a hole into the back, you can mount a candle and transform the deer into a candleholder.

Painted Shaker Table

To make this project, you have to use the band saw to cut curved and circular decorative shapes. The curve on the stretcher is made with a curved metal yardstick. (See Illus. 820.) You can cut the half circles either with a jig or freehand. This technique is discussed under the heading Partial Circles in Chapter 13. It is important that you plan ahead so that the piece swings away from the saw column. This table is painted a dark-green with milk paint.

Illus. 816. A tissue box with dovetail corners and a bookmatched top.

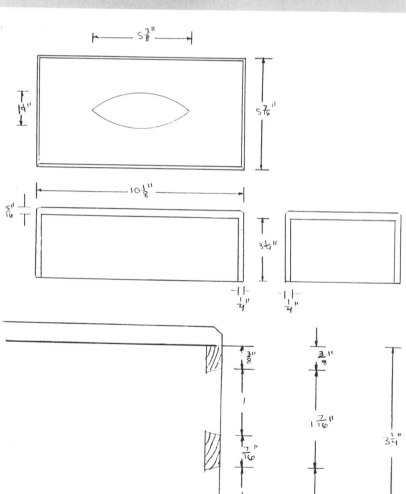

Illus. 817. The plans for the tissue box.

Illus. 818. A decorative deer made from butternut. A hole in its back is used to hold a candle.

Illus. 819. The plan for the decorative deer. Each square is equal to an inch.

Illus. 820. A painted Shaker table.

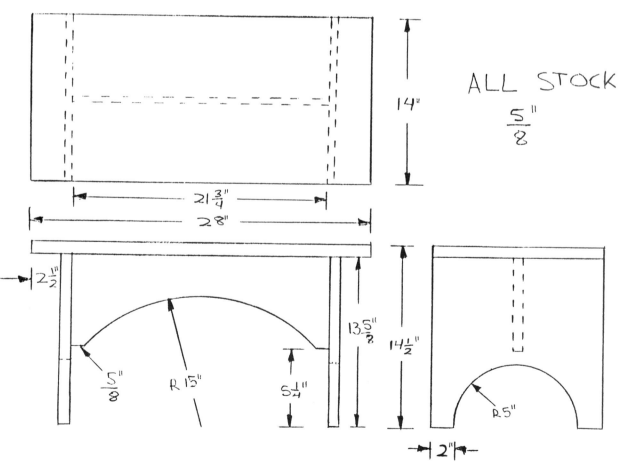

14"

ALL STOCK
$\frac{5}{8}$"

21$\frac{3}{4}$"

28"

2$\frac{1}{2}$"

13$\frac{5}{8}$"

14$\frac{1}{2}$"

$\frac{5}{8}$"

R 15"

5$\frac{1}{4}$"

R 5"

2"

Illus. 821. The plan for the painted Shaker table.

Wall Shelf

The wall shelf, which takes one day to construct, makes a useful present. (See Illus. 822.) If you want to cut the profiles of both sides at the same time, simply attach the sides together with double-faced tape. With the sides taped together, you can also sand their edges at the same time with a sanding drum attached to a drill press. The apron on the front of the shelf is an example of a half pattern.

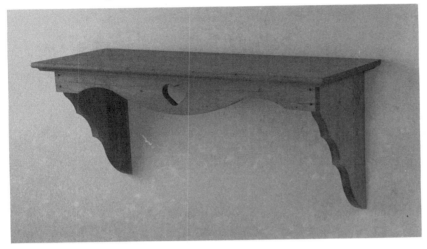

Illus. 822. A pine wall shelf.

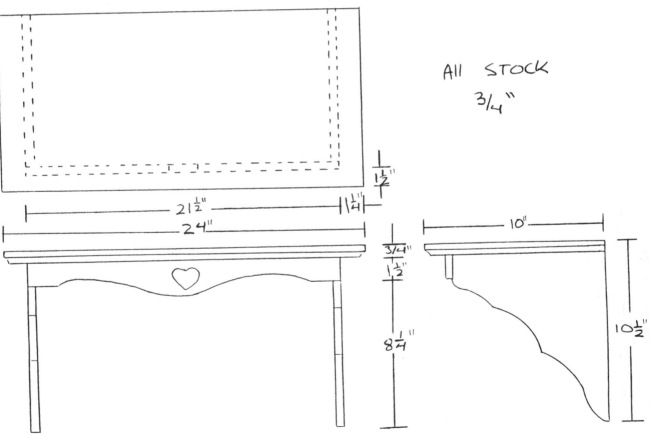

Illus. 823. The plan for the wall shelf.

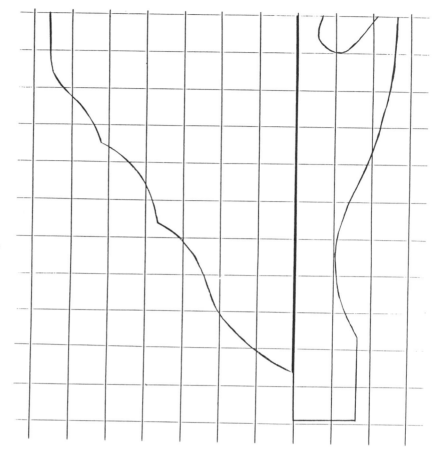

Illus. 824. The pattern for the shelf side and the half pattern for the shelf apron. Each square is equal to one inch.

Japanese-Style Marking Gauge

This is a very simple but useful project. In fact, you may decide to make a couple of these marking gauges.

The Japanese marking gauge has a design that is ideal. Its wide surface rests against the workpiece and is very stable. The knife is angled about two degrees, so as the gauge is pulled rearwards it is also pulled towards the stock. You can use an Exacto knife for the cutter. If you want to use a better cutter, make yourself a reground hacksaw blade. This makes a good knife because of its hardness. Use a 2-inch bolt with a wingnut for the tightening device.

Twin-Engine Plane

This is a good project on which to use scrap. (See Illus. 827.) The body has a double taper. The engines are made from ⅞-inch dowels. Using different colored woods makes this toy more interesting.

Knockdown Sawhorse

This is a design that is very easy to make with the band saw. Use a large taper jig to cut the angles for the legs. One of the legs for the one shown in Illus. 829 and 830 is made from halves glued together. Make the angled crosscuts on the stretcher by using a mitre guide on the band saw. Drill holes at the end of the slots. The holes should be slightly larger than the width of the plywood.

Illus. 825. A Japanese-style marking gauge. You can use an Exacto blade for the knife. You can also make a good blade by grinding a broken hacksaw blade.

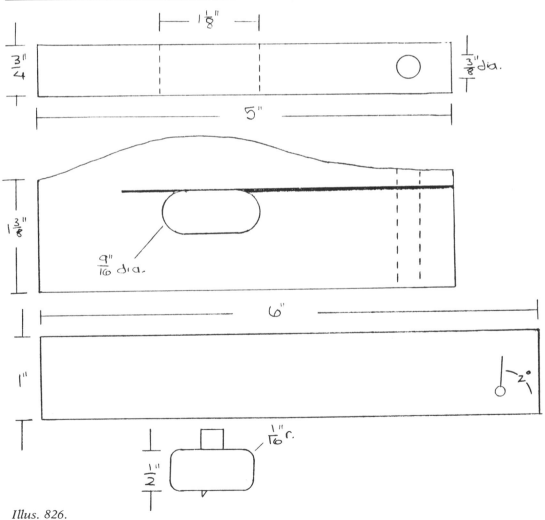

Illus. 826.

Illus. 827. A twin-engine plane.

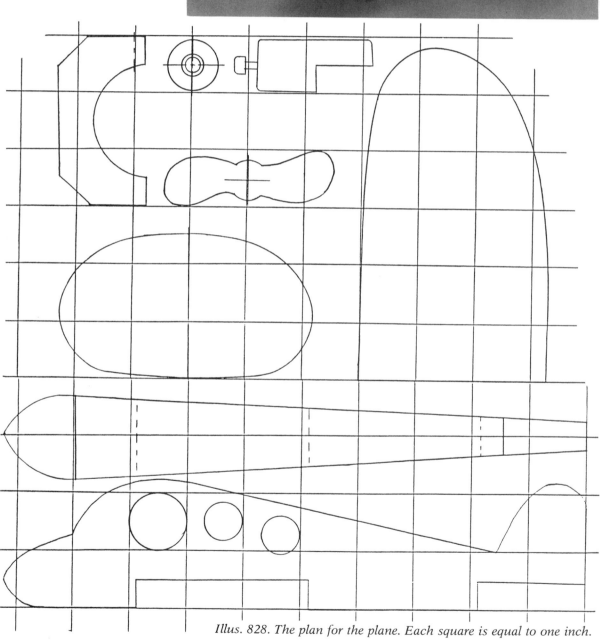

Illus. 828. The plan for the plane. Each square is equal to one inch.

Illus. 829. A knockdown sawhorse.

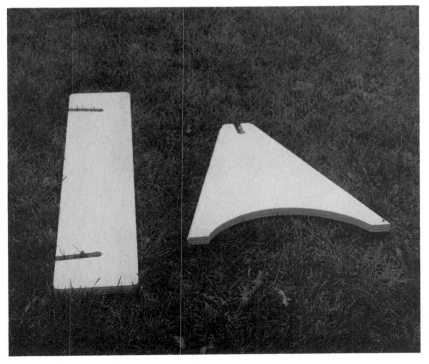

Illus. 830. The sawhorse stretcher and leg.

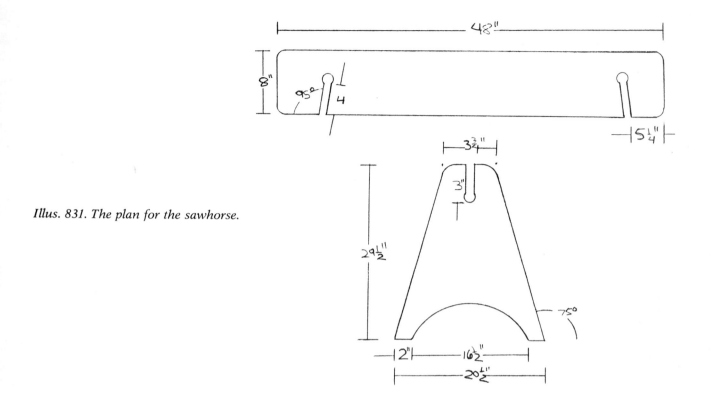

Illus. 831. The plan for the sawhorse.

METRIC EQUIVALENCY CHART

MM—MILLIMETRES   CM—CENTIMETRES

INCHES TO MILLIMETRES AND CENTIMETRES

INCHES	MM	CM	INCHES	CM	INCHES	CM
⅛	3	0.3	9	22.9	30	76.2
¼	6	0.6	10	25.4	31	78.7
⅜	10	1.0	11	27.9	32	81.3
½	13	1.3	12	30.5	33	83.8
⅝	16	1.6	13	33.0	34	86.4
¾	19	1.9	14	35.6	35	88.9
⅞	22	2.2	15	38.1	36	91.4
1	25	2.5	16	40.6	37	94.0
1¼	32	3.2	17	43.2	38	96.5
1½	38	3.8	18	45.7	39	99.1
1¾	44	4.4	19	48.3	40	101.6
2	51	5.1	20	50.8	41	104.1
2½	64	6.4	21	53.3	42	106.7
3	76	7.6	22	55.9	43	109.2
3½	89	8.9	23	58.4	44	111.8
4	102	10.2	24	61.0	45	114.3
4½	114	11.4	25	63.5	46	116.8
5	127	12.7	26	66.0	47	119.4
6	152	15.2	27	68.6	48	121.9
7	178	17.8	28	71.1	49	124.5
8	203	20.3	29	73.7	50	127.0

YARDS TO METRES

YARDS	METRES	YARDS	METRES	YARDS	METRES	YARDS	METRES	YARDS	METRES
⅛	0.11	2⅛	1.94	4⅛	3.77	6⅛	5.60	8⅛	7.43
¼	0.23	2¼	2.06	4¼	3.89	6¼	5.72	8¼	7.54
⅜	0.34	2⅜	2.17	4⅜	4.00	6⅜	5.83	8⅜	7.66
½	0.46	2½	2.29	4½	4.11	6½	5.94	8½	7.77
⅝	0.57	2⅝	2.40	4⅝	4.23	6⅝	6.06	8⅝	7.89
¾	0.69	2¾	2.51	4¾	4.34	6¾	6.17	8¾	8.00
⅞	0.80	2⅞	2.63	4⅞	4.46	6⅞	6.29	8⅞	8.12
1	0.91	3	2.74	5	4.57	7	6.40	9	8.23
1⅛	1.03	3⅛	2.86	5⅛	4.69	7⅛	6.52	9⅛	8.34
1¼	1.14	3¼	2.97	5¼	4.80	7¼	6.63	9¼	8.46
1⅜	1.26	3⅜	3.09	5⅜	4.91	7⅜	6.74	9⅜	8.57
1½	1.37	3½	3.20	5½	5.03	7½	6.86	9½	8.69
1⅝	1.49	3⅝	3.31	5⅝	5.14	7⅝	6.97	9⅝	8.80
1¾	1.60	3¾	3.43	5¾	5.26	7¾	7.09	9¾	8.92
1⅞	1.71	3⅞	3.54	5⅞	5.37	7⅞	7.20	9⅞	9.03
2	1.83	4	3.66	6	5.49	8	7.32	10	9.14

Index